Your Mother Should Know

Your Mother Should Know

From Liverpool to Los Angeles

by **ANGIE MCCARTNEY**

With Interruptions from Daughter Ruth

Probabilistic Publishing

Editor: Marshall Terrill
Assistant Editor: Lisa Derketsch
Assistant Editor: Nancy Winchester
Cover Design by Martin Nethercutt, McCartney Multimedia, Inc.

Copyright © 2019 by Angie McCartney and Probabilistic Publishing
All rights reserved.

Initial printing: November, 2019

Probabilistic Publishing
1702 Hodge Lake Ln
Sugar Land, TX 77478
281-277-4006

www.decisions-books.com
e-mail: dave@decisions-books.com

No part of this book may be reproduced, stored in a retrieval system or transcribed, in any form or by any means, electronic, mechanical, photocopying, recording, or otherwise without the prior written permission of the publisher or the author.

Written, designed, and printed in the United States of America.

Library of Congress Control Number: 2019955375

ISBN 13: 978-1-941075-09-8
eBook ISBN: 978-1-941075-10-4

To Ruth and Martin, family, friends, and fans of The Beatles everywhere

Contents

Foreword by Rikki Klieman xi

Back in the Saddle Again xiii

A Note About QR Codes xiv

A Note About UK Spelling xiv

Introduction xv

Prologue xvi

1 The Chemistry of Lennon & McCartney 1
    The Chemistry of Lennon & McCartney 1
    An Essay by Ruth McCartney 1

2 "You Should Write A Book" They Said 9
    Stopforth and Move Forward 10
    The Cannabis Revolution 14

3 In The Town Where I Was Born 17
    Hilbre Island 23
    More Childhood Reminiscences 27
    Religiosity, Music, and Other Messed Up Musings 29
    Thoughts While Folding Laundry 31
    My Big Sister Mae 32
    My Little Sister Joan 33
    Aunty Em 37
    Liverpool 39
    Ladies "Going to Bed" 41
    Fred Astaire and Ginger Rogers 42
    Her Majesty Queen Elizabeth II 43
    Racism 44
    Bessie Braddock, M.P. 46
    Football Clubs, Derby Games, Blood & Guts 48
    A Woman's Place 49

4 They Say It's Your Birthday 51
    Ruth Nearly Meets God 51
    Ruth and God 54
    Ruth Draws God 54

5 When I'm 64 57
    The Cotton Man 57
    Jim McCartney at the Movies 59
    Meeting Jim McCartney 60

Marriage and Marzipan	61
The Bells Were Ringing	63
HELP! I Need a Honeymoon!	66
Leaving Liverpool for the Wirral Peninsula	70
Michael (McGear) McCartney	74
Rembrandt Rocks	78
First Christmas in London	80
Good Ol' Freda	83
Dick James Honours Luncheon	88
Fanz, Fan Mail, and Customerz	89
Is The Doctor In?	91
RIP Jimmy Mac	92

6 John, Paul, George, Ringo & Friends 95

Liverpool's Lord Mayor's Civic Reception for The Beatles	95
Peter Archer	96
John Lennon	98
John's Aunty Mimi	101
Firestorm!	101
Ringo Starr	102
George Harrison	105
Louise Harrison	106
Brian Epstein	108
Ringo-isms that Resonate with Me	110
Come Back Milly	111
How I Won the War	112
Ray Connolly — Journalist	113
The Magical Mystery Tour Launch Party	116
Hey Jude	117
Blackbird (Singing in the Dead of Night)	118
To Malta with Milly	119
Lady Jane Asher	121
The Lovely Linda McCartney	123

7 All Things Must Pass 127

The Beatles Break Up	127
McCartney Family Outing	129
Wings Fun Club	130
James Paul McCartney at the Chelsea Reach Pub	131
Walking in the Park with Eloise	133
Four Lads Who Shook the World Statue	136
Joining the Circus	137
London Town	139
RIP John Lennon	141
Yoko Ono	142

   May Pang *144*
   RIP Linda *146*
   Pete Price *148*
   Down Under *150*

8 Here, There and Everywhere 155
   Dieter the Running Meter (aka Dieter Bockmeier) *157*
   Living in Germany *160*
   Kim Cooper (The Original Malibu Barbie) *163*
   San Fernando Valley *165*
   Nashville Here We Come *167*
   The Birth of McCartney Multimedia *169*
   Playa del Rey, You Say? *173*
   John Cleese *174*
   Wedding Facts from the Reverend Dr. Angie *179*
   Rikki Klieman and Bill Bratton *181*
   Tribute Bands *183*
   QR Codes *184*

9 Number 9, Number 9 185
   Celebrity Cookbook *185*
   Mrs. McCartney's Teas & Mrs McCartney's Wines *186*
   Dinner with the McCartneys *187*
   NASA's Dental Magician *189*
   Springboard South *190*
   HELP! In Obertauern, Austria *191*
   Turkey for Beginners *194*
   A Most Ebullient Gentleman *197*
   Around The World in 10,000 Bites *198*

10 With a Little Help from My Friends 203
   Art and The Beatles *203*
   Citizen Martin *204*
   Ellen DeGeneres *209*
   Farrah Fawcett Foundation *212*
   The Marriage of the Trans *214*
   James McCartney *215*
   Minerva Perez *216*
   Pamela Des Barres *218*
   Beit T'Shuvah *219*
   Sweet Alice *221*
   Val Camilletti *223*
   Arise Sir Richard Starkey *225*
   David Cassidy *226*
   Geoff Emerick *229*
   Anthony Bourdain *231*

    Mike Portnoy *232*
    Lawrence Gowan *233*
    Melissa Manchester *234*
    Strummer Hollis *234*
    The Nelsons *235*
    Gavin Scott *235*
    Ivor Davis *236*
    Christine Romeo *237*
    Jim O'Heir *238*
    Xavier Burgin *238*
    All Worn Out *239*

11 In My Life 241
    Big Data and Cryptocurrency *241*
    Artificial Intelligence *242*
    National Lampoon Lemmings Improv *243*
    Women and Credit in England *246*
    Swannies *246*
    Men Are Just Happier People! *248*
    Charity Begins at Home *249*
    The Man on the Moon *250*
    Liverpool *252*
    Happy Birthday and other Liverpudlian Stuff *254*
    Tea and History *255*
    2018 Capitol Records *258*
    TEAFLIX Tuesdays *260*
    Online Passwords *262*
    Robocalls and Other Digital Interruptions *263*
    The Changing Face of Advertising *264*
    Ticket to Ride *265*
    Ageing *266*
    Wet Behind the Ears *267*
    Tongue Twisters *269*

12 And in the End 271

Acknowledgements 274

Appendix 1: Foreword by Cynthia Lennon 279

Index 281

Publisher's Note 287

Angie's Biography 293

Foreword by Rikki Klieman

Angie McCartney is a force of nature. She swirls around you like a tornado and brings you into her orbit. Her energy is contagious. You are suddenly running alongside her, moving ever faster, gasping for air while she is telling you about all the new things you can do in your life and how you can make what you are already doing better. She is a friend, colleague, mentor, and a surrogate mother to so many people who want to ride on her wave of loving life. This tiny woman fills a room with enthusiasm.

For Angie, every day is a wonderful day because of the gift of life that she seizes with vigor. You want to be just like her when you are in your eighties. Actually, you want to be just like her right now! She is inspirational on so many levels and she makes you laugh in good times and in difficult times too. The term "role model" has almost become a cliché; however, it truly suits Angie because she is a role model for women and about how a life can be well lived into those late decades. When many people in their late eighties are moving slowly, talking about their ailments and never trying to do something new, Angie engages in a myriad of projects with the curiosity of youth.

I met Angie in 2002 when my husband, William Bratton, became the Los Angeles Police Chief. I moved from New York to share this episode of life and to find a way to continue my work on television and as a public speaker. A friend suggested that I create a website (which was a new idea in those days) and he referred me to McCartney Multimedia. My first meeting with Angie and her family is etched in my mind. Then and now, Angie takes over, directs, orchestrates, and pushes a project to fruition. I love being in her presence because she makes me a better person … and certainly makes me have fun.

Over these intervening years, Angie and I have been in constant touch for business since McCartney Multimedia runs my internet presence. However, far more importantly, Angie is always there to cheer me on and support me. She became a huge fan of my husband as well and was always at our policing and community events with Ruth and Martin, taking photos, cheering, and applauding.

When I see what she has done and is still doing, I am left breathless at the variety and depth of her interests. Her history with The Beatles is well known and I particularly adore the stories about Liverpool. But those are in the past. Meanwhile, she is working toward the future with Artificial Intelligence. How's that for spanning a century of development? In addition to creating a company, Mrs. Angie McCartney's Organic Teas, which are terrific, she somehow had time to obtain a Doctor of Business Studies, a Minister of Religion, host weekly live radio shows, a live Facebook show, and is about to embark on a monthly column for *Sensi Magazine*.

Who does all this at her age or at any age?

I truly love Angie. She is a blessing in my life each and every day. If I needed her in the middle of the night for an emergency, I have no doubt she would jump on a plane and be at my side. She lives her life in the spirit of gratitude and acknowledgement. I thank her for letting me express mine to her here. It is a privilege to tell the world about this remarkable woman.

Rikki Klieman
November 2018

To learn more about Rikki's career as a former prosecutor, legal analyst for CBS, and best-selling author, scan the code with your mobile device. Learn more about Rikki at her website (link):

Back in the Saddle Again

Looking back on our memory-filled trip to Liverpool for the launch of my first book, *My Long and Winding Road*, over six years ago, I realized that much has happened since that time, and that it was time to get cracking and jot down some more of my memories.

They have certainly been packed years with hopefully many more to come. I've promised myself that I am not leaving until I am at least 104, but the Good Lord will have the final say on that one.

My ambition is to get a telegram (or is it a Tweet now?) from the British Monarch on my 100th birthday. Be it Her Majesty or His Majesty – again, that is in the hands of our creator – and I can visualize poor, dear son-in-law, Martin, rolling his eyes at this point.

I'm a firm believer in the fact that a smile really is your umbrella on a rainy day, and I try to find something amusing every morning when I wake up, usually to find Sundance, my feisty little fur baby, pawing my face.

I'll swear that daughter Ruth and her long-suffering husband Martin send him downstairs every morning to check on me and report back to them to confirm that the old girl is still breathing.

Then I put the kettle on, check email (that's where the fun starts), and maybe, if I'm feeling strong enough, switch on the morning news to see who is after us, and off we go on another of life's jolly romps.

I am greatly encouraged by many of my Facebook friends (and discouraged by a few) who seem to think that my attempts at humour have some merit.

So fasten your seatbelts kids, here we go again.

Your Mother Should Know

A Note About QR Codes

This book uses SmartBook© technology, which, in simple terms, means that the codes that look like crazy crosswords you see throughout the pages can be scanned using a smartphone and any one of the free "QR Reader" applications (apps) you'll find in the App Store® or Google® Play.

1. Open your SmartPhone and navigate to the place you get your apps.
2. Search for "QR Reader" and any number of free apps will appear.
3. Download the app of your choice and when you wish to view the linked content from this book, and enjoy many more hours of entertainment, simply launch the app, hold your phone's camera over the code, and bingo!

This is the first book to use the SmartBook© Technology powered by McCartneyMultimedia.com (link).

Also, please note that the internet changes continually (people add and delete content), so please be patient if a link doesn't work.

Enjoy!

A Note About UK Spelling

As we were working on the book, one question that came up was whether to use UK or American spelling. Our editor, Marshall Terrill, correctly pointed out that many potential buyers live in America. However, Angie writes with the UK spellings. She, Ruth, and, of course, The Beatles are all English, so we decided that the original spelling would give the book flavor and color that otherwise would be missing. In some instances, the context favored American spellings, so you will find both spellings utilized, depending on context.

Here's a partial list of some of the words that are likely to be spelled the UK way: *colour, centre, theatre, parlour, humour, programme, ageing, whilst, flavour, organise, recognise, neighbour, favourite, amongst, encyclopaedia, anaesthesia, saviour* ...

Dave and Debbie Charlesworth, Publishers

Introduction

Since I published my first book at the ripe old age of 83-plus years, amongst the comments that I have heard is that there must be a lot of other things that have affected my perspective. Hence, this second book delves deeper into the people and events that have been important to me in the succeeding years.

I was fortunate enough to meet my new publisher, Dave Charlesworth of Probabilistic Publishing, in Texas. He was brave (or crazy) enough to take me on, and I hope you enjoy the results. And as I plan on living past 100, there might be a third book; you never know. I consider myself very fortunate to have Marshall Terrill oversee (aka edit) my ramblings, and try to rein me in and create some semblance of order out of my myriad thoughts.

I plan to donate a percentage of sales to the Linda McCartney Breast Cancer Research Centre in Liverpool, at the Royal Liverpool Hospital, as I do with sales of Mrs. McCartney's Teas and Mrs. McCartney's Wines and any other activities that generate funds.

We've added "QR" codes (which look like crossword puzzles), and if you go to the Apple Application Store or Google Play and download a free QR reader, you can simply launch the app on your phone, hold your camera lens to any one of these codes, and you will be transported to dozens of hours of video we have specially curated to go with the stories, and further paint the pictures in this book.

Thanks for your interest folks, and I hope you (and you smart phone) find something to tickle your fancy within these pages.

Angie McCartney
2019

Prologue

As anyone who knows me is quite aware, my darling daughter Ruth and I are joined at the hip. We are totally supportive of one another through thick and thin. And believe me, there has been lots of "thin."

That's why it wouldn't seem right to write this book without her collaboration. She is frequently the voice of reason when I go off on one of my rants and will show me an alternative point of view, then make me step back and recalibrate and see the other side of the coin. Why sometimes, I'll even agree with her!

And so ladies and gentlemen, without the aid of a net, I present to you my best pal, my favourite chef, my drinking buddy, my reason for living – my Ruthie. I can already envisage her rolling her eyes and saying, "Oh, Ange…"

Ruth and Angie in Playa del Rey, CA (2019). Photo courtesy Martin Nethercutt.

1
The Chemistry of Lennon & McCartney

> Many years ago my daughter Ruth wrote this piece, which I consider to be a worthy inclusion in our book. A few years ago when I asked Cynthia Lennon to write the foreword to my first book, *My Long and Winding Road,* she was so impressed by this essay that she even accused Ruth of having swallowed a dictionary. Sadly, we have lost Cynthia since then. She leaves a big gap in my heart.[1]

The Chemistry of Lennon & McCartney
An Essay by Ruth McCartney

"It's a drag, isn't it?"
Paul McCartney, December 8, 1980

My beloved step-brother was never one to deal with soul wrenching grief in a practical manner. He was brought up in the guilt-ridden Catholic mindset of "bury-your-head-in-the-sand.com," "Let's not talk about it son," a la father, Jimmy Mac.

He and the world had just lost someone very dear to them. I had lost my Uncle John, the myopic, misunderstood, manipulative, mystifying mop-top who had helped me to learn to ride a bicycle. Julian and Sean had lost a father; Cynthia, her knight in shining armour; Yoko, a fellow artist, contemporary, lover and house husband ... and Paul? Well, call me crazy, but he lost his

---

[1] We have included Cynthia Lennon's Foreword from *My Long and Winding Road* in Appendix 1.

first wife. I'm certainly not implying anything of a carnal nature here, but for almost all intents and porpoises (as John would have put it), what they had was a marriage.

Mark David Chapman's selfish quest for his Warhol-esque fifteen minutes of fame was the fatal wound to an injured relationship that had lasted almost 23 years. This unconventional partnership, much like a paradigmatic marriage, had endured its sundry situations ... its honeymoon period, its seven-year itch, the adoption of its offspring by Northern Songs and sometime foster parent Michael Jackson; the tender temptations of Jane, Cynthia, Yoko, Linda, May Pang, and others; the psychedelic side-trips; the jesters in the High Court; a very public airing of some dirty laundry lyrics, and finally, like two great lions in a butcher's shop who have matured enough to realize there's enough meat in the market for both of them ... a mutual, if grudging respect. It was a drag alright.

On a dank, blustery evening in October 1940, at the Oxford Street Maternity hospital in Liverpool, Julia Stanley Lennon gave birth to a bouncing bundle of boy joy whom she named John Winston. The boy's father, Alfred, a merchant seaman, was away on a voyage. He would return several years later and attempt to make amends with the young lad by offering to take him to New Zealand. Hitler's Luftwaffe was extremely interested in this industrialized zone with its munitions factories, rail network and busy seaport, but, despite the young John's pleas to Julia, Freddie was sent packing and John Winston was returned to the care of his house proud Aunty Mimi and dairy farmer Uncle George, at Mendips on Menlove Avenue, where he'd been living previously.

Almost 21 months after John Winston had screamed his first protest, a 32-year-old Mary Patricia Mohin McCartney would experience the same set of emotions and circumstances at her place of work – she was a nursing sister at Walton Hospital – the only difference being that her husband (a.k.a. "me Dad"), was there at 2.05 a.m. to welcome his first born, James Paul, into the world. The family grew within 18 months to include brother Peter Michael, and they resided in various houses in Allerton and Speke from Roach Avenue to Ardwick Road before finally settling at 20 Forthlin Road in 1955.

The following year, the boys' mother Mary died of breast cancer, leaving the emotionally immature Paul – in the opinion of my step-brother Mike – to use this pivotally catastrophic event to bury himself in his music, causing an inwardly devastated 14-year-old Paul to pour his passion and pain into his music, which paradoxically became a blessing for all of us.

Across town, John Winston would be the victim of the same disastrous occurrence just two years later. Julia was killed by a car driven by an off-duty policeman on July 15, 1958. The deprivation of his mother's friendship would affect John deeply and bond these partners in rhyme for years to come. Paul had already suffered the loss of his mother, and although two years younger and infinitely less experienced than John, it would prove to be a mutually morbid situation in which they could commiserate.

Almost a year before the sudden passing of Julia Lennon, a coincidental collision of cosmic proportions took place at St. Peter's Parish Church in Woolton Village.

On the afternoon of July 6, 1957, right across the street from the ossuary of a certain spinster called Eleanor Rigby, an unsuspecting schoolboy named Ivan Vaughn, lad about town, villain of Vale Street, and part-time tea chest bassist, took a chubby 15-year-old Paul McCartney to listen to local 'legends in their own lunchtime' – the band they called The Quarrymen. The group was headed by a sexy, sardonic closet nice-guy – the almost 17-year-old John Winston Lennon with his £17 guitar. Paul remembers: "It was at Woolton Village Fete I met him. I was a fat schoolboy and, as he leaned an arm 'round my shoulder, I realized that he was drunk."

Not a very glamorous account of an event that was to change minds, music, marketing, merchandise, and mania as we knew it. This completely unremarkable set of circumstances would lead to an alliance, that although nonconsanguineous, would ultimately disprove the old adage "blood is thicker than water." That may be, but crap is thicker than blood. And these guys went through their fair share of crap together.

To encapsulate their relationship, you most definitely "had to be there." I was very fortunate in that regard. I may have only been a child, but with the 20/20 vision of hindsight, I can safely say that even though I suffered the rigors of having my hair chopped off by teenage souvenir seekers as a tot, going to the school cloakroom and finding my raincoat and wellies missing because they had the name McCartney embossed inside them, and being told never to give my name or phone number to any strangers in case they were kidnappers, or worse, journalists. Growing up, I never knew if my friends wanted to play with me for me or if they had the ulterior "meet a Beatle" motive (and a jillion other put downs that have turned me into the psychotic, co-dependent mental case that I am today ... NOT!). Honestly, I wouldn't have missed it for the world. I would never have the memories of:

- John and Paul arguing out a song together in the attic at Cavendish Avenue,
- The honor of having "Blackbird" written for my maternal grandmother, Edie,
- The photos of a four-year-old me with Paul in the Bahamas on the location of *HELP!*
- The recollection of a "blind without his glasses" John waking up at our Wirral home (Rembrandt), to be told by mother Angie that they were number one on the charts – again,
- The birth of all my nieces and nephews,
- The look on Jim's face when he heard Paul had recorded his one-and-only musical composition ("Walking in the Park with Eloise") with Chet Atkins and Floyd Cramer,
- And a jillion other pick-me-ups too numerous to mention.

The reason I'm most grateful to have been there is, still to this day, that Jim chose to give me his name. It's a responsibility I take very seriously. McCartney is a fairly common name, as is Lennon, and if you look in any telephone book in most major cities in the world, you'll find a slew of us.

I remember Jim's words "toler and moder." This was code for toleration and moderation, and I try to live by them (except when it comes to buying shoes!). I clean my teeth, say my prayers, don't do drugs, don't smoke, TRY to pay my bills on time, and completely believe in karma. The significance of being there through the Beatle years is only just now beginning to dawn on me. Having finally realized the value and responsibility of "the name," I must say it's certainly a helluva perk to be related to Paul. But it's a helluva privilege to be related to Jim. Why? Coz there's no hairs on a seagull's chest!

Looking back across the years, the synchronicitous world events, the alignment of the planets, and a whole host of other spooky things – all I, with my high school education, can conclude is this: John and Paul were meant to meet, meant to create, and one was designed to play sturm and drang to the other's yin and yang.

One Romulus to the other's Remus. Ladies and Gentlemen, The Nurk Twins, live and without the aid of a net.

They were the product of a wartime town, a depressed economy, a "things-can't-get-any-worse-luv" society, and they struggled for years to become an "overnight success." There was something about being a Scouser that is still undefinable to this day. Our little city has spawned show business legends such as Sir Arthur Askey, Sir Ken Dodd, Glenda Jackson, Rex Harrison, Derek Nimmo, Willy Russell; even *Wayne's World's* funnyman, Mike Myers, grew up there. It seems that a free sense of humour kit is handed out at birth to every child born on 'Pool soil.

Is it stranger than fiction that the two Beatles, Stuart Sutcliffe, born in Edinburgh, Scotland, and Pete Best, born in Madras, India, who undoubtedly had an impact on both the group's look and sound, didn't stay the course? Certainly in the case of John and Paul, two English wartime babies, growing up without mothers in fairly, what could be considered upper working to middle class circumstances, the scouse glue bonded and stuck.

The combination of John's irreverence and Paul's naiveté; of John's panoply and Paul's privacy; John's perspicacious pessimism vs. Paul's seemingly obnoxious optimism created the oil and vinegar that tasted so good to our ears. The Brothers

Grimm of the musical manuscript. The Abbott & Costello of press conferences. The Orville & Wilbur of melodious travel.

That is not to decry the contributions of George and Ringo – it was all part of the phenomenal package that not only survived, but dictated the Zeitgeist. The two motherless boys certainly managed to find an "anschauung" – a way into each other's souls, bosoms, and brains; a way for one to discern the true nature of the other. Alike, yet different. Compatriots yet adversaries. I'm sure there's a fascinating psychoanalytical clinical explanation for their kinesis, but I just like to think of them as a needle and a thread in a haystack who were lucky enough to find each other and stitch together a tapestry of musical memories that has decorated the walls of the world, and, like those fine pieces of art, will only continue to improve with age.

Like the tragic deaths of Julia and Mary, and as the Death card in the Tarot signifies "change," the equally untimely demise of JFK left America in a depressed, emotional turmoil. The civil rights problems of the early 1960s, the social unrest after World War II and the Korean War served, in my opinion, to act as a tunnel from which it appeared there was no escape.

Then on February 9, 1964, Ed Sullivan shone the proverbial light on the boys for the viewing public's pleasure. The long night was over. The Beatles had conquered America. For the next two-and-a-half years, John and Paul (together with George and Ringo) would travel, eat, rehearse, write, play, record, and "sleep" (again, not literally) together.

The magic eventually had to wear off. On Monday, August 29, 1966, after endearing youth and enraging society, they played their penultimate concert together at Candlestick Park in San Francisco.

The Scouse glue was coming unstuck. Their next and final gig was to be on the roof of their Savile Row headquarters in London on January 30, 1969. The glue had turned flaky. The honeymoon was over. The divorce lawyers had moved in. But the legacy remains. From the four on the floor, skiffle inspired raw rock 'n' roll songs of the Hamburg days, to the sophisticated psychedelic tales of public works excavations in Blackburn, Lancashire – it's all still there for us to reminisce, regret, and rejoice over.

The Bonnie and Clyde of rock 'n' roll had pulled their last job. Busted. Caught red-handed with lives, wives, and children of their own. Finito. Sayonara. Later dude...

And so we move into the era of Spotify, Pandora, Burning Man, and inked-up groovy types with piercings in places I have to look up in a medical dictionary – but d'ya know what? Ask the songwriters of today who influenced them and eight out of ten will tell you Lennon and McCartney. So it goes, and in the end, the music you make is equal to the kudos you take. Now THAT's not such a drag after all!

Ruth McCartney

Then	**Now**
Friday night was bath night. Mother boiled the water. Put out the tin bath in front of the fireplace, poured the water in, added the children one by one, with the eldest first, youngest last. I was the youngest and had waist-length hair. Water cold and scummy. Not a happy memory.	Step into hot shower, adjust temperature, and wallow. Bliss!
An emergency: get small change, get dressed in warm clothing, go out to the nearest telephone box and hope phone is working, put your money in, get operator, and shout, HELP!!!	Open device, dial emergency number, sit tight and wait.
Plan visit to the theatre: dress appropriately, travel to box office, choose tickets, haggle, buy tickets, cash only, no checks or credit cards in those days.	Click on venue or act of your choice, select number of seats, price, date, enter credit card number, hit "send." Check email, open incoming, download tickets, hit print, and voila...

Ruth's Domestic Tips, Part 1

Prevent brown sugar from hardening

Help brown sugar stay soft and scoopable by tossing an orange peel or a slice of apple along with the sugar into an airtight container. For a quick fix, microwave brown sugar next to a small glass of water. The moisture within the microwave will help break up the block of sweetener.

Check if eggs are still (incredibly) edible

Gently place raw eggs in a bowl of cold water to see if they've gone bad. If the egg sinks to the bottom, it's a-OK. If it floats, it has seen better days. Over time, the liquid inside eggs evaporates through the porous shell, leaving a gas bubble inside. The floatier it is, the older it is.

Easily scoop out squash seeds

Remove seeds from vegetables, such as squash and pumpkin, with an ice cream scoop. Because the edge of the scoop is sharp, it cuts through the fibery, gooey stuff inside the squash easier than your hand, or a regular spoon, can.

Peel boiled eggs in a big batch

Peel multiple hard boiled eggs at a time by shaking them in a lidded container. The eggs won't be pretty, but they will be ready for an egg salad much quicker than traditional methods.

Make citrus fruits even jucier.

To get the most juice out of a lemon, refrigerate, then microwave it for 15 to 20 seconds. Bonus tips: Roll citrus fruits before squeezing, cut them lengthwise, and/or use a pair of tongs to squeeze, instead of your own two hands.

Make your own buttermilk

To make buttermilk when there's none of the real stuff in the fridge, add a tablespoon of vinegar or lemon juice to regular milk. The mixture won't get as thick and creamy as buttermilk, but it will help create fluffy pancakes and quick breads just the same.

2
"You Should Write A Book" They Said

I wish I had a penny for every time someone has said this to me. Without thinking, I often come up with some odd witticism and people take me up on it and say I should write a book. "I did," I told them. "Then write another," they said. So here goes.

For those of you who did not read the first one called *My Long and Winding Road* (2013), here's more of the same, and you've only got yourselves to blame.

Living in Los Angeles, every day brings something new, odd, and even weird. It just isn't possible to grow old and slope off into the sunset. Growing old I am indeed doing, but sloping off is not on my bucket list.

I wake up every morning thinking, *Oh, wow, I'm still here, isn't that great? I wonder what today will bring?*

There's the onslaught of media: TV, emails, Facebook, Twitter, Instagram, Netflix, Amazon, Hulu, and heaven knows how many more social media channels. Oh, and even the old-fashioned telephone, which some people still use. Although I have to admit that most of my calls are from people inviting me to have my penis enlarged or asking me to give them my bank account details so that they can send me vast amounts of money from some nice gentleman in Nigeria, or the Feds saying that the Marshals will be coming to take me away for unpaid taxes. This used to scare me, but not anymore.

Then there are those nice gents from India or Pakistan who say that my computer has a virus and I need to give them my login details so that they can help me.

Wouldn't it be terrific if these people applied their skills to do something productive instead of all this nonsense?

I have a friend who now answers her phone with: "Hello, FBI Field Office, Officer Rodriguez speaking. How are you related to the victim?" This tends to cut 'em off at the pass.

Oh and yes, I win countless cruises, trips to Florida, even vouchers for anal bleaching, which (so far) I have resisted. I have even been invited to view and select caskets for my potential demise, which doesn't exactly fill me with joy, particularly as I don't want a funeral. Cremate me, I say. Put my ashes into snow globes so that you can take me to all the parties. I don't want to be left out just because my bulk is not here anymore.

And we thought George Orwell was kidding.

Oh, when I'm cremated, I wonder what will happen to all the titanium in my knees? That must be worth a few bob. But, mortuary folks always side step that question. Who knows, I'm probably worth more dead than alive.

Stopforth and Move Forward

I was born in 1929, a far less enlightened age than we now share. I suffered from asthma as a child, which began when my dad died. I was seven years old. To assuage my grief, Mum bought me a puppy, Mickey, and it seems that I was allergic to him too. But in those days we had no knowledge of such things. I'm very happy to say that at 89 years of age I am still rocking on, working at least twelve hours a day and loving it, helping run McCartney Multimedia in Playa del Rey, California, a branding agency. I am a cat lady who does voice overs and weekly radio shows with England. I love life, music and movies, and am a general pain in the arse. But I'm still above ground.

Me, pushing a pram at about 18 months old in Hoylake. Photo courtesy Lucy Pemberton.

My dad, Bob Stopforth, was born in Liverpool, England in 1887. He was educated at St. Edward's College in Stoneycroft, a Catholic institution. Little is known of his family history other than it is suspected that they had some Spanish connections.

He had two adopted sisters, Emily and Mae Parsonage. I think they were distant cousins. But that's another story for another day.

Dad had two biological brothers. The eldest was Peter, who worked as an optometrist in the family business of Curry and Paxton in Liverpool. Then there was Richard (known as "Dick"), whose only claim to fame in my recollection is that he visited us at our house at 3 Carr Lane in Norris Green when I was a tot. He grandly presented to each of us kids a shiny half-crown piece as a Christmas gift. We duly put them into our piggy bank on the hall table, only to find after he left that he had taken said money box with him, neither of which was ever seen again.

His wife was a school headmistress. I later learned that Uncle Dick was an inveterate gambler, who had sold his wife's furs and jewels to pay off debts over the years. Other than that, my knowledge of him is sparse.

Uncle Peter was a small, bird-like man, who had suffered through several bouts of cancer. His battles resulted in some horrible surgery to his face and neck, which made him appear grotesque to most.

Then there was Dad's sister, Aunty Helen, who would hide bottles of gin in all kinds of places, including inside of her Wellington boots at the back of her wardrobe. I have a vague recollection of her. Tall with a very hairy face and a forbidding manner, she was known to everyone as "Aunty Tot."

I never knew how my parents met, but I had heard stories of Dad's time in the British Army during World War I when he was a Sergeant Major, complete with waxed moustache and auburn hair. (He was later dubbed "the red fella" at a clinic where he worked.)

Due to his previous experience in the field of medicine, which he had studied in hopes of becoming a doctor, he was drafted into a military unit that researched and produced mustard gas during World War I. This no doubt contributed to the throat cancer, which would take his life at the young age of 49. I am sure they didn't have hazmat suits or even masks in those days.

He failed his final exams to become a Doctor of Medicine as he was unable to complete the paperwork satisfactorily.

One of the stories that he passed along to me was when he was an apprentice at the chemical company, Evans, Lescher & Webb in Liverpool. He was told by his boss to go into a storage room, which was filled with boxes of these little rubber thingies, and stick a pin into every fifth one. They were, of course, condoms. At the tender age of 15 he had no idea what they were or what they might be used for. So much for his Catholic employer, who was doing his bit for population control.

Angie and Ruth, Butlin's Holiday Camp, Pwllheli, North Wales, 1963.

After the war, Dad, like so many others, found it extremely difficult to get a job. I would hear tales of him putting layers of newspaper into his threadbare shoes to pound the pavement in search of gainful employment.

Eventually he was hired by Dr. McAlpine, a general physician in Norris Green, Liverpool, to be his in-house pharmacist. It was there where he created tinctures, ointments, cough syrups, and ear drops from scratch. It was his firm conviction that only ingredients that came out of God's green earth should be used in these remedies, and for him, the idea of synthetic chemicals was totally abhorrent. He was one of the earliest compound pharmacists.

Even in those far off days, Dad would talk about hemp. He declared the future would prove it to be a valid remedy for many ailments. And lo and behold, here we are in the 21st century, with some people still needing to be convinced of its healing properties.

I remember hearing a story when he was hosting a card party at our house one night, and he decided to phone his boss, Dr. McAlpine, who lived nearby. He invited him to join the boys in a game of cards. However, the good doctor said, "I'd love to Bob, but I just got a case of syphilis in." To which my dad responded, "Oh, bring it with you, these fellas will drink anything."

I grew up with a very healthy resistance to over-the-counter medications, and to an extent, a suspicion of marijuana. I became well aware of the herb during my early days as stepmother to Paul McCartney. At the time, I was a young widow in my mid-thirties with a four-year-old daughter (Ruth). I married Paul's Dad, Jim McCartney, in November 1964 just as the Beatles phenomenon was beginning to storm the world.

Angie, Jim, and Ruth, the day after their wedding (November 25, 1964).

The Cannabis Revolution

Paul would visit our home on Merseyside, frequently bringing with him a selection of musicians and their "attachments." My husband Jim and I became more and more aware of the presence of various substances on our glass topped coffee tables, kitchen counters, and other smooth surfaces. I was the anxious mother who would swoop it all up and flush it down the toilet, worried stiff that my little daughter would discover it. I must have cost the boys a small fortune, but I would have none of it.

My initial awareness of marijuana was that it made them all mellow, sleepy, and then extremely hungry. I happily complied with the necessary food, ranging from deviled eggs to bacon butties, to soups, to cheese on toast ("prison toast," we called it, for some unknown reason), and tomato soup – at all hours of the night. Anything to keep them all mellow.

A few years later, having watched Jim suffer with arthritis, I gingerly tried a legal medical cream, and much to my delight, it removed the pain while nothing dreadful happened to me. So I began to research and discovered that there was so much more to all of this than my unenlightened mind had first thought.

I now have two titanium knees, a plastic hip, microchips behind both eyes, and a dental implant installed by a dentist who tends to astronauts when they return to terra firma. (It appears that their sojourn in space creates many dental and optical problems due to the effects of gravity.) My dental implant was affixed not by the usual post, but by a fiber optic connection.

So I am a bionic octogenarian. And if you know what's good for you, you won't get behind me at the airport screening area. I have a variety of identification cards to notify the TSA folks of my various spare parts, and it can sometimes have some pretty hilarious results.

I am so happy to have met with Tae Darnell, publisher of *Sensi Magazine*, who kindly invited me to contribute to their publication. I hope that folks who are hesitant and unaware of the helpful properties that CBD topicals can bring to their lives and make time a little easier and pain free will send me their questions. If I don't know the answers, I will research the hell out of it until I do. I am proud to be included in their masthead from time-to-time as a guest columnist; open the QR code and you will find me under "Ask Angie."

Old Age

Some people try to turn their backs on "odometers." Not me, I want people to know why I look this way. I've travelled a long way, and a lot of the roads were not paved. I have earned every darned wrinkle on this face of mine.

You know when you are getting old when everything either dries up or leaks.

Ah, being young may be beautiful, but being old is comfortable.

Lord, keep your arm around my shoulder and your hand over my mouth.

Litter Box

When people see a cat's litter box, they usually ask: "Oh, do you have a cat?" My answer is:

"No, it's just for company."

In these days of porch theft, use a Fedex box for your cats to litter in. When full, seal and leave it out on the front porch for thieves. Surprise!!!

Angie's Bucket List

1. Get a bigger bucket.
2. Make a sex tape. (It didn't do Kim Kardashian any harm.)
3. Exercise (other than jumping to conclusions).
4. Be tolerant (except with people who annoy me).
5. Smile at strangers (then run like hell before they come after me).
6. Persuade Elon Musk to take Mrs McCartney's wines into space.
7. Persuade Sir Richard Branson to take Mrs McCartney's Teas into space.
8. Win the lottery.
9. Buy a lottery ticket (Duh!).
10. Admit that item 3 was fake news.
11. Submit brain to Artificial Intelligence Lab.
12. Meet Dr. Ruth - Ask Dr. Ruth.

3
In The Town Where I Was Born

Hoylake is the little seaside town on the Wirral Peninsula across the River Mersey from Liverpool. I was born at home at 19 Grosvenor Road. In those days, the vast majority of working class women gave birth in their own homes. Hospitals were for the well off, or for people who were expecting to have difficult births.

Angie paying a visit to her birthplace, Hoylake, in 2013.

Hoylake still has lots of lovely little mock tudor-style gift shops, cafes, wool shops (called craft stores in America), and all manner of individually-owned antique shops and arty places. It has changed some, but not too much. Look it up on Google. It is a small peninsula between the River Dee and the River Mersey, flanked by the Irish Sea. There are lots of lovely walks and unexpected villages (and village pubs) here and there, and plenty of places for people to walk their dogs without traffic concerns. It still has a leisurely feel and, compared to the hustle and bustle of Los Angeles, it is like stepping back in time. It is wonderfully calming.

It's a bird watcher's paradise too, and has lots of peaceful areas. One of them is along the long retired railway tracks, and is called The Wirral Way. Our good friend, local legend and popular resort figure, Don Woods, has written a ditty about it as an ode to the last train that ran in 1956, called the 4-122.

You can see the video here (link):

Anyway, back to my first day on this planet … it was a foggy November day in 1929 (the 14th for those of you planning to send cards, flowers, and lottery tickets), and Mum was tended to by the local midwife and a couple of friends and neighbours. I was the last of the litter, the runt, or the "shakings of the box" as Mum used to call me. She was 41 and hotly protested to the doctor that she couldn't possibly be "with child" as they discreetly called it way back when. How to help your child grow up with confidence. She thought she was far too old to have another child. I have to say, I don't have any recollection of that momentous occasion, but, no doubt, my sisters Joan and Mae and brother Bob did. People took having babies much more in their stride in those days. They didn't do baby showers, give presents, send flowers or cards, or any of the commercial stuff that is so prevalent today.

When I was a couple of weeks old, Mum asked my dad to take me to the local Catholic Church to be christened. My godmother was to be her best friend, Lucy Pemberton. So off they trotted with my father firmly repeating that he would remember the names my mother had chosen – Angela Lucy.

However, when they got to the church, the priest said that there was no Saint Lucy, so he couldn't give me that name. But he suggested a compromise ... there WAS a Saint Lucia, so I finished up as Angela Lucia. Rather posh, don't you think?

When Dad got home, Mum was sitting up in bed and excited to have her officially baptized baby back in the nest. My dad, being a bit of a wag, said, "I couldn't remember those fancy names, so I got them to call her Mary Ellen." After the explosion, Mum insisted that he take me back and get it changed (like a pair of slippers that were too small or something). You see, Mary Ellen was the name generally given to the "shawlies" who sold fruits and veggies from barrows on the dock road or Clayton Square in the City Centre. Shawlies were usually very large ladies, frequently with bad feet, hairy chins and protruding warts, who wore great big black woollen shawls over their aprons. They used to vie for attention, out-yelling one another with the prices of their wares. It was a right kerfuffle. Mum told us kids that one of them would shout: "Ee-are, lemons, lovely juicy lemons, tuppence each, ask for three and I'll give you four. Ask for five and I'll blind yer." Or, "Buy me last three and I'll give yer four," and other compelling marketing ploys.

From Hoylake and West Kirby, you can see across the sands at low tide to Hilbre Islands, a gaunt forbidding formation of rocks that folks still hike across to today. You have to catch the tides just right though. The name is thought to derive from a chapel built on one of the three islands and dedicated to St. Hildeburgh.

We lived in a very damp area, in close proximity to the water. As a result, I began having asthma attacks, bronchitis, and pneumonia at a very early age. Dad, by this time, had a job working for Dr. McAlpine in Norris Green, Liverpool. He eventually found a Corporation House close to his surgery that we were able to rent.

This finally came to pass, and we moved over to the Liverpool side of the Mersey. Thus, we settled into 3 Carr Lane, Norris Green, just across from St. Teresa's Church and School.

On moving day, Mum and Dad and us kids, which included brother Bob, sisters Mae and Joan and me, traveled to our new abode via Mersey ferry boat and tramcar.

We were anxiously awaiting the arrival of the furniture removal van when there was a knock at the front door. When Mum answered, a young man standing on the step said, "Good morning, I have a message."

Mum eagerly asked him, "Oh, is it from Aunty Lucy?" Whereupon he solemnly replied, "No, it's from Jesus Christ." Mum collapsed in fits of laughter. The startled evangelist took his leave of us pretty quickly, no doubt thinking we were a bunch of heathens.

My early recollections of childhood are a bit of a blur, but I do remember that Mae took care of me most of the time. She, at sixteen years older than me, was the oldest child, with brother Bob five years younger, and Joan another five years younger. I was the last of the litter, the "runt" as they called me. She had me when she was well into menopause and didn't think it was possible to have another child. But there I was, and there I stayed.

Inevitably, Joan and I were enrolled in St. Teresa's. Joan started school at the age of five, but I was delayed until I was six due to my recurring chest problems (not that it mattered much). I hated school with a passion, a trait shared by all the Stopforth kids.

We were taught and disciplined (some might say abused) by nuns, dressed in their full length black habits, wimples and all, long heavy swinging rosaries hanging from their waists, and an obvious distaste for us kids. Every day was a challenge; however, I always managed to find something to laugh about, which was my downfall. I was often called to the front of class and regularly caned with a ruler on the palms of my hands. And silly me, I'd go home and tell Mum, "I got the cane today." Without missing a beat, she'd thwack me behind the knees with a hairbrush and say, "Well, you must have deserved it."

We had mixed classes of both girls and boys. I remember that when it came to the pecking order, there were always two boys – Casson and Downey (a bit like Butch and Sundance) – who got top marks in all subjects, followed by little old me.

It was a harsh day for me when the teacher handed out notes to select children to take home to their parents to ask if they would like their child to sit for a scholarship to a grammar school. When I realized what was happening, I raised my hand and asked if I could have one. I was sharply rebuked.

"No, your mother wouldn't be able to afford to buy your uniform and books," she said curtly. And that was that. By this time, Dad had died and Mum didn't get a widow's pension. She was in dire financial straits. The priests used to bring us food and the occasional bag of coal to help out. Britain's pension fund was new, and Dad had not made enough contributions for Mum to receive a widow's pension.

Another lasting memory of those days was when Father Murphy, who would examine us on religious knowledge every Friday afternoon, addressed the class. He finished up by saying, "Does anyone have any questions?" I gingerly raised my hand and was told to stand up and ask away. My question was, "Father, if Adam and Eve only had two sons, where did all the rest of the babies come from?" He narrowed his eyes, and hissed his answer to me.

"Sit down child, and don't try to run before you can walk," he replied harshly. All the kids giggled. I squirmed. I felt as if I had done something terribly wrong. And d'ya know, I still don't know the answer to that one!

When World War II came along and Hitler's bombs took their nightly toll on Liverpool, school was no longer an option by the age of eleven. We kids would assemble once a week at the home of Mrs. Farger, 3 Aconbury Close, near my home. We'd check the register (roll call as it's called in America), see who was present, then just have general conversation about whose house had been bombed, whose brothers or fathers had been wounded (or worse), and end with a little prayer. Then off we'd go until the same time next week. We each had to take a half-penny to give our hostess to put in her gas meter to warm up her front room where we met.

I officially left school around my fourteenth birthday. We did not leave empty handed. We received a certificate from the headmaster. I still have mine, which is one of the few possessions I have from my war-torn days.

When I was about eleven, I got a paper route and earned a few shillings a week. It helped pay for piano lessons with the

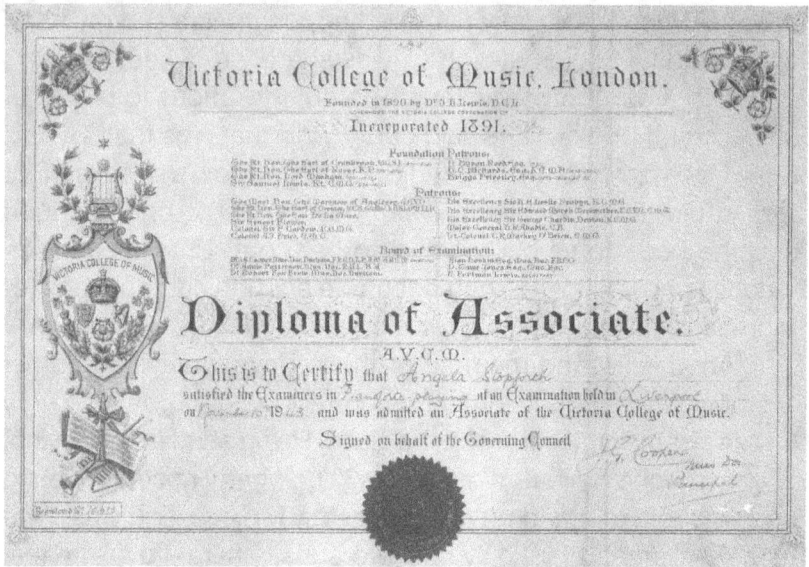

Angie's teaching diploma from the Victoria College of Music, November 10, 1943.

very patient Mrs. Foley, just across Carr Lane from where we lived. She was very kind to me and kept me supplied with sheet music and various tutorial books, and paid my entry fees to sit for my piano examinations with The Victoria College of Music. I was really pleased with myself when I obtained my teaching diploma from the Victoria College of Music in London just a few days before my fourteenth birthday.

I loved practicing. Funnily enough, I have a set of keyboards in our guest room where we live now. When I go in there to make tea in the mornings, I go through scales, arpeggios, and chromatic runs whilst I'm waiting for the kettle to boil. I long ago lost the confidence to play in front of people when my stepson, Mike (McGear) McCartney, said one night, as we were off to a family party, "Hey Ace, if they ask you to play the piano, leave it alone – there's only one star in this family." Up until this point, I had been very unselfconscious about it, and Paul and I would often bang out duets both at home and at parties, but, after that – never again. I'm sure Mike didn't realize what that meant to me, but it was as though my hands had been cut off at the wrists. I'm still working on that one.

Maybe I should send out an SOS to The Speakmans who cure all sorts of phobias!

Learn more about them here (link):

Hilbre Island

I remember when I was very young, we ventured on foot to Hilbre with Mum's friend, Mrs. Mulhearn, and our combined gaggle of kids. We went scrambling over the rocks looking for I can't remember what, whilst the mothers sat and chinwagged, glad to be out of the house for a while. The only problem was that we all forgot the time and, oops, in came the tide, and we were stuck there for the night.

Mrs. Mulhearn yanked out her rosary beads and began praying very loudly, as if she thought that God would be more susceptible to a higher volume of pleas or turn the tide back. For some unknown reason she had a supply of St. Christopher medals and doled them out to each of us, urging us to pray to Our Lord to let us make it through the night. Until then, we kids had been having a whale of a time, with no fears or thoughts of being in danger. It was just a great adventure to us. We found a cave and all huddled together. Mum kept tutting at us for giggling but we thought it was a great adventure. We didn't get much sleep and, as soon as the tide went out in the early hours of the morning, we trailed back across to Hoylake, looking like a right bunch of vagabonds. I haven't been there since. Turned out that Mrs. Mulhearn must have descended from King Canute.

If you watch this video you will be able to imagine how terrifying it was for us kids to be "stranded at sea" overnight (link)!

I did take a view of it last time we were over there, but only from a distance, when Pete Price took us for a trip down several memory lanes. He frequently walks over to Hilbre, and enjoys the solitude. Me? I prefer the bright lights of Sunset Boulevard, thank you.

Being back there a few years ago, I was reminded of the part that area played during World War II. My sister Joan's sister-in-law, Mary, was a lady soldier (just like The Queen), and was stationed a little further up the coast at Formby. She would tell us that when the Germans (a.k.a. zee Germanz) were getting too close for comfort in their submarines, the locals were asked to donate their petrol rations and take them down to the water's edge and set fire to them. This indeed happened and no doubt repelled Jerry[1] at just the right time. Talk about money to burn.

However, a German submarine (U-534) was salvaged in 1993, and since February, 2009, has been on display in Birkenhead as part of the ongoing U-boat story. The U-boat is one of only four German World War II submarines in preserved condition remaining in the world. A Royal Air Force bomber sank her on May 5, 1945 in the Kattegat, 20 kilometres northeast of the Danish island of Anholt. Since it was raised, it has been on display at the Woodside Ferry, on the Birkenhead side of the Mersey. Ruth's husband Martin (who was once a tank driver in the German Army when he was conscripted against his will) was most interested to see this item, which is a big tourist attraction. It certainly brought memories (of different kinds) for us all.

Angie and Pete Price in the Radio City tower studios in 2013.

1   "Jerry" was slang for Germans during World War II.

You can see the historical story here (link):

Another charming little area is Parkgate, which makes me think of Nicholls Ice Cream. Mmm ... Pete Price frequently taunts me with pictures of their lovely ice cream parlour. When Jim was alive, we often headed to Neston for potted shrimps, and then on to Parkgate for the famous ice cream, where we would sit on the sea wall and watch the boids!!! (Filthy, disgusting, lice ridden boids – okay, okay, that's a line from *The Producers*, one of my favourite films, "Springtime for Hitler" and all that.) We watched the birds and happily licked our ice cream cornets like a couple of kids.

Here's a look back at Parkgate over the last 90 years (link):

Ruth attended West Kirby Grammar School for Girls. Julian Lennon attended nearby Calday Grange Grammar School (for boys, of course). It was vastly different then. Ruth hated school with a passion (as did I), but that's another story for another day.

West Kirby is adjacent to Hoylake and has similar attributes. But Miss Ruth couldn't get out of school soon enough, and the day she left (at age 16 in 1976), she and I got in the car and drove to the New Forest in the south of England to visit with our Australian friends, the Crawfords, who had rented a cottage for the summer. I was fairly recently widowed at that time, and not quite sure what I was going to do with the rest of my life. Come to think of it, I'm pushing 90 and I'm still not sure!

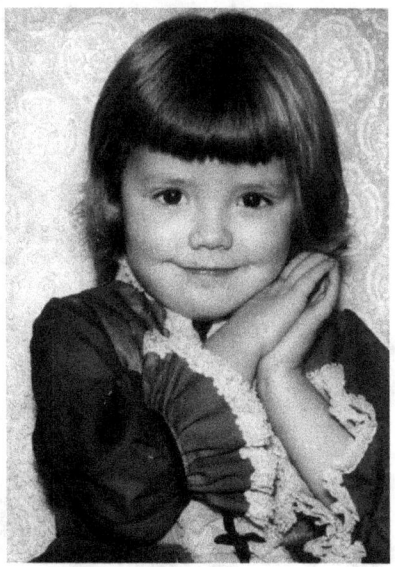

Ruth posing on top of piano in party frock, 1964.

Old schoolmates Ruth and Julian Lennon catch up at The Sunset Marquis in Los Angeles. Photo courtesy Martin Nethercutt.

I urge you, dear readers, to Google the Wirral Peninsula, which is where Rembrandt is, the lovely house that Paul bought for his Dad when he retired and, which, incidentally, he bought for a second time when Jim's arthritis got so bad that we needed to move to a bungalow nearby.

We were saddened to learn that our long-time gardener, Mr. Jack, chose not to stay with us after the move, as he thought we were lowering our standards, moving to a bungalow. Wow! He was a retired postman and part-time gardener. That really hurt Jim.

Ruth and cousin Geraldine with Julian and Cynthia Lennon at Rembrandt.

There was a lovely little park nearby, Dawstone Park, where I would take Ruth for picnics after school when she was a little tot. I can picture her now, making daisy chains and eating jam butties. Nowadays, I'm much more likely to be watching her cook a gourmet meal and choose the wine list! Life was so much simpler then.

Here is what Wirral looked like through her childhood eyes (link):

More Childhood Reminiscences

Recently, I was thumbing through some old photos to see if I could find anything else to add to this book. It set me thinking of my childhood and of the things that are still prominent in my memory.

One vivid memory I have is of a set of building blocks that I received one Christmas. They were all shaped like parts of a house: roof, chimney, front door, windows, garden path, grass and flowers, and white criss cross garden gate, which was exactly like the one at our house at 3 Carr Lane in Norris Green, Liverpool.

And there was a big thick wooden jigsaw puzzle of the three little pigs, which I loved. I am still a jigsaw puzzle junkie and every time I do one I remember my little childhood treasure.

One year I got a pair of miniature brown shoes: "brogues" as we called them in those days. They would fit on my fingers and I would devise little dances, and even do high kicks. Bob Fosse would have been impressed.

I think my favourite toy of all was Mum's green button tin. When clothes wore out, she would carefully remove the buttons and keep them "just in case." I don't recall her ever using any of them, but if there was a need, she'd have been able to rise to the challenge.

I used to tip them out, usually on the kitchen floor, and make all sorts of patterns and dream my life away. I was a little nerd even then.

But the most important artifacts were crayons and colouring books. In fact, I still have some of those today, but of a slightly more adult geometric style. No, you bad-minded people, I don't mean "adult" in that sense. Get your minds out of the gutter. Maybe I should just call them "mature."

As I got a little older, the dressing up box became my escape. I had a weird and wonderful assortment of feather boas, hats, net curtains, grown up dresses, beads, even high-heeled shoes which I would clump around in. I called them "hee highls." I know that sounds a bit Hitlerish, but we had never even heard of that monster in those days.

I also loved building houses of cards (long before the television series was even thought of). And Pick-Up Sticks. I'm sure today's young 'uns would think I was a nutcase. Maybe I was.

Sometimes when I see what parents spend on toys and devices for their kids, I harken back to my childhood and I'm sure I was just as happy with my little collection, if not more. Oh, and batteries didn't need to be included!

As time wore on, I progressed to crossword puzzles, to which I'm still addicted. I have crossword books beside my bed, on the porch outside my office, even in the loo (known affectionately as "the library").

So if the "engaged" sign stays on too long, it's probably because I am pondering over 17 across or 18 down. You may even hear me say, "Ooh, that's a hard one."

The mind is a strange thing – at least mine is. I recently saw a commercial for sweets and chocolates and, for some reason, it triggered a memory of Dad coming home on Fridays when we were kids. He'd bring us Milky Way bars, or were they Mars bars? I only know that we used to get my eldest sister Mae to cut them into slices with a sharp knife so that we could eat them sparingly, making them last as long as possible. Half your luck[2] doing that now – we seem to gulp them down in quick order.

In those days we didn't have the luxury of a refrigerator; that came much later in our lives. Anything we wanted to keep really cold, like milk, Mum would put into a metal bath contraption outside the back kitchen door in cold water with a damp cloth over the top. The Liverpool weather was not much of a

---

2 A British expression.

threat in those days, and it was usually pretty cold, so things would last quite a few days.

Also, we only shopped in very small quantities. Not only because that was all we could afford to do, but also because of the lack of space in our council house kitchen. It also housed the sink (cold water only), a four-ring gas stove, a gas boiler (for washing the clothes, in which Mum stashed her bottle of port or sherry when it was not in use), and a wooden unit with a marble top, which was great for pastry making.

Ooh pastries ... that made me think about the scones and almond slices that my sister Mae used to make. It's a funny thing, but when we recently began sampling Mrs. McCartney's Abbey Road Apple wine with a hint of almonds, it immediately brought back memories of the almond slices from childhood.

I'm very aware of the health and nutritional benefits of almonds, which can be a relief from heart and brain disorders and diabetes. Almonds are certainly our friend. They are so rich in vitamin E., calcium, magnesium, and high-quality protein. And it's good to know that California is the nation's leading producer of almonds (as well as avocados, broccoli, carrots, cauliflower, grapes, and many other nutritious foods). Another reason to love California.

Mum always used to have a handful of nuts in the pockets of her cardy, her dressing gown, even her jammies. And I do believe they really contributed to her long life and tenacity. That, and her amazing spirit.

Excuse me, I'm off to the pantry to get me a handful.

Religiosity, Music, and Other Messed Up Musings

My early schooling was spent at St. Teresa's Catholic School in Norris Green.

We were taught by both nuns and lay people. It is difficult to say which of them was the scariest. I had always been raised to be very respectful to all adults, people in positions of power, doctors, shopkeepers – in fact, anyone and everyone. It was a generation where "children should be seen and not heard." We spoke when we were spoken to, and usually in hushed tones.

That's not to say we had a bad childhood. Far from it. There was lots of music and laughter and fun in our household. Mum had been a choral singer and my father was an accompanist in the British Army during World War II.

He and Mum would regularly attend variety theatres in Liverpool, such as The Pavilion (the Pivvy), and The Shakespeare, (the Shakey). When they'd come home late in the evening, my father would get me out of bed, put a pillow on his lap, and lay me across his knees to listen to him playing the piano, picking up the tunes they had just heard. He was a wiz at playing by ear and instilled a love of music in me that is alive and well today.

He would say, "This little one may not be pretty (thanks Dad!), but by jove she'll be musical if I have anything to do with it." I guess he hit the nail on the head.

During World War II, when we spent most nights in the Anderson shelter in the back garden, I would re-enter the house when we got the "all clear" signal that it was okay to emerge in early daylight hours. Then I'd practice scales and arpeggios, much to the delight of the rest of the family. And then I'd be off to deliver the papers, followed by school (which I dreaded). However, I was always thankful that we had survived to see another day. That's always my first thought even now, when I begin to stir in the mornings. Yippee! I'm still here! At my age, every day above ground is a bonus.

Every Monday morning, school started with Sister Kieron towering over us with a big black book and marking up anyone who had missed mass the day before. And woe betide you if you didn't have a watertight excuse for not being there.

Then there was confession. We were supposed to go every Saturday. I would make up things to tell the priest when I didn't think I had committed any sins. Things like, "I was unkind to my sister," or "I thought uncharitable thoughts about one of my friends." It all seemed so false to me that I should be expected to ask forgiveness for something I had not even done. Bottom line: I was telling lies in confession. Figure that one out.

Thoughts While Folding Laundry

For no apparent reason, except for the weird machinations of my mind, I was folding laundry this morning and a thought popped into my mind. When I was just a snip of a girl, my brother Bob brought home a pair of stockings from his place of work, The Bear Brand Silk Stocking Factory in Woolton, Liverpool. He gathered us all around him to witness the unveiling of this wonderful new invention called nylon! It was made by some magical people in America called DuPont.

They do say that this thread is exceedingly strong and is only surpassed by the strength of a genuine spider's web. Evidently it is even bulletproof. What clever little creatures spiders are; they work every night outside my office window, creating their magic, which catches the sunlight in the early morning or glistens in the rain.

We watched, wonderstruck, whilst he poked his fingers into them, trying to make a hole or a ladder, without success. He said the world would soon be hailing this new fabric as the invention of the century. My sisters, my Mum, and I viewed this with a great deal of skepticism and made all the polite "oohs" and "aahs" as were expected, and promptly forgot about the whole thing.

How wrong we were. Soon nylons began emerging in the marketplace, even in wartime England. I can remember my sister Mae showing me an advertisement in the *Liverpool Echo*, placed by the great Woolworths. They were at that time billed as the "sixpence and shilling" stores, and sure enough, there they were on sale at sixpence a leg. Yes, for the princely sum of one shilling you could procure a pair of these new fangled stockings. In America, they were called the five and dime stores. Same difference.

That was still well before the days of pantyhose (I wonder, what did bank robbers do before their invention?). There goes that mind of mine again.

It's sometimes fun to look back on some of the things that have come to pass in my lifetime, from indoor toilets, to indoor lighting, to telephones, telegrams (from the Monarch when one reached the ripe old age of 100). Now we have artificial intelligence such as Alexa, who can listen to us and feed us requested information. There's also Siri on our phones, dating services, books you can read electronically, and even cloning. Driverless cars and cars you can buy online and pick up at a large vending machine. I wonder what will emerge in the next 90 years?

And most wondrous of all, I have just learned of a toilet roll made by Charmin with approximately 1,700 sheets, enough to stretch from the ground to the top of the Washington Monument. Now which focus group fathomed that one out? They are selling them together with a freebie chrome toilet roll holder which you can either have stand on the floor in the toilet (it'd need to be a flaming big toilet) or affix to the wall (ditto). Oh, and of course, you can have them delivered right to your door. This IS America after all. OK, I'm just being silly now.

If you're still not sure how to put your tights on, watch the carefully crafted instructions here (link):

My Big Sister Mae

My sister Mae was like a mother to me in many ways. Mum was in her early-forties when I was born, so by the time I was an active toddler, she was often tired, and Mae would take over the reins. She was a huge influence in my life.

Mae was beautiful, witty, a great cook, very artistic, and all in all, a wonderful person. I am happy to say that Ruth reminds me of her a great deal. Mae is gone now but I often feel her presence.

She could cook, decorate, garden, ballet dance, write hysterical stuff – it seemed to me there was nothing that she couldn't do. When our dad was going to London to be operated on for throat cancer, his last words to her were, "If anything happens to me, I want you and Ralph (her fiance) to get married and keep the home together."

Two weeks later, he was gone. We never saw him again. Mum brought his body home on the train to the Lime Street Station in Liverpool.

Within a short time, they carried out his wish. Ralph Butchard married Mae Stopforth at St. Teresa's Church in Norris Green, and then moved into 3 Carr Lane with us, where she bore three lovely children: Bobby, Jill and John, all of whom now live in Brisbane, Australia, with their growing families. Thanks to Facebook, we are constantly in touch. It really seems that they are never so far away.

Mae first introduced me to The Goons on British radio. Also to Tommy Handley, Ted Ray, Arthur Askey, the Crazy Gang, and scores of other comedians and entertainers. I would learn many years later that George Martin, The Beatles' producer, made some of The Goons' early records, introducing their brand of zany humour to the public.

I still have some of Mae's cookbook recipes for scones, almond slices, and lemon curd, which I have passed on to "Chef Ruth," who never fails to amaze me with her culinary skills. I have long since given up cooking and am merely her cleanup crew.

We spend lots of happy hours in the kitchen together.

My Little Sister Joan

Born five years apart, my sister Joan and I would fight and scrap, pinch each other and pull one another's hair as little 'uns. Dad used to call us the snarling cats.

I was always a thorn in her side, she being older than I am. I suffered from asthma and was always wheezing and sneezing. When she wanted to go to the park, Mum would say, "take Angela with you. The fresh air will do her good." Joan would reluctantly drag me into the bathroom and scrub my face with a nail brush (ouch). I have often said that it's her fault that I have one arm longer than the other from when she used to drag me.

I remember one Sunday afternoon after lunch, she and her friend Lily Gould took me upstairs, stood me on Mum's bedside table, draped a piece of net curtain over my head, put rosary beads on my hands and said, "Stay there … you're Our Lady." They promptly went out into the garden with their comic books and forgot all about me.

Much later, Mum wondered where I was. Then she came upstairs and found me. In response to her, "What on earth are you doing?" I was swaying, almost asleep. I whispered, "Shhh, I can't talk. I'm Our Lady." I didn't think it was funny. But over the years I've taken to being photographed in locations around the world in the same position. By now the bedside tables need to be well fortified to hold me. Maybe a coffee table book is in my future? What do you think of, "Our Lady and the Bedside Tables?"

After we were slung out of our first married home, first husband Eddie Williams and I lived for a time with Joan and her husband Peter Archer in their Malmesbury Road Corporation house in Norris Green. But that's another story.

Peter's legendary Thursday nights out, with the lads from work, were like a reality show. Thursday being payday in those days, off the boys would go for a few pints in downtown Liverpool, followed by a trip to watch wrestling at The Stadium. The big favourite "baddy" was Jackie Pie, who would not only pulverize his opponents, but would yell obscenities at the audience and make very rude gestures. "Dirty Pie" the crowds would boo him, which made him even angrier. It was nothing to see beer bottles being hurled into the ring.

Peter and his mates would be in fine fettle when they got out of there. They then went in search of whichever pub might serve them a last pint before taking the tram home.

Joan and I were usually in bed before he got home, but on occasion, he'd wake us up, banging on the front door if he'd lost his house key. I remember a night when he tired of trying to get in through the front door and went round the back, finally climbing into the big dog kennel with their two red setters, Pal and Ricky, where he slept it off. He was a splendid sight in the morning when Joan unlocked the kitchen door and let him in. He was wearing his brand new overcoat too, completely covered in dog hairs, which didn't go down too well with Joan.

On another of his attempts to get in through the back door late one Thursday night, he ran at it, crashing it open, landing on the washing machine, which had casters. It took him for a ride through the kitchen and into the hallway, smashing dishes and pots and pans, and making us think we had been invaded by aliens. The cleanup crew (Joan and me), swung into action and finished up laughing at what could have been a tragedy.

On another occasion, I heard him yelling, "Joan, let me in; I've brought my friend to see you." We finally opened the front door to find him standing there with his friend, Frankie Flynn, plus a very large brown horse with a rope around its neck. This was the new friend that they had found in a field on the East Lancashire Road, "... all by himself" as he put it. Joan yelled at him to take it back to where he'd found it and not to bring it back. After much persuasion, he and Frankie tottered off into the night with their equine friend.

Joan and I would have what we called "settling up" night at the kitchen table on Friday evenings, an exercise in financial wizardry. I would pay her something towards the household expenses for rent, electricity and she'd pay me for shared grocery shopping, toilet paper, and other household goods. I would pay her for my Freeman's catalogue installments and she would pay me for my outlay for other miscellaneous items. The "I owe you, but you owe me" procedure would become hilarious, especially as we usually fortified ourselves with a little drop of nasty, cheap wine to help the proceedings along.

Eddie was eventually awarded a low rent house on the Kirkby Trading Estate by his employer, Concrete Utilities. He only had to pay them five pounds a week out of his wages, and we moved away to Southdene where we lived at 3 Spinney Close until Eddie was killed in a car crash in 1962. Within a month of his death, we were forced to get out of there so that the man who took over Eddie's job could have the house. Tough times.

After Joan was widowed in 1993, she continued to live in the same house where we had so many fun times in years gone by. I still remember the address: 26 Malmesbury Road in Norris Green, Liverpool.

In more recent times, Joan and Peter visited us in several of our locations in America and enjoyed our trips to all the tourist spots, which included the Hollywood Bowl, Universal Studios, Disneyland, Malibu, and The Ingleside Inn in Palm Springs, which was one of her favourite places. Over time it became mine, too.

Ruth and I had the pleasure of visiting her in Norris Green when we were in Liverpool early in 2015. The last time I spoke with her she'd just been to see Barry Manilow at the Liverpool Arena. She had fun wagging her light stick and singing along to all of his popular songs. Funny, but I could always tell what the weather was like in Liverpool when I called her. If the sun was shining, she answered with a bright and chirpy, "Hello, this is Joan." But if the weather was its more typical dull and gloomy, the tone of her voice would be lower. It's interesting how the climate has such an effect on people. That's one of the reasons why I love living in California. We may have a few earthquakes and drive-by shootings, but sunshine we got!

Joan was at my first book launch at The Royal Liverpool Philharmonic Hall on January 30, 2013. She was accompanied by her daughter Geraldine and grandson, Paul Archer (look up his great art on Facebook).

Angie, Ruth, and Joan, Liverpool, 2015. Photo courtesy Peter Archer.

Sadly, Joan left us on July 20, 2016, passing away peacefully in her sleep and surrounded by her loving family. She left behind many happy memories, lots of fun stories, and photographs galore.

Because she so loved The Ingleside Inn in Palm Springs, I buried a token piece of her jewelry in the gardens there on a later visit.

On the day of her funeral over the pond in Liverpool, Ruth, Martin and I were all sad and reflective. Friends insisted on taking us out to lunch. When we got home, Ruth was reaching into the back of the car to give me her hand when we both heard a tinkling sound. We looked down and there at our feet was a British two-penny piece with the Queen's head on one side and the traditional emblem on the other. I plan to have it made into a medallion that I can wear around my neck.

Martin said it must be "pennies from heaven" – one each for Ruth and me – compliments of Joan. That really unleashed the floodgates. I also heard from family members that after the Requiem Mass at St. Teresa's Church, as they proceeded to Anfield Crematorium, they heard Joan's voice singing a tune from a CD she had made at her church club a couple of years before. So we all felt that Joan was still well and truly with us. We've been comforted by the outpouring of love that has been unleashed from around the world.

Our Joan Maureen will never be forgotten.

Aunty Em

A lady who made a great impression on me in my formative years was my dear old Aunty Emily, known in the family as "Em." She was larger than life and an imperious character who took no prisoners.

Emily McClarty was my dad's cousin. She and her sister, Mae, were adopted or fostered by Dad's parents in their youth. The Stopforths and the McClartys all grew up together.

By the time I got to know her, she was living in London in somewhat impoverished circumstances with her sister Mae. Her husband had moved on.

She was tall, austere, and had a booming contralto voice. She looked very much like Queen Mary, and had a fantastic wardrobe and a collection of paste jewelry acquired during her days as an opera singer. She used a lorgnette with sweeping gestures and addressed people, "Look here, young man/young lady," or whatever befitted the occasion. Imperious is the best way to describe her.

Mum used to take the train to visit her occasionally, and the two of them would tarry forth into central London and have a rare old time. Mum would come home with hilarious tales of their doings. One time they had afternoon tea at the Dorchester Hotel, and when Emily saw the bill, she was prompted to go into the ladies' room and take down a gold coloured velvet curtain and stuff it into her voluminous carpet bag. She figured it was her due in light of the price she had just paid for their refreshments.

Another time, they attended a movie matinee, and a man sitting behind her asked Aunty Em to remove her hat, as it blocked his view of the screen. It was big enough to have had its own zip code. She withered him with a glance and replied, "Sir, if I take off my hat, my bloody hair comes with it. Go and sit somewhere else." He did.

During World War II, when food was rationed, Aunty Em was waiting in line at her local butcher's shop when she heard a young woman who was being served say, "Please charge it to my account; I am Mrs. McClarty." Upon which the incensed, forsaken wife of the philandering Mr. McClarty belted out, "No you are not! I am the only Mrs. McClarty. You are the slut that's living with my husband."

You just can't make this stuff up.

She stayed with us in Liverpool one time and asked my sister Mae to take her to our local hairdresser on Scargreen Avenue in Norris Green. When the hairdresser asked her, "Madam, have you ever bleached your hair?" She replied, "Young lady, I have had my hair every colour but heliotrope, and I hate heliotrope." The poor gal quivered and had to excuse herself for a few minutes. Such was the effect that she had on people.

But I think her most classic yarn was of the time she gatecrashed the Princess Royal's Wedding at Westminster Abbey, in February of 1922.

She arrived by taxi, and had discovered from combing the pages of Debrett's Peerage, that there was no current Lord Inverclyde. She made her exit and told the first policemen that she encountered, "I'm Lady Inverclyde, my husband has already gone ahead, and he has our invitation. Please escort me to him." The unsuspecting cop, who couldn't leave his post, called out down the line, "Lady Inverclyde," and it was repeated and repeated, the echoing chorus "Lady Inverclyde" until she reached the military guards at the entrance to the Abbey. She was ultimately ushered into the historic building. Once inside, she slipped into one of the rear pews where she witnessed the entire ceremony before slipping out again at the end, mingling with the cheering crowds and finally making her way back to her one-bedroom flat, by taxi, at the end of a very exciting day.

Liverpool

Wartime Liverpool was vastly different from the vibrant city we know today. We lived a few miles outside of the City Centre in a district called Norris Green. It was full of council houses, but with electricity and indoor plumbing, so it was a step in the right direction. We lived just across the road from St. Teresa's Church and School, and the 14 tramcar ran beside us, going all the way down to the pier head. It was a place that dreams were made of.

One of my earliest recollections is attending Sunday mass in the morning, sometimes with rain and hailstones rattling on the corrugated tin roof of the church.

When I was five, my dad took me on his shoulders to King George and Queen Mary's appearance at the opening of "Kingsway," a.k.a. The Mersey Tunnel. I recall standing across the road, in a big crowd, and watching King George deliver a speech and declare the tunnel open. Although this was generations before "selfies," Dad bought me a long stick, with a mirror on the top, so that I could hold it up above the crowd to better see what was going on.

After the dedication, the public was allowed to walk through the tunnel, which our family did. My only lasting memory of that is that my oldest sister, Mae, lost the heel off one of her shoes and completed the trek in bare feet. How we got back I don't remember, but we probably took the ferry back to the Liverpool side.

How that occasion forever changed Merseyside. Later, in 1971, the Kingsway Tunnel was built. I made the trip (both ways) through the Mersey tunnels on my visit to Liverpool in 2013, when my first book was launched. That was a memorable trip in many ways.

Here is a video (link) of the day the Queensway Tunnel opened in July 1934. See if you can spot me!

When September 1939 came around and World War II broke out, my brother Bob donned his Territorial Army uniform and went off to the local barracks to sign up. We saw him off on the number 14 tram, crying and waving our handkerchiefs at him (none of your Kleenex nonsense in those days, my girl), and heard our first Air Raid Sirens, and watched a barrage balloon going up over Scargreen Avenue Shops (the Strand) a few yards away.

How anyone could have imagined that these contraptions would have deterred the German planes from coming to bomb the bejeezus out of us, I can't comprehend. But they did. Likewise, with the Anderson shelters, our little corrugated metal paradise that the soldiers erected outside of the back kitchen door where we dutifully spent our nights.

We just took it in our stride (being vewwy Bwitish), and whiled away the hours doing crossword puzzles, singing, quizzing one another on spelling bees, and chanting our multiplication tables. Boy, we sure knew how to have a good time.

We had, by this time, been turfed out of school, which was housing less fortunate folks whose houses had been bombed.

In the early mornings when the "all clear" sounded, sister Joan and I would go back into the house, have a wash, brush our teeth and hair, and set off on a daily walk around the area to see what damage had been done overnight.

Sometimes, when I see wartime movies on TV, a rush of memories come flooding black.

The good part was that we didn't go to school any more. One day a week we would assemble in a local house. (I have written about this separately.)

The centre of the city was badly bombed. I didn't go down there often during those times, but when I did, it made a lasting impression on me. One of the things I remember most is the smell and the smoke, which spiraled and curled upwards for days after a building had been demolished.

Maybe Liverpool should have been renamed Phoenix, another place that rose from the ashes.

Ladies "Going to Bed"

In my youth, there was never a mention of anyone being pregnant or "with child." Instead, gals in the pudding club were referred to as "going to bed." I often used to wonder what was wrong with all these lazy bitches in our circle who were partaking of this pastime until, eventually, I came home one lunchtime from school to find the local midwife's bicycle parked at our gate. Bear in mind, I was eleven years old and, apart from some hushed conversations between my Mum, eldest sister Mae, and various friends who visited, with the kitchen door firmly shut, I had no idea there might be something afoot. Boy, was I in for a surprise!

I remember an overwhelming smell of Dettol in the house. It's a strong antiseptic that makes me gag to this day. Mum came bustling through and asked me to come upstairs as she had a surprise for me.

Indeed it was a surprise to walk into my oldest sister Mae's bedroom, totally unprepared to see her sitting up with a little white woolly bundle in her arms, containing my first nephew – Bobby Butchard. My initial reaction was of shock and anger, that this little red-faced creature had taken over my territory. I was convinced that nobody would love me anymore.

I can't stress how important it is to share these things with other family members, as it made a mark on my already delicate psyche that has never fully healed. When little Bobby was a toddler, I had no time for him at all. It was really unfair as he was a sunny natured little boy, but, as the years wore on, we became friends rather than adversaries. He lives in Brisbane, Australia now with his lovely family. Through the wonders of cyberspace, we are in touch constantly. He respectfully refers to me as his "Tatty Aunty."

I guess my mother should have known!

Fred Astaire and Ginger Rogers

Although I personally never met the legendary Fred Astaire, I was a huge fan of his films, especially the ones where he paired up with the great Ginger Rogers.

When supermodel Twiggy (now Dame Twiggy) was visiting with us at Rembrandt one time, she told us that when she was at the zenith of her fame, she was entertained by Astaire at his Bel Air home. She said she was mesmerized to be in the company of this charming man. She told us it was a memory she would forever revisit when, as she said her goodbyes and left, he not only accompanied her to the front door, but danced her down the steps to her waiting limo.

Many years later, my daughter Ruth found herself stopped at a traffic light in Beverly Hills alongside the great entertainer, who was driving his brown Rolls Royce. She made a gesture of bowing to him, and he responded by doffing his Fedora in her direction, with a gracious smile. She too was bowled over, and said she drove home about six inches above the ground.

Why don't we have any stars like this anymore? I recently watched a lovely documentary about Ginger Rogers on Turner Classic Movies that was narrated by Nigel Lythgoe. The documentary contained several fabulous clips of her stints with Fred Astaire, as well as many other roles in dramatic movies. She made 73 movies in all and yet is mostly remembered for the ten she made with Fred Astaire.

You can see a snippet here (link):

On one of my first visits to Palm Springs some years back, I went on a tour of the stars' homes. One of the stops included the lovely, but simple, home of Ginger Rogers in Rancho Mirage. She spent her retirement there and became a prolific painter. She belonged to the Church of Latter Day Saints and lived quietly after two strokes had left her wheelchair bound. According to her assistant, Ginger still liked to have friends over for movie nights.

There is a famous quote about the two entertainers: Ginger did everything Fred did except backwards and in high heels! She has stars both on the Hollywood Walk of Fame and the Palm Springs Walk of Fame. I know she is remembered worldwide and still beloved.

Her Majesty Queen Elizabeth II

From a very early age, I have followed our royal family, by whatever means possible, be it newspapers, magazines, and, now, electronically. I have always been fascinated by our royals and their activities.

During World War II, we were inspired by our present Queen's parents when they would get out in London in the mornings after being bombed by Hitler night after night. They walked amongst the rubble and the ruins to talk to the people, giving them what little comfort they could, encouraging them to hang on to their good old British grit and determination. Theirs was the kind of support that money couldn't buy.

Our Queen's father, King George VI, had so much to face when he was plunged into the monarchy by the abdication of his brother, the Prince of Wales, who abandoned his royal duties to marry divorcee Wallis Simpson in an unheard of dereliction of his duties.

His ultimate death plunged his eldest daughter, Elizabeth, into the monarchy during a safari in Kenya with her husband, Prince Philip. She had to don black clothing and fly back to England and step off the plane as Queen Elizabeth II, a noble position that she carries to this day with grace, dedication, and total loyalty to her sovereign leadership. I consider this lady to be an incredible human being, ruler, mother, and all-around inspiration to her loyal subjects.

Consider the changes that have taken place in her lifetime: mind-boggling to say the least. From the simplicity of communications to her making her first radio address to the nation, and then on to television; the media onslaught that has become part of her daily life; the changes in social media and communications; scandals, divorce, and all that comes with it. She now has a Twitter account. Imagine that.

Her children and grandchildren have been a large part of guiding her into what we now know as the digital age. At her advanced age, she is still so communicative and inspiring to her subjects, old and young alike.

She was even persuaded to appear with Daniel Craig, who was playing "007" in a filmed spoof during her Silver Jubilee celebration.

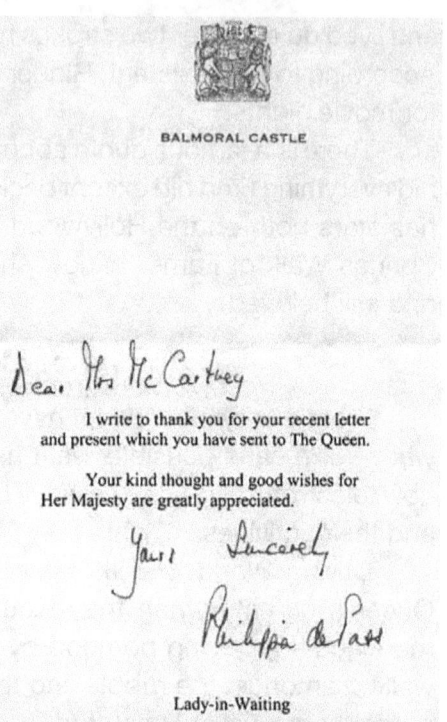

Upon sending Mrs. McCartney's Teas to Her Majesty, I received this thank you note.

I find it endearing to learn that Prince Philip's favourite nickname for her is "Sausage."

God save our gracious Queen.

Here is a lovely look back though 90+ years of our magnificent Monarch (link):

Racism

Way back when I still lived in England, Jim and I used to watch a lot of American TV. I didn't fully dig some of the humour, traditions, and social situations, but once I came to live in the United States, that really changed.

I was also never really aware, or had seen racism up close until I came to the United States. Liverpool is a seaport city with a population of many colours and creeds; nobody thought much about it. Everyone lived and worked together with no problems whatsoever.

This was brought home to me one day when I picked up four-year-old Ruth from Kirkby Day Nursery (kindergarten) on the outskirts of Liverpool. As she left, a little black girl was tearing up and waving "bye bye" to Ruth. As we walked away, I asked her who was that? Her response was, "Oh, do you mean the little girl with the striped socks? She's my friend." That was the only thing in particular she had noticed that set her apart from all the others. It was interesting to me, and I realized that, until we start putting labels on people, young kids don't even think about it.

I was pretty shocked when I lived in Southern California some years later, a historically liberal state, and discovered that it was an issue – and it still remains such. I guess I will never understand.

Merseyside had had its brush with slavery in the early days when the ships from Africa would pull in to Liverpool to take on fresh supplies. In nearby Neston and Parkgate, across the river Mersey, there are big rusted metal rings where they tethered these poor souls when they brought some of the slaves ashore to sell them before setting off on the final stage of their journey to America.

Liverpool was a major trading port and its ships and merchants dominated the transatlantic slave trade in the second half of the 18th century. The town and its inhabitants derived great civic and personal wealth from the trade, which laid the foundations for the port's future growth.

The precise reasons for Liverpool's dominance of the trade are still debated by historians. Some suggest that Liverpool merchants were being pushed out of the other Atlantic trades, such as sugar and tobacco. Others claim that the town's merchants were more enterprising. A significant factor was the port's position, with ready access via a network of rivers and canals to the goods traded in Africa – textiles from Lancashire and Yorkshire, copper and brass from Staffordshire and Cheshire in the North, and guns from Birmingham in the Midlands.

Even though the shame of this dubious past is still a part of Liverpool's history, it has led to a great melting pot of cultures, cuisines, and music. I am proud to say that in my hometown, diversity is not a dirty word, and no matter where your ancestors came from – Africa, the Caribbean, Scotland, Ireland, or China – we can all put the kettle on and sit and talk football over a nice cup of tea. It has also led to a very diverse sense of humour.

But, when it comes to intolerance, don't let the football supporters get started on that one, either in Liverpool, Manchester, London, Scotland, or many other places. Start up those discussions and people will be asking you, "Do you like hospital food?"

Bessie Braddock, M.P.

Bessie Braddock ("Battling Bessie") was one of my earliest recollections and example of a powerful woman. She was originally a member of the Communist Party and later shifted to the Labour Party in Liverpool. This, at a time when it took iron courage for a woman to even attempt to enter politics.

She represented one of the city's toughest areas, and was very outspoken when it came to pushing for the rights of the working classes. She was also a big supporter of boxing, a sport made popular through the Catholic churches, which would encourage young boys to join after school activities to keep them out of trouble. In the early 1940s, both parents were mostly out working in order to make ends meet, leaving an army of "latchkey kids" to roam the streets.

When Bessie Braddock became a member of Parliament, she was up against the good ol' boys network of better educated and rather snobby folks in the House of Commons. Her adventures in Parliament were the stuff of legend. She wasn't afraid to stand up for herself. She was the first woman ever to be suspended from the House for her constant attacks on the Speaker of the House when she would vehemently oppose the procedures. But she just wouldn't back down. After a time, she even received grudging appreciation from the members on both sides of the aisle for being so persistent in having her issues considered.

I became aware of her through the *Liverpool Echo*, but my personal experience kicked in many years later.

After my first husband, Eddie Williams, was killed in a car crash in February 1962, I was left as a single parent with two-year-old Ruth. We lived in 3 Spinney Close, a house on the Kirkby Trading Estate outside of Liverpool. It belonged to his employer, Concrete Utilities. I had to vacate it about a month after he died in order for Eddie's replacement to move into the property, which was a condition of the post.

After unsuccessfully applying to 47 addresses from ads culled from the *Liverpool Echo* every night, I was at my wits' end. In those days, people would bluntly say, without even inviting you inside, such gems as, "We don't take kids" or "Is she yours? Sorry, we don't want kids." It was brutal.

One day after I finished up at my Mum's house, I related my tale of woe. Unbeknownst to me, Mum wrote to Bessie Braddock at the House of Commons in Westminster, telling her of my plight. She even fessed up to the fact that I didn't even vote for her! Within a couple of days, Mum got a personal letter back on official House of Commons notepaper, telling her to direct me to the Liverpool Housing offices. Then, on presentation of this missive, they would give me the keys to a flat on the Kirkby Trading Estate.

Mrs. Braddock used her influence for someone down on their luck, and luckily for us, we had the security of a roof over our heads once more. As a side note, the man at the Housing Office tried to kiss me across the counter, in the tiny cubicle, even with little Ruth beside me. I was only in my early thirties then and my reflexes were quite sharp. I grabbed the key and got the heck out of there faster than a small dog on fire. Thinking he had the last say, his parting words were, "I'll be coming to see you one of these nights." My first task was to have the locks changed, and I was nervous for a very long time.

I was so broken in those days. If it were now, I'd be giving him a quick swipe with my handbag. But, of course, things like that no longer happen to me! I guess 89 is the new cut-off for these guys.

But then again – have a look at how it was for women in the '60s with these unbelievable sexist "contests" for "birds." There was no #metoo back then!

Scan this code for a look back (link):

Football Clubs, Derby Games, Blood & Guts

As far back as I can remember, there has existed a tremendous rivalry between the supporters of Liverpool and Everton football clubs.

It's a rivalry which originated, as so many British soccer teams do, from Catholics versus Protestants. This is not isolated in Liverpool, but many other cities base their support on similar beliefs and values. Celtic vs. Rangers, Manchester United versus Manchester City; the list goes on and on.

I became even more aware of it when I worked for Littlewoods Pools, first in Edge Lane, and then Walton Hall Avenue in Liverpool. I was shocked to find that supporters of one team would not even sit at the same canteen table as their rivals, so strong was the animosity between them.

Incidentally, the Edge Lane Littlewoods building was later going to become a great Liverpool Film Production facility, but was stopped in its tracks by a massive fire in mid-2018.

There was a tendency for fathers to name their male offspring with eleven names of the current "A" list players of their chosen team. Poor kids. Imagine growing up with that legacy!

I'm sure you don't need me to tell you that red is the Liverpool colour, and blue represents Everton.

That reminds me of the comment someone recently made that parents only give their children a middle name so that they'll know when they are REALLY in trouble.

But I digress.

The Merseyside derby games were a time for caution. There was much bottle hurling and riotous drinking before, during, and after the game. There were monumental punch-ups after the final whistle blew. I had a friend who was a barman at a Yates Wine Lodge in Liverpool who told me that a man, riding a blue and white striped donkey, tried to ride him into the bar when they had won a derby game against Liverpool FC. He quickly had to call the "bizzies" to avert a bloodbath.

The origin of the derby is unclear. It is thought that it might originate from games played in Darby, for centuries, three days before Ash Wednesday, with hundreds, yes, hundreds of players on both sides.

I suppose that's appropriate, as the derby borders on religion.

You can view Gerry Marsden getting a thunderous reception when he appeared and sang You'll Never Walk Alone at Liverpool FC, Anfield, to celebrate their hometown heroes' success in Spain in June 2019. That's when they won the European Championship for the sixth time. It was certainly a hot time in the old town (link).

A Woman's Place

It's incredible how much life has changed in the span of my years on this earth. In my childhood and youth, women were to be seen and not heard. Wives and daughters were expected to be totally submissive.

In our household, manners were of supreme importance, but feminine matters were taboo when the men and boys were around. I can remember the day when I began my first menstrual cycle. I was at a matinee at The Regal Cinema on Broadway in Norris Green, Liverpool, and realized that something had happened to me. When I got home and told Mum, she "shushed" me and hustled me upstairs into the bathroom to clean up. She gave me a big ugly pad of cotton wool to stick inside my undies and brought up newspaper to wrap up the offending items and put them in the dustbin in the back garden (plastic bags had not been invented then). I had the feeling that I had done something rather shameful. She told me never to speak of it around Dad or brother Bob, and to make sure that they never saw any evidence of my condition.

The only thing she said was that my body was changing and getting ready for the day when I would be able to have children. Perish the thought! If this was any indicator, I didn't want to know about any of that other stuff.

Obviously, sex was never mentioned in our house. I was 26 when I married my first husband, Eddie Williams. On the eve of my wedding, Mum said to me, "I suppose we should have a talk about what you are going to have to face." (Sounds like my dad must have had a groovy sex life.) I politely said that I thought I knew as much as I needed to and would deal with it.

But one sage piece of advice she did give me was that the way to a man's heart was through his stomach. She certainly got that right.

After we got married, Eddie and I took the train from Liverpool Lime Street Station to London to stay in a pub owned by a friend of his. Once there, we celebrated with the locals in the bar until closing time. Then we got to trying out Hula Hoops, which were all the rage, and then finally tottered upstairs to bed. We were both pretty far from getting into anything ambitious, so the night drew to a fairly uneventful close.

I really didn't know that much about "it" and, to this day, people laugh in my face when I say I was a virgin until I got married at the ripe old age of 26. I'd probably get my own reality show now! Hey, maybe that's not a bad idea.

The word pregnant was never uttered out loud, nor on the telly. I can remember our next door neighbour, Mrs. Kelly, telling Mum that so-and-so was "going to bed." I couldn't for the life of me imagine why that would have to be shared with the hand covering the mouth in hushed tones. Aha, she meant that person was in the pudding club!

Great Truths that Adults have Learned

- Raising teenagers is like nailing jello to a tree.
- Wrinkles don't hurt.
- Families are like fudge, mostly sweet, with a few nuts.
- Today's mighty oak is just yesterday's nut that held its ground.
- Laughing is good exercise. It's like jogging on the inside.
- Middle age is when you choose your cereal for the fiber, not the toy.

4
They Say It's Your Birthday

In the late stages of my pregnancy, I had left my permanent job at Pure Chemicals and was working part time, mainly from home, for an insulation firm on the Kirby Trading Estate, GB Insulations. I had been having blood pressure problems and my general practitioner figured it would be safest if I was admitted to Walton Hospital early to avoid complications.

The lovely people tried all the things to try and coax little Ruth to make her appearance, but that didn't seem to be working. So they waved their magic wand (or was it a catheter?) and set me on the road to being induced.

And so the real adventure began. I believe I was some twenty hours or more in the process of delivering this little person on February 15, 1960, who would become the most important human being in my life. I have a woozy recollection of them finally taking her from me, slapping her butt, wiping her down, and putting her in my arms. I know it sounds crazy, but I still remember the final moments of her being born, an incredible moment, and her little cry as she blinked her way into the world. I even dream about it sometimes.

Ruth Nearly Meets God

Do I believe in miracles? Indeed I do.

After I was widowed for the first time and life was bleak, I decided to do something to cheer us up. I joined a travel club through the *Sunday Express* in England, and divvied up a few bob here and there until I had enough saved to book us a cruise.

We set sail out of Southampton on *The Empress of Britain*, bound for the Mediterranean, with several ports of call on the agenda.

A young man I knew was a crew member and, although we were unable to meet up much due to staff regulations, at least I knew I had a friend aboard. I had a strange sort of premonition that this was going to be a life changer.

The trip itself was fabulous. I think I paid 64 British pounds for the ship, plus our train fares to and from Liverpool, and an overnight stay in a cheap bed and breakfast the night before we boarded. It was so exciting. Yet all the time, little Ruth was her usual quiet self, not reacting very much to anything but cuddles and bedtime stories. I made some lovely friends: Carys and Gwen, two Welsh girls who were fun, friendly, and loving with Ruth. We all went ashore together at each port of call and it really was like a wonderland. We went ashore at Malta, where I remembered with fondness their bravery in World War II. In Tunisia, we were warned not to travel as ladies alone, but to ask a crew member to watch over us. We even visited the Casbah, which I had only seen in films. At Gibraltar, we saw the Barbary apes leaping about crazily. In Sicily, our shore trip included seeing an amazing American marching band, which further whetted my appetite to visit their amazing country. And we finally made it back to Southampton.

With so much sunshine, we were regularly advised to protect ourselves from its rays, and we all complied. And whilst we girls all got a nice golden tan, little Ruth remained pale. I had that gut feeling that something was wrong.

When the trip was over, I immediately took her to our local general practitioner for an examination. He said he couldn't really find anything wrong. By this time her hair was coming out in tufts, and I was convinced something was seriously wrong. I insisted that he give me a note of authorization to take Ruth to Alder Hey Children's Hospital for further tests (talk about trusting your gut feeling). Thank God I did. They drew blood, and within a couple of hours, she was admitted as a patient and scheduled for surgery immediately to remove her diseased right kidney. The next few days were a blur. The nurses arranged a bed for me in an office at the end of the ward. I went home to Spinney Close in Kirkby, packed a few things, made a quick side trip to Mum's house in Norris Green, and got back to the hospital as quickly as possible. There was no extra money for taxis in those days, so buses were the order of the day. My boss, David Oakes at Pure Chemicals on the Kirkby Trading Estate, was most kind, offering me use of a company car and driver to help me.

The surgery was quickly scheduled for Sunday, May 17, which was a bank holiday weekend. They couldn't carry this out until she had been given four pints of packed blood cells. That will tell you just how close to death she was. I was almost out of my mind with fear and anxiety. Not my baby, not my lifeline. I remember my brother Bob turning up at the hospital briefly, and I was impressed that he had driven all the way from Yorkshire. He had an idea of what I was going through, having experienced a similar patch when his first born, Margo, was diagnosed with polio.

Margo, by the way, is another miracle child. She is a proud mother and grandmother, still braving it out in Yorkshire. And she is still the big Kahuna of the Stopforth and Hanstock families.

But, back at Alder Hey Children's Hospital, Ruth began to emerge from the anaesthesia. I was beside her, together with a few of the nurses, who, by this time had come to love her.

Nurse Ruth at Liverpool's Alder Hey Hospital, June, 1964.

She put her hand on my cheek and sang the song, "I love you because…" We had often heard it on the radio, sung by Jim Reeves. When she got to the end of it, she shut her eyes and drifted back to sleep. You can imagine what we were like. Tears flowing, hugging one another, and that was the moment that I truly believed in miracles.

Little did I know what life held in store for us, and that within a few short months I would meet Jim McCartney, become his wife, have him adopt Ruth, and give her his family name. He made us feel secure and sheltered for the first time in our lives.

So do I believe in miracles? Hell yes!

Ruth and God

When Ruth was discharged from Liverpool's Alder Hey Hospital in June, 1964, after having a kidney removed, we visited my mum on the way home to our little one-bedroom flat on the Kirkby Trading Estate.

She was still very frail, pale, and her hair was coming out in tufts. But she was very excited and alert to be going home, and I remember her tightly clutching her teddy bear, Mr. Ted. We stopped off at 3 Carr Lane to see my Mum.

As we were about to leave, her loving Nanny said to her, "Now don't forget, tonight when you say your prayers, thank God for making you better." She pondered for a few moments and then piped up, "Why, Nanny, I didn't shout at Him for making me sick?"

"Out of the mouths of babes and sucklings hast thou ordained strength." (Psalms 8:2 Bible)

"Out of unconscious lips of babes and sucklings are we satirized." (Mark Twain)

Take your pick!

Ruth Draws God
By Ruth McCartney

When I was about three, I was a kindergartener attending daily whilst Mum went to her day job to earn a whopping five pounds a week. One day, the teacher gave us all paper and crayons and asked us to draw God.

Now that was an interesting assignment

Since I couldn't quite conjure up what God looked like, I decided to go a bit "abstract" as it were. I coloured in the whole page with navy and black and then smushed some white and yellow blobs on top and handed it in. I know, smart arse, right?

When it was my turn for the "show and tell" bit, the teacher, clearly bewildered by my approach, just handed it to me and said "Go on, then…"

Quite indignantly, I explained to her that, as no one in our class had ever actually MET God (yet), I had drawn the night sky to represent God's blanket. When asked "How is this a blanket?" I explained quite simply that since God was sooooooo old, there were BOUND to be holes in the blanket that the stars shone through at night, which was, in my considered opinion (at three mind you), why the twinkling lights were in the sky at night – as the sunlight was shining through said holes.

So there you have it. The cosmos solved. Sorry Stephen Hawking. Move over Neil deGrasse Tyson. It's all just an old blanket.

Ruth's Domestic Tips, Part 2

Foam milk without a frother.

So maybe you don't have a fancy-schmancy espresso machine with attached milk steamer. We can't help you on the espresso front, but we can tell you how to get frothy, creamy, delicious milk foam on the cheap! All you need is a small jar with a lid. Fill the jar with a little milk (no more than halfway) and shake what your mama gave you (or your leftover jam jar) until the milk has doubled in size. Pop off the lid and microwave the milk for about 30 seconds.

Save fresh herbs for later use.

Use an ice-cube tray or muffin tin to freeze fresh chopped herbs in water, olive oil, or stock for later use as a seasoning agent.

Cool down coffee without diluting it.

Fill an ice cube tray with leftover coffee (cooled to room temp) and let the cubes set in the freezer. The coffee cubes will keep an iced cup of joe from becoming watered down. You can even customize the cubes by adding milk and sweetener.

Remove icky cooking smells from your hands.

Neutralize garlic- or onion-scented hands by rubbing them with lemon juice, baking soda, or stainless steel. Why stainless steel? When you touch the material, the molecules in the steel bind with the stinky-stanky-causing molecules (such as sulfur from garlic).

Keep wooden cutting boards looking new.

Scrub a wooden cutting board with coarse salt and massage with half a lemon to clean away food particles and food smells. Rub the board with food-grade mineral oil (find it at a hardware store) to condition the wood once a month.

Use frozen sponges for cheap lunch box ice packs.

Soak several sponges in water, then seal them in separate Ziploc bags. Freeze, then pack them in lunch boxes for a quick, and inexpensive ice pack. The sponges will melt, soak up the water, and freeze over and over again!

Interesting tips you may consider:

- Adding 1/2 a teaspoon of baking soda to the water before you boil eggs makes them easier to peel.
- Use empty Tic Tac containers for spice storage.
- Did you know that eggshells help rose bushes to grow? The nutrients contained in the shells are a great benefit, especially if you crush them up and deposit them under the surface of the soil surrounding the bushes.
- If you are going to beat egg whites for a recipe, let them sit at room temperature first for about 30 minutes, and then they will beat up to a much higher volume.

5
When I'm 64

The Cotton Man

Due to a fall in which he broke one of his eardrums, Jim McCartney was unable to join the military during World War II. Instead, he was an ARP Fireman, patrolling the streets at night during the regular bombings of the Merseyside area.

However, Jim's condition led to him having more hearing perception in his good ear than the average person.

He worked for Hannay & Co., cotton merchants in Liverpool, who would send him down to the docks to meet the incoming ships bearing cotton from various points around the world.

I never realized, until listening to Jim, that Liverpool was so influenced by the cotton trade, but its history is steeped in it. Evidently, during the early 19th century, brokers from all over the world lived in Liverpool, from places like Germany, Russia, India, USA, Greece and many more.

A lot of Liverpool's early wealthy people made their fortunes from cotton. Many of them lived in fine houses, mainly in the Sefton Park area.

The power behind the trade were the dockers, the clerks, and boys who ran around passing messages from company to company, the warehouse men, and many more. These people were all of a much lower rank and earned far less money than their bosses.

There was a rumor that cotton bales formed the foundation of The Liver Buildings, but I guess we will never know if that is true.

As far back as the 17th century, cotton arrived in Liverpool via London from places such as the Middle East. This later extended to Brazil, Egypt, and India. By the middle of the 19th century, cotton accounted for almost half of the city's trade. It's been recorded that one and a half million bales were imported.

From there, they went to the Lancashire mills to become finished goods, and Liverpool then exported about half of the recorded exports by 1901.

There's an area in the city called Exchange Flags. This is where many of the brokers opened their offices and, whilst there was an official Cotton Exchange building, many of the merchants preferred to do their trading out of doors.

By 1906, a purpose-built Cotton Exchange was commissioned with new technology of the time, such as telephones and telegraph lines, which played an immense part in the progress of the trade. They even boasted having direct cable access to the New York, Bremen, and Bombay cotton exchanges.

You can learn more by visiting the Maritime Museum site of Liverpool. For real history buffs, this contains a mighty amount of information so we can have a peek into how life was in our beloved city in those far off days.

According to our Mike (in his informative, and now highly collectible book, *Thank U Very Much*), his dad took a train journey from Liverpool to Manchester's Cotton Exchange every couple of days, having moved up through the ranks from being a sample boy, earning 6 shillings a week. Then, in 1930, after 14 years on the job, he progressed to cotton salesman. Imagine the feeling of pride that it gave him when Paul bought him Rembrandt, a lovely mock Tudor house in the upper class area of Heswall on the Wirral Peninsula. He couldn't believe his good fortune.

While other inspectors would need to do extensive testing to determine the grade of the cotton, Jim could merely break off a small piece, hold it to his good ear, rub it through his fingers, and know immediately, from the sound, what staple or grade it was. This was a terrific advantage for his employers, who could decide immediately whether to buy or not. He was much respected by them, as he was such an asset to their marketing techniques.

Shortly after Paul began to see some of the financial benefits of his membership of The Beatles, Jim was able to retire.

Angie walking down memory lane outside Rembrandt in 2013.

Many years further down the line, when Jim's arthritis made it necessary to move to a bungalow, Paul decided to buy Rembrandt for a second time, which he retains today, and stays whilst in the Liverpool area.

Here is some history on the Liverpool Cotton Exchange (link):

Jim McCartney at the Movies

I've seen so many changes in my lifetime, including what's happened with the movies. When I was a little kid in Liverpool, we could go to a Saturday matinee at the Regal Cinema on Broadway in Norris Green for a penny. Yes, you heard that right... one penny!

Then, gradually, as technology progressed, that all changed to the whirlwind of choices that we have now.

My late husband, Jim McCartney, used to play the piano in the orchestra pit at the Clubmoor Cinema in Liverpool. He had to totally ad lib to the silent films, having not seen the picture before its current showing. He looked back at a time when he was completely stumped. It was the funeral of The Queen of Sheba, a very solemn scene. While the audience was whimpering and crying at the sad state of affairs, all he could think of to play was a music hall ditty of the day, "Horsey, Keep Your Tail Up." Fortunately, as they were so distraught, the audience didn't seem to notice.

Ever resourceful, Jim would go into the auditorium after the early performance ("first house" as it was called), and scoop up all programmes that folks had dropped. He'd race back home to Scargreen Avenue in Norris Green on his bike, iron them with his Mother's flat iron, and dash back in time to re-sell them for three-pence each for the second house. We always knew he'd go far!

Today, we have so many outlets. In addition to network television, there's streaming devices, cable television, Netflix, Amazon, Roku, Hulu, and heaven knows what else. And still we hear people say all too often, "There's nothing to watch."

Meeting Jim McCartney

Meeting Jim McCartney opened the door to a new and exciting life. We were still picking up the threads of our life, since Ruth had had a kidney removed earlier that year. I was struggling to keep a job and pay our way when the earnings rule in England was £5.00 a week. If I earned more than that, I had to go to the Social Security office and declare it, and have my next Widow's Pension payment reduced accordingly.

Then, meeting Jim and deciding to make a life together, seemed like the dawning of a new day, and indeed it was. He was kind, considerate, patient, and ever "gentleman Jim," taking little Ruth into his heart. Beyond that, he legally adopted her, giving her his name, and freeing us from the anxiety of our financially tricky times.

That period in our lives taught us so many things, and took us to so many places around the world that we had previously only dreamed of ever visiting. This enabled us to make lasting friendships, experience other cultures, and gave us exposure to the entertainment business. Truly an experience that money couldn't buy.

Marriage and Marzipan

My first meeting with Paul McCartney was on the night that Jim had proposed to me. Ruth was tucked up in bed at Rembrandt.

It was a modest four-bedroom house, with incredibly only one bathroom. The house was in a very nice neighbourhood and certainly more "posh" than I was used to.

Jim and I had sat on two long black "pleather" couches in the lounge room. It also had long burgundy velvet curtains, dark green carpet, and a central fireplace. We talked for hours about what we wanted to do with the rest of our lives. Mine had been somewhat difficult since Eddie's deadly car crash. Jim was also widowed eight years earlier, when he lost his beloved wife (and the boys' mother), Mary from breast cancer. He was pretty isolated, living in this lovely, but lonely house, with views of the River Dee and North Wales. It had a half-acre back garden, where Jim could grow vegetables and flowers, and a greenhouse with vines for making wine. But a house is not a home.

However, the constant trail of fans made it difficult for him to go out of the front of the house, and he relied on his sisters, Milly and Ginnie, to come every Monday to look after him. They did his laundry, changed the beds, cooked, and did all the work of a housekeeper. He had never learned to drive, so daily routines like grocery shopping, visits to the post office, and visiting family and friends were a chore. The onset of arthritis hindered him from being as active as he would have liked.

We talked a lot about our lives, our loneliness, and our need to take the next step. Whilst I was playing the piano, Jim came behind me, and put his hands on my shoulders.

"I want to ask you something," he said. I looked up at him and said, "The answer's 'yes.'" He laughed and said, "I haven't even asked you the bloody question yet." I guess that was as close to a proposal as I was going to get. So we toddled back over to the couch, and Jim said, "We both know we need to do something, but what would you like to do? Do you want to be my housekeeper? Or do you want us to live together? Or do you want to get married?"

I said I would only want to consider getting married, as I was concerned about little Ruth growing up with a mother who was living with a man that she wasn't married to. I was pretty old fashioned, and looking back, it served me well. This sat well with Jim, who said he would need to let Paul know, as his son provided him with his lovely home.

It didn't take long. A little later, the phone rang. It was situated in a little cubby hole under the stairs. Jim picked up the phone, and it didn't take a genius to figure out who it was.

"Hello son. Yes, she is. Yes, I have. Yes, we are. Just a minute son, I'll put her on the phone," Jim said. My knees were knocking. Paul was obviously checking up on a) whether I was there, b) if his dad had asked me to marry him, and c) if we were going to do the deed.

I'm not sure who was more nervous on the phone. I said a timid, "Hello" and he countered with, "Hello, this is Paul." Then he said, to break the ice, "You sound nice," or something equally fatuous. He said he was going to hop in the car and drive up. In those days it usually took a good three hours to drive from London to Merseyside. So drive he did, and when Jim heard the Aston Martin roaring up the noisy gravel driveway, he nipped through the kitchen to open the garage doors so he could drive straight in, douse the lights, and come into the house through the kitchen. Mind you, by then it was the wee small hours of the morning when there weren't any fans lurking. But that was rare.

I was washing teacups when he came in, and we exchanged fumbling greetings. Of course, I put the kettle on again. We chatted, and then he asked me to get Ruth out of bed. She was in her little pink flannelette pajamas. I sat her on his knee, she was rubbing her eyes, and when the penny dropped, she said, "I know who you are! You're on my cousin's wallpaper." I was mortified. My niece, Geraldine, had a little Wendy house at the bottom of their garden in Malmesbury Road, Norris Green, with

Beatles wallpaper. That sure broke the ice! Then Ruth lifted up her pajama top and showed him her scar, where she had had her kidney removed just five months earlier. Paul told her that Ringo had appendix scars too, and in no time, it was like we had all known each other forever. It was a surreal moment in time to watch my young daughter chatting away with a Beatle as if she somehow knew we all just put our pants on one leg at a time. She's still the same to this day.

Jim and I planned our nuptials promptly. The next day Jim sent a car through the Mersey Tunnel for my Mum to come and stay with us as a chaperone for a while. Paul had to go back to London for recording commitments. Whilst we were finishing his laundry and he was packing his things, Mum made him some sandwiches ("butties") for the journey. A couple of hours after he left, Paul called from a payphone in Brownhills in the West Midlands. Cellphones? Never 'eard of 'em. This was in the days before the M6 and the M1 used to actually connect. Paul asked to speak to my mum. He thanked her for the marzipan butties. She didn't have her glasses on when she'd whipped them up, and had thought it was cream cheese.

On our wedding day a few weeks later, Paul sent us a telegram. It read: "Wishing you long life and happiness...and lots of marzipan butties."

The Bells Were Ringing...

Jim and I married on November 24, 1964, after taking a taxi from Rembrandt on the Wirral to a little chapel in Carrog, North Wales, where the Rev. Buddy Bevan performed the ceremony.

Jim had phoned ahead and set up the ceremony with Buddy, and we first drove to St. Asaph Cathedral to pick up the licence. On the way there, we asked the taxi driver if he would be willing to be our best man. I'm sure he was asked many things during rides, but this request had to throw him for a loop. However, when we arrived at The Rectory in Carrog, those plans were ditched in favour of another strange idea. It was suggested that Grif Jones, the local gravedigger (affectionately known as "Grif The Grave") be our best man. Mary Bevan, wife of the rector, was going to be my matron of honor. Grif was dispatched

Rembrandt, the day after our wedding, November 25, 1964.

home to clean up, and duly returned in his Sunday best. I will always remember his long hands dangling from the sleeves of his navy blue suit.

To my chagrin, no photographs were taken of the ceremony. Buddy's wife, Mary, also served as the organist. As we walked down the aisle, in true Beatles fashion, she played one of their songs. It appeared that she was all too excited to play something more traditional. We did at least get "The Wedding March" on the way out. Mary was the sister of Mike Robbins, who figured in our lives monumentally.

After the ceremony was done and dusted, we had libations across the road at The Rectory, and returned to Rembrandt in the taxi. When we got back, my mum, Edie, along with Jim's sisters, Milly, Ginnie and Edie, were all ready and waiting (yes, two Edie's for the price of one). Ruth was dolled up in her party frock, which I had bought from the local dress shop the day before. Bette Robbins, Jim's niece, who had introduced us lovebirds, was also there.

They had conjured up a wedding cake and some champagne from The Victoria Hotel in Heswall, just down the road from Rembrandt. A small celebration ensued, and guests left early in the evening. We put Ruth to bed and sat in the lounge, awkwardly finishing off the last of the champagne.

After the famous "marzipan" telegram arrived from Paul, we were also touched to receive a nice congratulatory telegram from Beatles manager Brian Epstein, wishing us both a great future together. Where was a scanner when you needed one?

When Jim and I retired to bed, it wasn't long before we were aware of noises, and lights flashing up at the bedroom window. The back garden at Rembrandt at that time led on to an empty plot of land, and the journalists and fans had somehow got wind

Angie and Jim in the garden at Rembrandt, 1967.

of the event. For some reason they were flashing their lights at the house. Fortunately, Ruth was sleeping at the front of the house, so she wasn't aware of the activity. I did then, and for a long time after, try to keep her shielded from the circus that would become Beatlemania.

A *Daily Mail* journalist, whom Jim had dealt with before, got through on the phone, and arranged to come by next morning to do an interview. This was all a little bewildering to me, and rather exciting. I had no idea how this would develop as time went on. The day after Jim and I were married, we spent time at Rembrandt with the press, going through all the usual hoops of questions, and pictures. I was a real novice at all that stuff in those days. Jim had told me to be very circumspect and guarded in my answers to their questions. I made pots of tea and poured whiskies and beers for them all, and tried to be the unassuming wife and submissive partner that I knew was my expected role.

I was horrified to find when the press boys were visiting, one of them actually followed me out to the kitchen and tried to hit on me! Today I would have smacked him in the kisser, given him a few choice words, then dared him to print that for his story. At that stage I was so afraid to put a foot wrong that I shrugged it off, loaded up a fresh tray of refreshments, and took it through to the lounge.

I found that when it came to all things Beatles, it was wise to keep your best foot forward. And your lip zipped.

HELP! I Need a Honeymoon!

Two months after Jim and I were married, Jim asked Alistair Taylor, Brian Epstein's personal assistant, to book us a trip for a honeymoon.

Early in February, 1965, he arranged for us to fly to Nassau, Bahamas, where the boys were filming *HELP!* It all seemed very exotic to me. At that time, Ruth was a co-member of my British passport, under my former name of Williams.

We flew from Liverpool on BOAC to London, then transferred to our international flight. We were very distressed to

When I'm 64 67

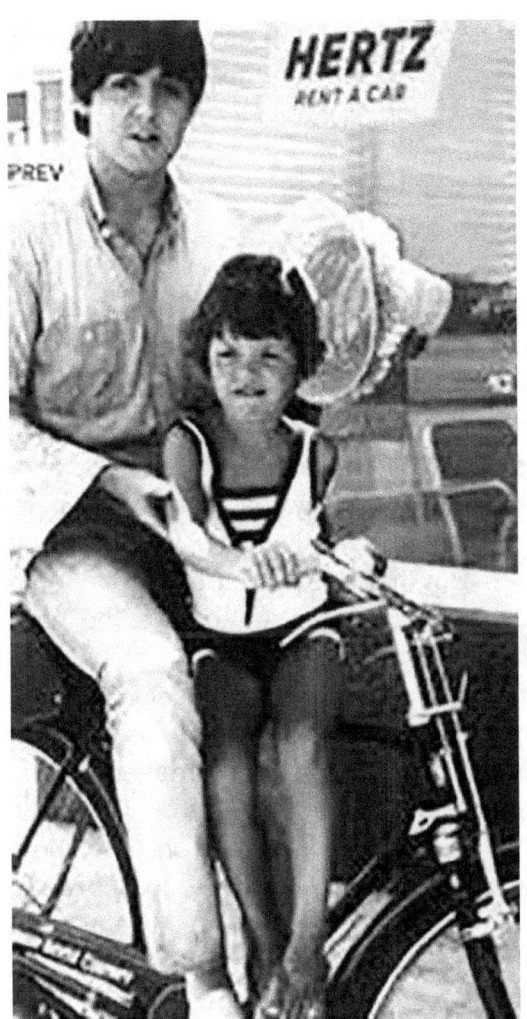

Paul, Ruth, and a bicycle...

find that Ruth didn't appear to be on the passenger list. I was listed as Mrs. Angie McCartney and she, as Ruth Williams. Somehow this had slipped through the cracks. After some explanations, it was remedied, but Jim was very upset.

"This is bullshit!" he muttered under his breath. He then vowed to legally adopt Ruth when we returned home and put McCartney at the end of her name. This he did with all haste.

We were well taken care of at the wonderful Balmoral Club, where Ruth celebrated her fifth birthday on February, 15, 1965. The chef, a German man whose English was not exactly on the ball, made her a special cake. It read: "Happy Birthday Ruth, Jah, Jah, Jah!" We assumed "Jah" was German for "Yeah, Yeah, Yeah!" This was one of many occasions which, on reflection, should have been recorded on camera. But at least we still have our memories.

Ruth was befriended by a lovely little American girl, Robyn. I can't remember her last name, but she took Ruth under her wing, and guided her through the delights of the swimming pool. I wonder if she will ever read this and check us out. She was very lithe, and had lovely long blonde hair.

Whilst at The Balmoral Club, we witnessed the arrival of Senator Ted Kennedy, who was sporting a neck brace. He had been in a plane crash a few months earlier. Being a greenhorn from England, I was not aware of who he was. There was a flurry of his "people" making the arrangements for luggage.

The history of his crash is here (link):

We were sitting in the lobby at the time, waiting to be picked up by one of Brian Epstein's drivers, to take us to the filming location. The manager of the resort served tea to everyone. I remember us making small talk with the dear departed Senator Kennedy and his wife, Joan. Wow, if only I had known about my future plans for Mrs. McCartney's Teas, I could have really done a bang up PR job on him. But that was yesterday…

Brian was most solicitous during our stay, despite the many duties he had regarding the movie's production. One night as we dined under the stars and palm trees, the local wandering musicians came to our table and played "Yellow Bird (Up High in Banana Tree)." Jim gave them a more than ample tip. From that point on, any time they saw us, they made a beeline in our direction, even following me to the ladies room one evening. I distinctly remember them playing that flaming song outside of the window whilst I relieved myself. I still laugh to this day when I hear it, and remember their pursuit of me in the loo.

Brian sent a car for us each morning to go to the location where the boys were filming, and it was fascinating. There was one particular scene where they were on bicycles riding around in a circle. Paul had the line, "A man's gotta do what a man's gotta do." For some reason, the sound was not being captured to director Richard Lester's liking. I was flabbergasted at how many takes they had to go through in the blazing hot sun until Lester was satisfied.

Filmmaking is not as easy or glamorous as most people think. So much of it is "hurry up and wait," sitting around in the trailers or whatever other shelter they have, often in makeup, costumes, and wigs. Makeup artists also had to stick around to do touch-ups to keep the film's continuity. In those days, they had to take Polaroids to keep track of how everyone looked and to ensure everything was as exactly as before.

It appeared to me that there was no real rapport between the boys and actress Eleanor Bron, who was the female lead in the movie. While they were nice to her, she was more middle-class and well-educated than they were. I remember seeing her shoot a scene where she and Ringo had to dive into the water. She was wearing a cloak, which spread out in the water and covered her head. Ringo seemed to just flail about, and later told Dick Lester that he couldn't really swim. But he was certainly game enough to go for it.

We didn't ever see Eleanor in the evenings, either in the restaurant, or the bar, so I guess she must have retired to her room early, probably to prepare for the next day.

I recollect that the boys were pretty laced on something most afternoons. I think it's been well documented they were smoking a lot of pot, even whilst working, which seemed fairly acceptable. Poor Dick Lester would have to do take after take, whilst the lads were giggling their silly heads off. But he was very patient with them, although I can't imagine how much footage was wasted (like the lead actors).

Dick and his wife brought their little son with him. The boy was very hyper, and perpetually running around on the set. I remember that Jim, ever the strict disciplinarian, was horrified at how little control the parents had over his behaviour.

We had some great evenings in the bar with fun people like Roy Kinnear and Victor Spinetti, who was an absolute hoot. After a few refreshing adult beverages, his Welsh accent would become more and more pronounced, causing great hilarity. Journalist Donald Zec was often on the scene, and he too had lots of funny anecdotes to add to the mix.

British Actor Leo McKern (the baddie) regaled us with stories of his many adventures in stage and films. Because of his persona in the movie, the boys hissed and booed whenever he came into the bar. A real Bahamian pantomime scene. He was a very jovial man and such an experienced actor, and everyone was a little in awe of him.

He was an Aussie by birth, but had come to prominence on the London stage, appearing in all the classics, from *Uncle Vanya* to *A Man for All Seasons*, and later in the television series, *Rumpole of the Bailey*. He made no bones about having a glass eye. He had lost an eye in an accident when he was fifteen and came to terms with it, even finding it a distinct advantage in many cases, as it singled him out from many other performers. He didn't seem to be at all embarrassed to talk about the loss, even threatening to take it out one night in the bar for a bet. I left before that line of chatter got any more out of hand.

Many happy memories of that memorable trip. Certainly a honeymoon to remember.

Scan this code for a look back at the film scene of the boys departing for Nassau (link):

Leaving Liverpool for the Wirral Peninsula

Once married to Jim in November of 1964, Ruth and I moved from Liverpool proper over to Heswall on The Wirral. When people read about Liverpool, they usually think of The Cavern, The Liver Buildings, and all of the iconic touristy things that relate to The Beatles. But, what many people don't realize is that, across the other side of the Mersey ("over the water" as they say), is another very different area. It's a more green grass, horsey type of place. It's where Paul bought his dad a house called Rembrandt, on Baskervyle Road, Gayton, Wirral, in Cheshire County.

My old friend and songwriter, Don Woods, has made several lovely videos that you can find on YouTube.com about the many faces of Merseyside. I urge you to take a look. There are many lovely little villages tucked away in unexpected places, trails to hike, horses galore, training stables, and sweet old fashioned shops. You will find thatched roofs, country pubs; places that seem as though the 21st century has passed them by. And, in my book, that's not a bad thing.

If you didn't scan the code on page 18 with your mobile device, you can do so here and wander along the Wirral Way with dear Don (link):

Ruth, Angie, and Pete Price at the scene of the crime in Parkgate.

Oh, and then there's Nicholls Ice Cream in Parkgate. Mmm... I can't write about that place without drooling. Pete Price frequently taunts me on Facebook with pictures of their latest creations, such as whisky flavoured and caramel and raisin ice cream. A pox on him for that!

It was the kind of area where, when Ruth was growing up, she was safe to ride her bicycle to her friends' houses. Once there, they would play out in the garden, with such simple pleasures such as dressing up, swinging on the backyard swings, creating little concerts for themselves and families and friends, and indulging in the really simple life, which is all but gone now, sadly.

Ruth went to the Heswall Village School called The Puddydale, and later to Gayton County Primary School, which was just paces away from our home at Rembrandt. We often went to Dawstone Park after school for picnics, to make daisy chains, and spend time being calm and uncomplicated. I so often wish we could revisit those days. But time marches on.

Her later spell at West Kirby Grammar School for Girls was a period in her life that she tried to forget. Ruth hated school with a passion. That's something else we have in common.

I used to go every Friday morning to Malcolm, a hairdresser in the lower village (I believe he is still there), and would smuggle in a bottle of sherry to share with my friends Gill Rowlands and Betty Thomas, being the first Real Scousewives of Lower Heswall. In fact, Malcolm turned up to my book launch at the Royal Philharmonic Hall in January of 2013. We shared a few memories of those old days, I can assure you.

Ruth and Paul on the porch at Rembrandt.

Another recollection I have is of Ruth's friend, Sheena Moylan, whose father was interested in the history of Hitler. He had watched several documentaries on the dictator, and his pet parrot picked up some of the sounds of the madman, which he would spout out when you walked into their house. He would yell "Heil Hitler!" and frighten the bejeezus out of us all. He had the exact guttural delivery of The Fuhrer, too. That was a great conversation opener.

My stepson, Mike (McGear) McCartney, was married to a lady also named Angela, and we had accounts at the same shops in the village. You can imagine how that lead to endless complications with our bills. Although we both had different addresses, (they lived in Lower Heswall), the locals had a job wrapping their heads around this, and we were constantly setting them straight. And, of course, need I say more, than that Ash & Nephew, the

Angie and Paul at Aintree Racetrack to watch Drake's Drum.

local wine shop, were utterly confused, particularly as we both did so much entertaining. Our bills from this establishment could almost equal the national debt.

Drake's Drum, the racehorse that Paul bought for his dad, was moved from his Yorkshire training facility with Colonel Lyde, to a local establishment called Crossley Farms. I recently found out the place employed none other than Freda Kelly (yes, "Good Ol' Freda"), but we had no knowledge of that, because it was after she had ceased to work for Brian Epstein and The Beatles.

After Jim died, I figured that the best thing to do was to give Drake's Drum back to Paul, and he relocated him to the South of England where he and Linda could keep an eye on him. She was very knowledgeable about horses. I have a photograph hanging on my office wall of Jim, with Drakey, in the Crossley Stables. Drakey knew I was afraid of him, and he often took advantage of this, nibbling at my hair, or even biting the button off my butcher

Jim with Drake's Drum at Crossley's Farm.

boy cap one time. This was the only time in my life that I was in proximity to such a large animal, and his size and strength used to scare me. But he was mostly a gentle creature, and brought much happiness to Jim.

Michael (McGear) McCartney

My dear stepson, Mike McGear, is one of the gentlest, kindest, and most artistic people on the planet. Yet, being born as the second son to Mary and Jim McCartney, he has never been fully recognised for his many facets and God-given talents.

When Jim and I decided to get married, at very short notice, Mike was away on tour with The Scaffold.

The Scaffold was a satirical group that consisted of Mike, Roger McGough, and John Gorman. They were three diverse and brilliant minds. They played clubs, small theatres, universities, and The Edinburgh Festival, and had a very interesting career in theater and television. They also made a couple of successful records.

The Scaffold even made it on to talk shows in America, and unfortunately for one guest, who was touting the ridiculous "Paul is Dead" nonsense, Mike was in the audience as a show guest that day and here is how – in a nice British manner – he took the guy to pieces! Scan to watch Mike talking about the old days, singing in Forthlin Road, and lots more family musical history (link).

The Scaffold's hits included chart-toppers such as "Thank U Very Much," "Lily The Pink," and another called "Dance The Do," for which he invited his young stepsister Ruth to be the choreographer. This involved her taking a solo train to London to demonstrate her steps to the BBC's dance group, Pan's People, who would perform the dance for the video clip. This was quite an adventure at her young age.

I didn't realize until later that Jim never really told Mike about us. So it must have been an awful shock for him to find he was getting a new stepmother and stepsister, and we would all be living together at Rembrandt. Much to Mike's credit, he never showed me his shock, dismay, or whatever he was feeling at the time. He arrived home late one Saturday evening, with fellow group members and their (then) lady manager. The house was crowded with aunts, cousins, and my Mum, all there to celebrate Jim's engagement and impending nuptials. Mike took it all in his stride, but I would have been horrified had I known that this was his first knowledge of the plan. I still don't know what transpired between Jim and Mike on the subject of our marriage.

A couple of days later, Mike had to go on the road again. He was not around when we finally tied the knot.

I never quite understood, at first, what exactly it was that Mike did. He had, by then changed his name to McGear in an admirable move, so as not to appear to be riding on the coattails of his big brother Paul.

One Saturday morning when Mike was having his first pot of tea with us at the kitchen table, he told us he had met a young lady the previous night at a local club, also named Angela. He said he would be bringing her to meet us that afternoon. Angela Fishwick was a local girl, and we got on splendidly. Her parents, Edith and Frank, and Jim and I formed a great bond. In no time, the family was just automatically extended. Frank played the piano, as did I, and we had many musical evenings at our house, their house, and Frank's golf club in Leasowe.

When Mike and Angie arranged their wedding, it was in the same place where Jim and I tied the knot – the Parish Church in Carrog, in North Wales. Paul and Jane Asher stood for them as Best Man and Maid of Honour. They bought Ruth a pageboy outfit (yes, why would they do anything as conventional as a bridesmaid's dress?) and she attended them, carrying Angie's favourite stuffed toy, Piglet, to be a part of the celebration. They too were married by the Reverend Buddy Bevan, brother-in-law to Mike Robbins, keeping it all in the family.

We held the reception at Rembrandt with a cast of hundreds. They included Tony Barrow, the PR man for The Beatles, and lots and lots of colourful celebrities. I recently found a photograph that one of the family members took in the back garden.

They moved just a few blocks away to their own dear little place called Sunset, in the Lower Village of Heswall, where Angie proved to be a wonderful cook and homemaker. They had three lovely daughters, Benna, Theran, and Abbi, who, through the wonders of the internet, can now communicate with me from across the pond and across the planet.

Outside the chapel in Carrog after Mike and Angie's wedding, June 8, 1968.

Sadly, their marriage didn't stand the test of time, and they moved on to other partners, other lives, and other pursuits. But I will always remember those times with Mike and Angie as happy ones, and his delicious sense of humour and whimsy.

I remember Tim Rice (then partnering with Andrew Lloyd Webber) telling me that he thought Mike's talent even surpassed that of Paul's. But, with his older brother's monumental success having come first, the world would never learn this fact.

Paul produced an album for Mike in 1974 called *McGear*, and enjoyed their collaboration. Paul had also given Mike a camera for his 21st birthday, which began his love of photography. I'm happy to say it has continued, leading to many successful books, exhibitions, and tours right through to the present. Long may he reign!

Angie (Fishwick-McCartney) has left this mortal coil, but her spirit lives on through my grandchildren. Mike is again happily married to a sweet lady, Rowena, and they have three beautiful and talented sons: Josh, Max, and Sonny. The circle of life continues.

We were delighted to learn that he was included in the Queen's Birthday Honors list of June 2019. Our dear Mike was awarded a British Empire Medal for his services to Merseyside in arts and culture. I can only imagine how proud Jimmy Mac would have been to know that both of his sons have been honoured by The Queen of England.

Mike also celebrated the re-mastering and June 2019 re-release of his *McGear* album (a new deluxe edition), which was produced by big bro Paul at Strawberry Studios in Manchester. This was marked by a ceremony at LIPA in Liverpool a few days later, attended by fellow Scaffold member John Gorman, and emceed by Pete Price.

This is available on Amazon.com and all fine record stores.

Recently, I delved into my treasure trove, and was glad to find my copy of the original vinyl album, together with the press release, lyric sheets, and welcoming letter that was issued with our family copy. This has traveled around the world with Ruth and me over the years. Linda was also featured on the record, along with the esteemed Brian "Saxophone" Jones, who is still going strong and does a lot of work for local charities. He also worked with us on the various Gary Glitter tours, which he writes about in his recent book, *Sax and Drugs and Rock n Roll* (available on Amazon.com and Brian's website, briansaxjones.com).

Ruth and I always call Mike on his birthday on January 7th, whether he needs it or not! We also keep tabs on him virtually, as he is finally getting "with it" on the cyber front, so we can follow his activities on his website. He even Tweets now...clever boy.

Listen to UK radio personality Richard Oliff interview Mike in 2014 (link):

Rembrandt Rocks

You could truly say that from 1964 to 1976, Rembrandt rocked! Mike McGear often came home to Rembrandt with various friends and hangers-on. Let's just say those moments never failed to entertain.

I remember one night when Jim was away in Mexico, at his nephew Keith McCartney's wedding, and my mum, Edie, was staying with me. We were awoken in the middle of the night by loud music and the distinct smell of bacon. Mum and I donned our dressing gowns and went downstairs to investigate. Imagine our surprise and horror to find two very tipsy young girls with frying pans on the stove burning the heck out of bacon, whilst sloshing down glasses of wine. We offered to take over before the house was burned to the ground.

That was the night that we found the hilarious and utterly brilliant late, great Freddie Starr in the lounge, making an appearance from behind the long maroon velvet curtains that shielded the bay window area from the main room. He was doing a very unseemly impression of Marlene Dietrich, singing "Falling in Love Again." Trinity member Brian Auger was there, and playing the piano in a masterful manner.

Watch Freddie's "best of" impressions (link):

On Ruth's seventh birthday, she came home from school in the afternoon to prepare for a tea party with her chums. But she went upstairs to find a supine Rod Stewart fast asleep in her bed! She has oft been heard to make comments to the effect of, "When Rod Stewart was in my bed…", of course, always failing to mention that she was a seven-year-old child at the time.

Another one of Mike's memorable house guests was Billy Connolly. That was after Mike had married Angie Fishwick and moved into Heswall Lower Village. It was at a Christmas party at Rembrandt, and the house was overflowing with guests. At one point Billy decided to jump out of the upstairs landing window with a little plastic Batman parachute from a cereal packet. How he managed to land on the gravel without hurting himself, I will never know. Maybe that parachute really slowed his fall.

The next morning, Boxing Day, Angie McGear called and asked me if she could borrow some items for their breakfast. So Ruth and I headed over to dispense a few goodies. As we pulled up the driveway, there was Billy Connolly, in red boxer shorts, attempting to vacuum up the snow on the front porch! Ah, those were the days. Here is the "best of" dear Billy (link):

Mike also brought Dusty Springfield and Madeleine Bell to Rembrandt one night. I distinctly remember it was the first time I had ever tasted vodka, but certainly not the last. Mike asked me to be sure to buy some vodka for Dusty. When they arrived, for some unknown reason, they both sat under the grand piano in the living room. I remember being appalled when the supremely glamorous Dusty whipped off her wig to reveal a flattened down and plain head of hair in a stocking cap. That was a fun night.

Mike was also friendly with Paul Jones of Manfred Mann. They and The Scaffold once played a gig at The Liverpool Playhouse, and Ruth and I went to the show.

The next day, Paul Jones visited us, and it was the first time he ever met Ruth. He obviously took a shine to her, as he used to send her the odd postcard from London every now and then. She was very impressed. We also had a lovely evening with Paul and Barry Ryan of The Ryan Twins, who were very popular at the time. They were also charming house guests.

First Christmas in London

It was December, 1964 and, with great excitement Jim, Ruth, and I travelled by train from Lime Street in Liverpool to Euston Station in London to spend our first married Christmas with Paul and the Asher Family.

Paul met us off the train in his Aston Martin, and drove us to our hotel in Russell Square. I remember that, as we were cruising along, Paul and his dad were busily chatting. We were in a traffic jam as he slowly glided into the car in front of him. He lightly touched the bumper. It wasn't a big collision, but the lady driver jumped out in a great state of wrath, and stormed towards the car.

She banged on the window, which Paul slowly lowered. It was amazing to see how quickly her demeanor went from "What the hell?" to "Ooh, can I have your autograph, please?" He quickly complied, and she tottered back to her car in amazement. As the traffic moved away, she kept looking back over her shoulder. She just couldn't believe her luck, both good and bad.

On Christmas morning, Ruth and I took a taxi to mass whilst Jim relaxed at the hotel. While we were stopped in traffic, a very inebriated man opened the door of the taxi and staggered inside. Ruth clung to me in fear. The driver immediately got out and slung the guy out onto the street.

When we got to our destination, I proffered the driver what I thought was an adequate tip. It evidently was not, as he threw it on the pavement.

"Here lady, you keep it!" he said. "Obviously you need it more than I do." Oops. My first real taste of the big city.

Christmas Dinner was served at the home of Dr. Richard and Margaret Asher on Wimpole Street, an elegant section of London. They were the parents of Jane Asher and the household was where Paul was living at the time. The place was a yuletide dream. I had never seen such a massive Christmas tree. The fireplace was roaring, and lots of presents were sitting under the tree. There was a long, magnificently laid table, with crystal, beautiful place settings, decorations, Christmas crackers, candles, and all. Margaret Asher carried in the turkey, Richard carved it ceremoniously, and all the trimmings were laid on the table. After that, we had brandy soaked, lighted Christmas pudding, with sixpenny pieces and little trinkets buried inside. It was like a true Dickensian Christmas.

In addition to the presence of Dr. and Mrs. Asher and their daughters, Jane and Clare, was their son, Peter, with his musical partner Gordon Waller, who sadly passed away in 2009. At the time, Peter was dating a young lady called Betsy Doster, the publicist for recording artist Sam the Sham. It all seemed very exotic to me. Peter & Gordon. Jane Asher. A Beatle. A far cry from paper hats and roast chicken back in Norris Green.

Ruth's face was a sight to behold. This was like a fairytale to her. We sang carols, ate, drank (well, the grownups did anyway), and were merry. They had presents for us all under the tree. Even the wrappings with beautiful paper, golden ribbons, and tinkly bells, were a sight to behold. After the meal was over, we all traipsed down to the basement to burn the Christmas paper in the boiler.

Jim had great affection for Richard Asher, who spent time with him up North at Rembrandt. They used to go for walks together in Heswall Lower Village and sit in the back garden and do crossword puzzles. As a memento of his visit, Dr. Asher sent Jim an Oxford English dictionary, which I still have. It was one of Jim's most treasured possessions.

As a sparsely formally educated man (although very gentlemanly and worldly wise), Jim was extremely flattered to have the attention of a man of such great intellect and good standing, both in his community and the medical research field.

Richard Asher was a physician at the Central Middlesex Hospital. He'd combined clarity of thought, deep understanding of the everyday problems of medicine, and possessed a sparkling wit. It was he who gave Munchausen's syndrome its name in 1951, after the famous Baron who travelled widely and told tales that were both dramatic and untrue. In 1947, he was amongst the earliest to identify the dangers of institutionalization.

His wife Margaret was a professor at the London Guildhall School of Music, and taught George Martin to play the oboe. She also taught Paul to play the recorder whilst he was living on the top floor of their house in Wimpole Street.

We were indeed privileged to be so hospitably received in their magnificent home. I remember as I walked in, thinking that I had never seen so many books in my entire life. The hallway was lined with beautiful leather-bound books.

On Boxing Day, Paul picked up Ruth from our hotel mid-morning, and took her to visit Alma Cogan, the very popular musical star, whose name, at one time, was linked with Brian Epstein. Ruth recalls that it was like a palace out of a picture book. Alma's apartment was the scene of many parties around that time. It was said that she was England's highest paid female singer in the 1950s and '60s. She played host to such diverse people as Noel Coward, Tommy Steele, Danny Kaye, Princess Margaret, Michael Caine, Roger Moore, Cary Grant, Sammy Davis Jr., and countless other stars.

There was even a little buzz that John Lennon may have had a little something going with Alma for a time, which even Cynthia Lennon thought might have been true. There was an even less likely buzz that there might have been something between Alma and Brian Epstein.

Scan this code (link) to see John Lennon introducing Alma singing "Tennessee Waltz:"

After that, it was back into the car and off to the Hammersmith Odeon for the Beatles Christmas Show. No rest for the wicked!

You can see their silly greeting by scanning the code (link):

While all good things must come to an end, London in the Sixties was a magical time, and Ruth and I were privileged to have had a taste of it.

Jim's Gems

Jim had many funny sayings, which were usually prompted by a question from Ruth. It went something like this:

"Daddy, why does...?"

He would reply, "Cos there's no hairs on a seagull's chest."

Or, if Ruth would ask a particularly hard question, then Jim would say, "It's imposausigable."

He used to say that the two most important words were: "tole" and "mode" – meaning toleration and moderation. It was how he thought one should live one's life.

Another ditty was, "If you can't say anything nice, don't say anything at all."

Another amusing anecdote he told me was that, when he was a kid, his father brought home tobacco from Cope's Tobacco Warehouse, where he worked. He sent Jim to deliver some 'baccy' to a neighbour and to say, "If my Dad asks me how much did you give me, what shall I tell him?"

He had not only a great sense of humour, but also a great sense of right and wrong. He was so humble, appreciating his financial position once Paul had reached fame. Paul bought him a house and promised to take care of him financially, which, in turn, made Jim generous to a fault. He was the only person I knew who would tip the cashier at the entrance to the Mersey Tunnel!

Upon reflection, I think Jim tried to overcompensate for his good fortune, having had such a frugal upbringing and so many tough times raising his two boys after Mary died, trying to be both father and mother to Paul and Mike.

Well done, Jim. Well done.

Good Ol' Freda

A couple of days after Jim and I were married, he showed me boxes and boxes of mail from all over the world, stored in the garage. It was mostly fan mail for Paul. Some were simply addressed: Paul, Beatle England, or Paul, Liverpool. Somehow the British Post Office knew where to deliver them.

Up until then, Jim had been taking the mail through the Mersey Tunnel by taxi to Freda Kelly at NEMS offices in Liverpool. Freda was The Beatles Fan Club secretary, having been moved up from being Brian Epstein's personal secretary when the boys' career began to take off.

So I decided to get a system going. My secretarial instincts kicked in quick-smart. Already, I was beginning to wonder what I would be doing with my time outside of the normal domestic things. Jim was making rumblings about me getting help in the house, a process which had to be very carefully considered due to the need for confidentiality when Paul came home. This we eventually remedied, first with the addition of Nancy Bates, who came highly recommended from our local lady councillor, and later supplemented by her friend, Margaret Stewart, who took on more duties as Jim's health became more of an issue.

I rounded up a load of empty shoe boxes from a local store, and labelled them with the names of countries. Then, with the help of five-year-old Ruth, we arranged them geographically in our dining room at Rembrandt. I combined this as a sort of

Angie and Freda, 2013.

geography lesson for her. The Australian mail went on the floor (Down Under); the letters from Japan, China and other parts of Asia went on the window ledge on the right (the Far East).

In the way of fan mail, Ruth's first task was to open it and paper clip the envelopes to the letters. I quickly learned that Brits and Europeans were the only people who wrote their home address on the actual letters – all the others merely wrote it on the envelope. It seems funny to recall that we didn't even have a stapling machine in those days, let alone a typewriter.

Ruth often reflects on how this influenced her, and inspired her to start our now successful service of McCartney Multimedia called iFanz. It's a service for musicians and artists to communicate with their fans, assemble their profiles, and find out what they really, really want (I sounded a bit like a Spice Girl right then, didn't I?).

Long story short, after it had all been sorted and any enclosures removed (i.e. chewing gum to be chewed by Paul and mailed back – yuck!), pairs of panties (I won't even tell you about those requests), pictures, and other memorabilia to be signed, I would periodically drive through the Mersey Tunnel to Liverpool and pass it onto Freda, who was already besieged with tons of incoming mail.

It is to Freda's credit and dedication that, after leaving their employ, she took the remaining letters home and personally responded to every single one of them. It must have taken her years, and a lot of her personal money for postage. (Hey Freda, I dare you to invoice Apple!)

Freda was about 17 years old at that time; a happy cheerful lass, with a work ethic that would blow your doors off. Especially today.

As the years went by and our lives moved on, we lost touch for some years. That is, until Freda ran into Pete Price, Liverpool's famed radio presenter at City Talk a few years ago. She asked if he could put us in touch. He did so, and off we set again! She's one of those friends that you just take up with as though you've never been apart.

We reunited at the launch of my first book, *My Long and Winding Road*, at The Royal Liverpool Philharmonic Hall on

January 30, 2013. We hadn't seen one another for so long, but the years just melted away.

Freda invited me to take part in a documentary about her life that was in production called *Good Ol' Freda*. Director Ryan White and his crew came to our house in California and filmed me talking about the old days. Later, Ruth and I were delighted to attend a screening of this award-winning film in Los Angeles on Hollywood Boulevard. It has been screened all around the world, and Freda has been able to attend many showings, attending her engaging Q & A session at the end of the screenings.

On reflection, we were so happy that Freda and director Ryan White had included a segment with the late Tony Barrow, who was such an integral part of the whole Beatles story. Sadly, Tony left us in 2016.

The documentary also included Billy Hatton, formerly of The Fourmost, one of Liverpool's premier groups, whom Brian Epstein also managed. Billy and Freda were friends since she was a teenager. Billy passed away suddenly in September 2017. I was last with him at the launch of my book at The Liverpool Philharmonic, when a rollicking good time was had by all. He and Martin periodically slipped away to The Philharmonic Pub to down an adult beverage or two, and regale one another with stories about the music business and other adventures from their past.

As a side note, Ryan recently directed a documentary about champion tennis player Serena Williams, and an award-winning series on Netflix called *The Keepers*. He is a charming and dedicated filmmaker, and I know he is going places. His latest venture is a documentary about Dr. Ruth, another delightful and inspiring piece of filmmaking.

We enjoyed having Freda come and stay with us, in a charming Airbnb in Vienna. We were there to film segments of our "Magical History Tour" show, whilst Freda attended screenings of *Good Ol' Freda* in other locations. Klaus Voormann was also along to screen his fascinating movie *All You Need is Klaus* and to answer questions following the presentation.

We filmed in Obertauern on the 50th anniversary of when The Beatles filmed their ski scenes for *HELP!* We met Herbert

Lurzer, who was Paul's double for the ski segments – although Paul did actually film some of it himself, too. Herr Lurzer invited us to visit his ski lodge one afternoon, and said he would send a ski taxi for me. Naive old me, I thought it would be akin to a chairlift. It turned out to be a snowmobile kind of contraption and I had to be bungee corded to the driver, who sped up the mountain. Martin had my back on the way up, and Raimund Carl (McCartney Group GmbH Division chief in Vienna) on the way back down.

There's a video clip of this adventure on YouTube.com (link):

That was one riotous afternoon. Hundreds of skiers were up there drinking and dancing, even up on the table tops. I noticed that when we finally reached the village again, the orthopedic surgeons were sitting in their vehicles, waiting for new customers with broken limbs to come their way. Talk about supporting home industries. One of the few hours off in between gigs, we got to visit the studio of Austrian fine artist VOKA and see some of his larger-than-life paintings, including this one of Paul. Wish

Ruth, Angie, and artist VOKA in Vienna, Austria (2013).

it would have fit in the overhead bin! Not that I could afford it, I'm sure!

We had some fun on that trip, I can assure you. And Freda and I sat up and burned the midnight oil (jet lag be damned) and caught up on so much that had happened to us both since the crazy Beatle days. I'm so glad that Freda Kelly finally got her close-up.

Scan this QR Code (link) to see the movie trailer:

Dick James Honours Luncheon

In the brand new year of 1965, when Jim, Ruth, and I were spending time in London, we were invited to a luncheon honouring Dick James, the Beatles' music publisher. It took place at The Café Royal, a posh spot on Regent Street.

We were picked up in a limo from Cavendish Avenue, and the emcee was in the car. He took an immediate shine to little Ruth because she told him a very corny joke on the way there.

Freda Kelly and Angie at Julien's auction house in Beverly Hills, December 2015.

It was about a rich man from the Middle East who had a thick accent. He came to England and wanted a big house built with lots of gardens, a lake, swans, chandeliers, and "a statue in every room." When the big day arrived and the builders were putting on the final touches, he arrived in his chauffeur-driven Rolls Royce. He inspected the staff on the steps, then entered the house to be shown around by the designer. He seemed very pleased with everything except that he was a bit puzzled with the big alabaster and marble statues of nymphs, angels, gargoyles, and all manner of massive pieces. When he asked the designer, "But vot are deese?" He was informed, "But sir, you asked for statues in every room." "No, no," he replied, making a mime of speaking into a telephone, saying, "I meant, 'Hello, stat you?'"

Jim and I had heard this a dozen times and shrugged it off, but the event host was tickled to pieces. He was the master of ceremonies at this celebrity and press-ladened event, which had already had a spot of excitement before he took the stage. Paul, recovering from a heavy-duty holiday party season, asked for cornflakes and milk for his breakfast, and not the smoked salmon, champagne, and other high-falutin' stuff that the guests were being served. Of course, a runner was promptly dispatched to get the necessary breakfast staples for Paul, and later, when things got under way, it was announced from the stage that a little guest (Ruth) had something to tell them. So he got Ruth to stand up on her chair and present her little story. She got her laughs, and no doubt it gave her a taste for the limelight.

When we left the hotel that day, there was a mob of fans outside. Word had spread about the star guests, and it was the first scary experience we had of them rocking the limo from side to side. Alf Bicknell, their trusty driver, together with the security guys, pushed Ruth down on to the floor to keep her away from the screaming girls who were clawing at the windows as our brave driver negotiated a way out of there. A baptism of fire for sure.

Fanz, Fan Mail, and Customerz

In the early days of my marriage to Jim, through opening Paul's fan mail, I discovered a long-time fan of Paul's named

Cristy Trembly. She has kept in touch over the years and worked in television, mainly with CBS. She has been involved in production on several of the popular series, including the highly popular *Dancing with the Stars*.

In the mid-1960s, she wrote to Paul at the Heswall address. After a time, I began to recognise many of the recurring addresses. So one of Ruth's tasks, in order to earn her pocket money, was to open letters, paper clip the envelopes to them, sort them into countries, and file them in shoe boxes that were all over and underneath our long dining table at Rembrandt.

As I previously mentioned, the boxes roughly represented geographical locations. Australian mail went on the floor (down under); Asian and Pacific mail on the window ledge (far East). This was a geography lesson, as well as the beginnings of Ruth's awareness of the fan culture. This guided her in forming our current service, www.ifanz.com, which caters to over six million people who want to circulate their information to "fanz" and "customerz."

When I personally responded to Cristy, she sent Ruth a lovely little rag doll with a porcelain face, which she treasured.

When Ruth and I were speaking at a Beatlefest in Los Angeles many years later, Cristy was in the audience, and we made personal contact for the first time. She is one heck of a lady, and has traveled the world.

Another memorable connection was with two Japanese girls, Tomoko and Katuko. They once sent Ruth an enormous Geisha doll on a wooden plinth. It was magnificent. Unfortunately, it became a casualty during one of our many house moves after Jim died when we had to move from place to place during our "survival period."

Another interesting (and somewhat alarming) thread of fan mail was from a young lady whose postal addresses kept getting closer and closer. This culminated in a phone call one night from the Dockside Police in Liverpool. She had been discovered as a stowaway on a freighter, which had just arrived. She said she was invited to the home of Paul McCartney. Paul was home at the time and spoke to her on the phone. I can't quite remember the chain of events, but it ended up with her arrival at Rembrandt. We fed her, made tea, made her call her parents in America, called her a taxi, and booked her a room at a small Mount Pleasant Hotel in Liverpool. However, it did take a little negotiating to get her to leave. Arrangements were duly made the next day to get on a flight back to the United States.

Years later, I remember Linda telling me that this girl was a constant visitor to their Cavendish Avenue house, and even took the kids to the local park. Linda had met her in a grocery store and I guess she didn't feel as if she were a threat. We were all just a little more innocent then. She sent me several pictures of Heather, Mary, and Stella taken on the swings and roundabouts at a park in St. Johns Wood with this young lady. After I told Linda about her turning up in Liverpool, she became a little more wary.

Is The Doctor In?

Jim had weekly visits from his general practitioner to keep an eye on his overall health and condition. Tuesday afternoon was a ritual – a pot of tea, two bottles of beer, and a drop of scotch.

The doctor checked Jim's pulse, blood pressure, and, from time to time, prescribed various medicines to ease his arthritis pain.

Jim had the old-fashioned working class respect for the medical man, and used to give him an annual Christmas gift of three hundred quid. We were quite taken aback one year when he asked Jim if he could double up on the amount because he wanted to buy a colour telly! Jim acquiesced, and had me prepare a check for £600.

In the early days of our marriage, Jim and Paul had a joint Barclays Bank account. Paul would make regular deposits, which were fueled by his substantial songwriting royalties. Jim was particularly prudent with this money, and appreciative that his son helped make his life comfortable in his later years.

Our yearly allowance from Paul's office at that time was £7,000 per year, payable every April (the beginning of the new tax year in England). I meticulously kept a note of all our expenditures to verify how I was spending my £125 a week housekeeping budget. Often times we would go well over that amount when various relatives would ask Jim for help to avoid them having their electricity or phones cut off. I would run around the area, dropping off checks, or cash, to take care of such matters.

I still have all my diaries from those days, and when I look through them, I am amazed to see how much of my time was spent taking folks to doctors, dentists, and going to railway stations. Jim was so generous that he would not have considered ever refusing to take care of his family in this way, as he felt that he was the privileged one with an allowance from his son.

I sometimes smile when I see that I meticulously recorded every little expenditure, even shoelaces, and other minutiae. My diaries have accompanied me on my peripatetic meanderings around the globe.

Every week, I drove Jim to Liverpool to pay his betting account with his bookmakers in cash. He loved to have a flutter on the horses, and watched them on the telly with great interest. He spent a considerable amount of time studying form. He only bet in a very small way, but he really loved it, and soaked up all the "form" of the horses and their trainers.

That is why it was such a thrill when Paul gave him a racehorse, Drake's Drum, for a birthday present. Paul was a very good son. He took care of his father financially until the day he died.

RIP Jimmy Mac

Jim's health deteriorated over a period of several years, with the onset of arthritis just before we met in 1964, to his sad passing on March 18, 1976.

Bless him, Jim was willing to try anything that was suggested in order to bring him relief. Treatments ranged from hot hand waxes, to foot baths, to acupuncture, to calcium injections, to many oils, treatments, and medicines. He even tried gold injections and physiotherapy to see if it would ease his painful joints.

When we first met, he was still pretty active and loved to putter about in his garden and greenhouse. He'd also go for walks every day down to Heswall Lower Village, with maybe a stop off at The Victoria Hotel for a Bell's scotch and water. Then, when Paul bought him a cottage in Carrog, North Wales, he loved his fishing trips on the River Dee. Problem was, the river was down 100 steps from the house – in fact, I snapped these candid pictures of Paul and Ruth there on one of those idyllic weekends.

But, as his illness progressed, and Jim became less able to do these things, he retreated to his armchair and watched a lot of television. He loved American programs like *Rowan and Martin's Laugh In* and other similar shows. However, he was happiest watching afternoon racing from the various English tracks. This still gave him the opportunity to have a "flutter" (a bet on the races), which would precipitate a phone call to his Liverpool bookie. Then, periodically I would drive him through

Paul, Ruth, Martha, and Hamish at Afon Ro, Carrog, North Wales.

the Mersey Tunnel, to either collect his winnings or pay his debts. Usually, it was the latter.

After his knee replacement surgery, it took Jim a long time to rehabilitate. A lovely man named Ken Kessie would come to the house to help Jim with physical therapy. There was also another gentleman, named Roger Waterworth, who was blind, whose wife used to drive him. They both did wonderful work to try to help Jim, but we couldn't stop the progress of the pain. Of course, the weather in England didn't help. There was lots of rain, fog, and dampness. If we had only known what we know now, maybe he could have asked Paul to buy him a little place in Arizona or Palm Springs, where the dry desert air would have been beneficial. It was so sad to watch him deteriorate and lose his independence.

There was a lot of difference of opinion from immediate family members as to how Jim's final time should be handled. Jim repeatedly told me that he wanted to die in his own bed, and not in some hospital. I could understand that some of the older generation of the Mac family thought I should be asking Paul to pay for a nursing home. I tried to explain to them that I was following Jim's wishes, and in their grief, they just couldn't accept that. It resulted in some unfortunate attitudes, and a few cross words. The bottom line was that we were taking care of him and they weren't. We did have a night nurse for the last week of Jim's life, mainly so that I could at least get a few hours of sleep. But at distressing times like that, sleep seems to evade one.

Mike's first wife, Angie, was with Ruth and me and sitting at Jim's bedside when he finally left us, along with her youngest daughter, Abbi. As he exhaled his last breath and finally stopped, little Abbi said, "Oh look, Poppy's stopped."

Out of the mouths of babes.

I had never actually seen anyone die before, and no matter how prepared you are for it, it comes as a terrible shock. We all kissed him and said a little prayer, hugged one another, and wept. The cycle of life had finally ended, but Jim was surrounded by many of his loved ones.

And that's how I want to go, too.

6
John, Paul, George, Ringo & Friends

Liverpool's Lord Mayor's Civic Reception for The Beatles

The Beatles landed at Speke Airport and had their triumphant ride through the Liverpool streets to the Town Hall balcony to receive the Freedom of the City from Mayor Louie Caplan at a huge civic reception on July 19, 1964. I was there in the crowd on Castle Street, looking up at them, not knowing that one day I would be "family," or at least "married in." I was accompanied by a young man that I worked with at Pure Chemicals. After the event, we walked uptown and had a drink at The Eagle. Once inside, we discovered that the landlord was Paul McCartney's uncle, Bill Mohin, and I met his lovely wife, Dilys. Little did I know that night that she would later on become one of my champions further down the line when I was integrating into the McCartney family.

Their pub was packed to capacity and, come closing time, Bill delivered his usual speech.

"I've had your money, now sup up and sod off," he said, then clanged the bell and ushered the excited crowd out of the bar.

By Christmas I'd be back in the same pub; this time, not as a customer, but as a member of the McCartney family. And, years later, I would stand on that very Town Hall balcony myself, with none other than the Lord Mayor Gary Millar after my private tour of this stunning building in 2013.

Angie and Lord Mayor Gary Millar, 2013.

See the chaos I'm describing by scanning the QR Code (link):

Peter Archer

My nephew, Peter Archer (who is also my godson), was one of the earliest Cavern Club, and saw The Beatles transform into a worldwide sensation. I think his membership number was six. He treasured his card, but unfortunately it was stolen from his home when he lived in East Grinstead (which we used to call Clint Eastwood). It has probably travelled through Ebay by now and is in the hands of some lucky collector.

I asked him about his recollections of the Cavern in 1962. He is quoted below:

"Started to go every Friday night. There were always five bands, introduced by Bob Wooler.

"The sound was raw, noisy; the groups were brilliant. The Cavern was always very hot, with condensation streaming down

Angie and Fourmost singer, the late Billy Hatton in Liverpool in 2013. Photo courtesy Martin Nethercutt.

the walls. The toilets were constantly overflowing, so you needed waterproof shoes in there if you wanted to keep your feet dry.

"The entrance was down some steep, slimy stone steps, then a small landing, then further steps down to the cellar. There was no fire escape, and the air was thick with ciggie smoke.

"There were chairs set out in the middle, which were soon pushed to one side for the dancing. There was a strange dance, which became known as the 'Cavern Stomp.'

"In one night, you would see The Beatles, Gerry and the Pacemakers, The Big Three, Faron's Flamingos, maybe. The groups were endless. The Mojos – Lewis Collins, one of their members went on to be an actor; he starred in a TV series called 'The Professionals.' The Undertakers (including Brian "Saxophone" Jones), The Chants (an all black group), and The Hollies. I think I saw them more times than any other group. I didn't even know they were from Manchester. And then there were Freddie and The Dreamers (another Manchester group), Wayne Fontana and the Mindbenders, The Searchers, and Billy J. Kramer and the Dakotas. The girls all loved him. To be fair to them, they all made some really good records and had quite a few chart hits.

"Rory Storm and The Hurricanes was another group I saw a lot. I'm not sure but I think Ringo was with them at that time, before he took over from Pete Best in The Beatles.

"Then there were The Swinging Blue Jeans. I had a mate at school (St. Edwards College), Ralph Ennis, whose brother Ray was the lead singer. When 'our kid' was on at lunchtime, we sometimes bunked off school to go and see them. We'd get in for free.

"The Beatles aside, I think my favourite groups (we didn't refer to them as bands) were The Big Three, Faron, The Fourmost, and the Blue Jeans.

"One of the Fourmost, a big guy named Mike Millward, got cancer and passed away in Clatterbridge Hospital 'over the water.' He was about 22 and a lot of people were affected by his death. It was such a tragedy. I was 16 at the time.

"October 1962 became a real turning point when The Beatles reached the national charts with 'Love Me Do.' For many, it was a turning point for the better, but with hindsight, it was for the worse as far as I was concerned. Their fame spread quickly and The Cavern became a place everyone wanted to go to. It was never quite the same after that. Now we had to share them with the world."

Indeed.

To see a BBC archive of the original Cavern Club video, scan this code with your phone or iPad (link):

John Lennon

What can I write about John Lennon that hasn't already been written? Having first known of him as a famous celebrity and then having him in my home as part of an extended family and house guest was a bit surreal.

Yet, he was not the big, bold, acerbic guy that the world often saw. I knew he could be sarcastic and was a very complex man with a brilliant mind, but from my perch, I saw him as a frightened little boy. His fame had created an invisible wall around him, and nobody can ever know what their experiences may have been like unless you lived through the madness as they all did.

Jim was always a little wary of John, and even Paul at times was aware of the need to tread lightly in his presence, so great was their competitiveness. Yet they shared a strong bond – the bond of sharing their loss of their mothers at a young age. It was worse for John than for Paul because Paul had the continuity of living with his dad and brother Mike. Poor John literally had his mother ripped away from him several times throughout his life.

I have fond recollections of the time he and Paul spent a few days with us at Rembrandt when Paul decided they should go to nearby Chester on a little shopping spree. Jim suggested that I either drive them or order a taxi. Paul insisted on a real adventure and wanted to take the local Crosville bus, which they did. They also "disguised" themselves in a couple of ratty old raincoats that Jim used to keep in the greenhouse and trilby hats (Fedoras) and old pairs of Jim's glasses.

John Lennon's star on The Hollywood Walk of Fame.

They evidently had a fine old time, and when they came home late afternoon, Paul said I should expect a few deliveries. John bought a huge crucifix, a Bible, some candlesticks, old books, and various other items from an antique shop. Paul purchased a pine-framed bed, which was riddled with woodworm and threw me into a right old panic. I got one of the local handymen to come around and spray it with some foul smelling remedy, which I hoped would kill the little critters.

John was very patient with Ruth, who was a lively young girl at the time. He did silly things and pulled faces to make her laugh and read to her at night. He had a very serious conversation with her about her teddy bear, "Mr. Ted." Good old Ted still lives in a chair in the corner of her bedroom in California, and wears a black bow tie, which belonged to Jim.

I remember Jim telling me (in 1964) about one very special April morning when Brian Epstein called from London. He said that The Beatles were numbers one, two, three, four, and five on the American charts. He made the inevitable pot of tea, went upstairs and wakened the boys, as John was staying at Rembrandt at the time. He finally got them down into the kitchen to tell them the news. Naturally, they were chuffed.

Cynthia once related to me how John respected me for chiding him on his manners. Once, he absent-mindedly handed me his empty cup and saucer, waggling it to indicate he wanted another cup of tea.

"We have a word in this house," I sternly told him. "That word is PLEASE."

I wasn't going to let anyone, not even him, misbehave in front of little Ruth, who was being raised in a household where manners were a top priority. I remember getting looks from Jim and Paul, who were shocked that I would take the great John Lennon to task. But he evidently understood my motives.

As the years went by, we didn't see very much of John, except when we went down south. Paul once took us to Kenwood, his house in St. George's Hill in Surrey. I remember there was a suit of armour in the hallway, and some very ornate pieces of furniture. It seemed like a mansion to me. And, of course, we would see him, along with the others, at various concerts, and in the Bahamas during the filming of *HELP!*

To view inside Kenwood today, scan this code with your smartphone or iPad (link):

After her breakup with John, we didn't see much of Cynthia and Julian for some time. That is, until she moved to North Wales and then back to the Wirral, Hoylake, where Julian went to school quite close to Ruth. He was at Calday Grammar School, and Ruth at West Kirby Grammar School.

It was nice to be neighbours again.

John's Aunty Mimi

Before first meeting John's Aunty Mimi, I anticipated she'd be a rather stern lady. Her reputation preceded her. She reminded me of Barker & Dobson's toffee – a bit brittle on the outside – but with a soft centre. She always had John's welfare at heart, but wanted him to be a lawyer or a doctor; anything other than a rocker. Of course, she was extremely proud of his success when it happened.

She occasionally visited Rembrandt with Louise and Harry Harrison, and we'd sit in the back garden and enjoy a leisurely afternoon tea. She said she didn't really like mixing much, and was a very private person. That said, she and Jim hit it off and would meander off down the garden to look at his rose garden, his vegetable patch, and, of course, his beloved grapevines.

But she seemed to carry a certain sadness about her. Maybe because she had never had a child of her own, just her tenuous relationship with the gifted John.

It's interesting how things like music and gardening can bridge many gaps.

Watch the video of her on board a BOAC flight with The Beatles in Australia by scanning the code with your smartphone or iPad (link):

Firestorm!

Rory Storm was a famous Liverpool vocalist for whom Ringo once was the drummer. His band, The Hurricanes, was one of the most popular and exciting acts on the Liverpool and Hamburg club scenes during their existence, although their attempt at a recording career was sadly not so successful.

They released only two singles (and one additional compilation track) during their early 1960s heyday, and none of their material made the charts. Their second (and final) single was a version of the *West Side Story* song "America," and was produced by the Beatles' manager Brian Epstein.

More about Rory and his fascinating history with Liverpool, Hamburg, Allan Williams, and Ringo, as well as his tragic death, can be seen on Wikipedia by scanning the code in this chapter with your mobile device (link):

We thought it was hilarious when Paul told us that, during a meal in a posh restaurant, Rory Storm's mother Violet panicked when the chef, preparing crepes suzette at their table, thought the place was on fire when he poured the brandy on the dish. She promptly grabbed a syphon of soda water and doused the meal. And the Chef.

Whenever I'm in a restaurant featuring flambé dishes like they do at one of my favourite haunts, Melvyn's at The Ingleside Inn in Palm Springs, Violet Caldwell always springs to mind. I manage, however, to resist the temptation to bring the proceedings to a speedy and damp conclusion.

Scan this QR code with your phone or tablet to see what Liverpool and the Mersey Sound were like in the '60s (link):

Ringo Starr

I first met Ringo Starr when Paul took Jim, Ruth, and me to visit him and his wife Maureen at Sunny Heights, their lovely country home in St. George's Hill, a lush Surrey suburb.

My lasting recollection is of a tree house, a go-kart track in the grounds, and my special favourite: a beautiful dishwasher in the kitchen.

Ringo's son Zack was just a toddler then, but now he is a world-famous drummer in his own right, including touring with his dad's All Starr Band.

At that time, I had been trying to wheedle Jim into letting me have a dishwasher. Technological advancements be damned! Jim said the invention was "stuff and nonsense," and that we'd always washed our dishes the old-fashioned way – by hand. Or rather, by my hand. I quietly told Ritchie this, hoping he might say something. He then he took us on a tour of the house, including the kitchen, and did a pitch to Jim about the dishwasher. I was eternally grateful to him for that.

Soon after we got back home, Jim said softly, "I suppose we should get one of those new fangled things." Until he saw Mo and Ritchie's, he had always assumed that the dishes went round and round, much like a clothes washing machine.

So I got my wish, and boy, was I glad, considering the amount of entertaining that followed over the years. It came in handy when Paul came home and invited lots of family, or Mike was in town and brought home many of his fellow performers and their various companions.

Scan this QR code to see a funny interview with Ringo and George talking about the old days on Michael Aspel's show (link):

In the early days of my marriage to Jim, I had the pleasure of meeting Elsie and Harry Graves, Ringo Starr's mum and stepfather. Talk about two lovely people. They sometimes visited Rembrandt where we would all chew the fat about the old days in Liverpool, before it was turned on its ear by these four mop-topped lads.

Ringo bought his parents a lovely bungalow in Gateacre, on the outskirts of Liverpool, where we would sometimes go over and visit them. Harry loved working in his garden, and they both lived simply. He and Jim liked to talk about plants and gardening, whilst we women and little Ruth always found plenty to chat about. We were not such slaves to TV then as people tend to be now.

She told us of her early struggles as a single mum before she married Harry, a dear sweet and kind man. She was often afraid to open the front door in case it was the rent man. So she'd tell young Ritchie to bend down and look under the gap

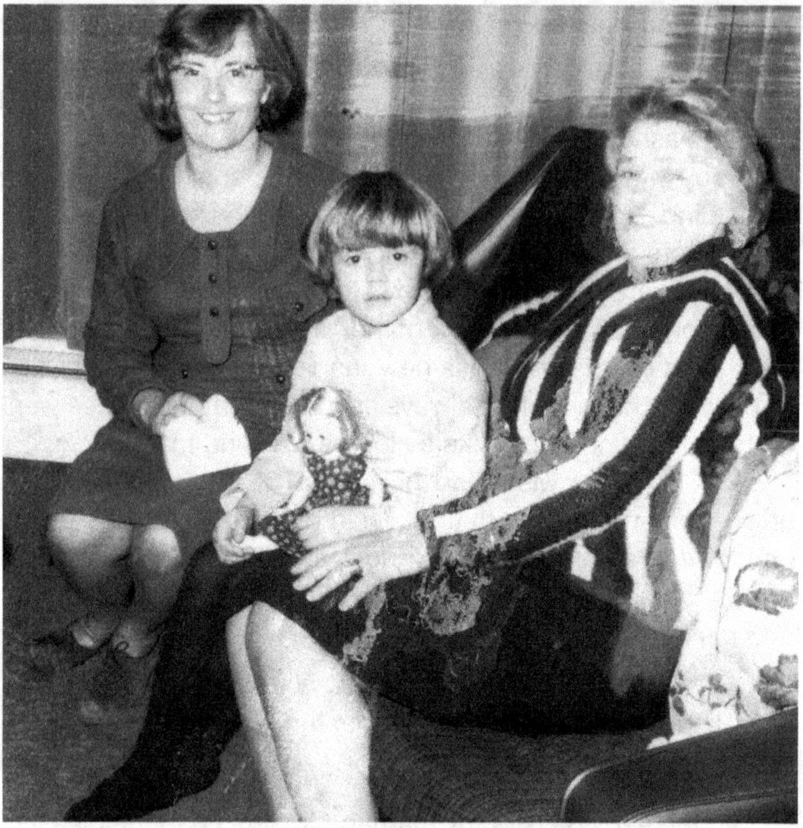

Angie, Ruth, and Elsie Graves (Ringo's mum).

at the bottom of the door to see if it was a pair of boots. If the answer was yes, then she knew it was the dreaded rent man and not to open it.

Elsie told me that Ritchie gave her an allowance, just like Paul did with Jim. Every time she received it, she put 10 quid into a post office savings account for Ritchie in case it all ever went away and he needed the money. Bless her heart, if she only knew. She was very proud of him, and never failed to cut out clippings from the papers and magazines and keep them in scrapbooks.

Then again, as parents and step-parents, we were all proud of our Beatle Boys.

Here they are in a long lost interview. Scan the code to reveal all (link):

George Harrison

George was an occasional visitor at Rembrandt, and was very fond of his "Uncle Jim" as he addressed the elder McCartney. His first greeting was usually, "Hello Ange, put the kettle on." It seems that in every phase of my life, tea has always been center stage.

He also loved Jim's custard, and whenever he popped in, that was another order of the day. George wanted to know the secret of how Jim could make custard without it forming a skin on the top. The funny thing is, Jim would never tell him. He did, however, tell me, and whenever I make custard or trifle, I always do it the Jimmy Mac way.

Ruth was taking piano lessons, which she hated. One afternoon when I picked her up from her music teacher's house, she was grumpy on the way home, but she lightened up when she saw that George was in the lounge. She plonked her music case down and he asked her how she was getting on. Sensing her lack of delight for her music lessons, he sat her down at the piano, and took a seat on the bench beside her. He taught her a raga and explained the rudiments of Indian music. That certainly got her attention.

I also remember we had a nice afternoon at Kinfauns in Esher, the home where he and Pattie lived, on one of our trips to London. It was a bungalow, with psychedelic murals painted on the outside. Pattie was very sweet and made us most welcome.

After our paths went different ways over the years, I didn't see much of George or Pattie until Louise Harrison's (his Mum) funeral in July 1970.[1] Then, years later, Ruth and I were at an Indian restaurant on Ventura Boulevard in Sherman Oaks and ran into Pattie with her then husband, Eric Clapton. When I think back over the years, we have all put a lot of miles on our clocks.

Pattie published a best-selling book, *Wonderful Tonight*, which contained some of her beautiful photography. A few years ago, she did a book signing at The Ingleside Inn in Palm Springs. Unfortunately, due to clients keeping me busy, I wasn't able to

---

1 George Harrison's mother and sister were both named Louise.

go. Then, a little later, she did another one at Catalina Island, which is just a hop, skip, and a hydrofoil ride away from here. Friends of mine attended and really enjoyed it. Her personality is still very warm and engaging.

And once again, Pattie has ventured down the path of matrimony and looks very happy.

To see the last interview with George Harrison, scan the code (link):

Louise Harrison

My friendship with Louise Harrison, George's older sister, goes back to the very early days, when we would meet at Beatles premieres and other such events.

"Lou" has lived in the United States for many years and has always been a champion of The Beatles, even long before they came to America.

She was a radio show host, which was pretty rad for a woman in those days. She urged Brian Epstein to send her copies of their first records, which she duly touted around radio stations and was met with a great deal of hostility. Why on earth would a WOMAN be coming in with promotional materials? Yes, it was that bad. But she persevered and got things moving.

Louise went "green" way before it was fashionable. She is a devout environmentalist and, even now, when I brush my teeth, I don't let the water run, such was her influence when we met up during our time living in Nashville.

She came to visit us, and we ended up driving together to South Carolina, where she was appearing on a cable TV show run by Beatles aficionado Ken Barker. In fact, we almost missed her call time as we had not given much thought to the time zone change, but she made it on time.

Ken also became a good friend. He and Ruth travelled to England together some years later to film some segments of people such as Bob Wooler, Cynthia Lennon, Neil Innes, and Billy Hatton. This footage has still not seen the light of day but we have it archived and hope to use it in the not too distant future.

Martin, Ruth and Angie with Marty Scott (George Harrison) of Liverpool Legends at Club Arcada in St. Charles, IL.

Louise manages a fantastic tribute band called Liverpool Legends, who are based in Branson, Missouri. We shared a stage with them when we co-hosted an evening at the fabulous Arcada Theatre in St. Charles, just outside of Chicago. Ruth and I told some Beatles stories in between the band's sets, whilst they changed costumes. It was a great experience.

Louise, Ruth, and I sat on a panel at a Beatlefest some years ago, together with Neil Innes, Pauline Sutcliffe, and Gerry Marsden. I remember that Neil said something that tickled her, and she collapsed in gales of laughter. It became so infectious that all of us on the panel were in a state of disarray and the poor emcee had one heck of a time trying to control us. We acted like naughty children.

She has published a great family book, *My Kid Brother's Band – a.k.a. The Beatles*. It contains a lot of stories you won't find anywhere else, and some great old family photographs. Louise, like the book, is a real treasure.

Scan to see Lou on the Grammy's Red Carpet when she was nominated for Best Spoken Word album in 2012 (link):

Brian Epstein

Brian Epstein was an exceptional person in almost every way. He was a great businessman, and a very courteous and mannerly young man. He served The Beatles well as their manager.

Brian had taken all the right steps in getting Jim to sign Paul's contract when The Beatles' negotiations first began. Jim was very impressed with him, and also his parents, Queenie and Harry.

When we spent time in the Bahamas on our honeymoon, Brian was constant in his regard for our comfort, transportation, and lodging. He even took us out one evening to a nightclub, which all seemed a little weird to me with people smoking huge joints and fire eaters and limbo dancers on the scene. Nevertheless, Brian did everything in his power to take care of us.

We were so shocked when he died in August 1967. Jim, Ruth, and I had spent the day at Bangor University, where the Beatles and the other George Harrison, a journalist with the *Liverpool Echo* (I know, I know. Two George Harrisons. What are the odds, right?) attended a seminar with the Maharishi Mahesh Yogi.

We all had lunch in a canteen-like area at long wooden tables, where simple fare was served. It consisted of salads, water, bread, and fruit.

As we got in our car to drive back to Heswall, Paul came out and stuck his head in the window to bid us farewell. While we were talking, George Harrison (the journalist) shouted from the steps, "Paul, Brian's on the phone. He wants to speak to you about tomorrow." So Paul left to take that call.

It was a bank holiday weekend and traffic was heavy. We stopped on the road for a bite to eat and to let Hamish, our little Scotty dog, have a run and a wee wee.

As we opened the front door at Rembrandt, the phone was ringing. It was Louise Harrison, George's mum. She said that Brian had committed suicide, or that it might have even been murder. She had heard something on the pirate radio station, Radio Caroline, and, at that stage, the news was very garbled. We were in complete shock. It was many hours before we could reach any substantial conclusion.

It had to be something else, perhaps an accidental overdose. He had just spoken to Paul to say he would join them the next day.

What a void his death left in so many lives.

The Beatles didn't attend the actual Liverpool funeral in deference to Brian's parents, who felt their presence would have turned it into a media circus.

The service at the graveside was held by Rabbi Norman Solomon, who said disparagingly that Epstein was "a symbol of the malaise of our generation." The comment shocked and saddened many in attendance, for it was completely out of line and uncharitable.

A few weeks later, on October 17, all four Beatles attended a memorial service for Epstein at the New London Synagogue in St. John's Wood, located near Abbey Road Studios. It was officiated by Rabbi Louis Jacobs. The service was attended by many of Brian's friends, family, and clients. The mourners included Cilla Black, Gerry Marsden, The Fourmost and Billy J. Kramer, and the Beatles and their ladies. I also remember meeting Lulu for the first time that day. She wore hot pants with suspenders (braces to the Brits) holding them up! Over-the-knee boots and a big floppy hat. She was certainly the most stylish mourner.

History seems to have downplayed Brian's role in the Beatles' success. For those of us who were there and in the know, none of it would have been remotely possible without Brian Epstein's participation, persistence, and passion.

Godspeed Brian ... Godspeed.

Scan the code to see Brian on the "The UK Tonight Show" from 1964 (link):

Ringo-isms that Resonate with Me

Ringo Starr certainly has a way with words. He's highly entertaining, even when he doesn't mean to be. Here are some Ringo-isms that have resonated with me over the years:

"I feel the older I get, the more I'm learning to handle life. Being on this quest for a long time, it's all about finding yourself."

"That's all drugs and alcohol do, they cut off your emotions in the end."

"We've got children, so we have to deal with each other because we have to deal with children's problems, you know, and our own problems. But some days it's fine, and then some days we just are at each other's throats."

"I've never been able to sit round on my own and play drums, practice in the backroom; never been able to. I've always played with other musicians. It's how I play; there's no joy for me in playing on my own, bashing away. I need a bass, a piano, guitar, whatever, and then I can play."

"We will miss George for his sense of love, his sense of music, and his sense of laughter."

"First and foremost, I am a drummer. After that, I'm other things ... but I didn't play drums to make money."

"I ... don't remember all the bombs, though they did actually break up Liverpool, you know. I remember when I was a little older, there were big gaps in all the streets where houses used to be. We used to play over them."

"And I came back and it was great, 'cuz George had set up all these flowers all over the studio saying welcome home. So then we got it together again. I always felt it was better on the *White Album* for me. We were more like a band, you know."

"Gene Autry was the most. It may sound like a joke – go and have a look in my bedroom. It's covered with Gene Autry posters. He was my first musical influence."

"So this is America. They must be out of their minds."

"I never studied anything, really. I didn't study the drums. I joined bands and made all the mistakes onstage."

"Drumming is my middle name."

"For me, God is in my life. I don't hide from that ... I think the search has been on since the Sixties."

Amen to that.

Come Back Milly

When the Beatles performed "All You Need Is Love" on the BBC's *Our World*, it was transmitted literally around the globe, with millions watching. Ruth made a big cardboard sign that read, "COME BACK MILLY." The BBC estimated that the June 25, 1967 broadcast reached approximately 400 million people. That was quite something in those days. You can see it to this day on YouTube.com, in the beginning of the video clip.

Here's the backstory: Paul and Mike's Aunty Milly had recently gone to Australia to visit her son, Jim Kendall, and family in Adelaide. She was badly missed by us all.

Mike took the sign to the studios and held it up to the cameras. Milly told us that she had just arrived at her son's home, where the telly was in the next room. They were sort of half watching the screen, when suddenly this placard came up. They were all flabbergasted, because it was a real time link between our two hemispheres. I think it was a turning point that made Milly plan to return to base as soon as possible.

It could be argued that it was the first Snapchat or Skype session.

Subsequently, an annual event has been dedicated: Global Beatles Day, on every June 25th. The fans play Beatles music all day and celebrate in various ways. Their music now spans several generations, and will no doubt continue for many more.

If you scan this code with your mobile device and watch for it carefully, you'll see the very sign that made Milly turn around and come home (link):

How I Won the War

On October 18, 1967, Jim and I attended the premiere of *How I Won the War* at the London Pavilion. It co-starred John Lennon, and was directed by Dick Lester, who guided the Beatles in *A Hard Day's Night* and *HELP!*

The film was a hilarious fun poke at war. It starred Michael Crawford (before his career as a serious singer), comedic actor Roy Kinnear, and even Neil Aspinall had a small (and uncredited) part as a dead soldier.

After the performance, we were all invited back to Cilla Black and Bobby Willis' Portland Place apartment.

Little Ruth, Angie, Jim, and Paul, June, 1967, St. John's Wood, London. Picture courtesy Barbara Burton.

That was the night that we climbed out of the limo to enter the building. We were greeted by a very tipsy gent in top hat, white tie and tails (no, it wasn't Fred Astaire), who staggered up to John Lennon. He asked in a very plummy accent, "I say, aren't you one of those Beatle chappies?" John nodded in agreement. Then the man thrust a notebook and pen in John's hand and rudely said, "Then give me your autograph. It's for my daughter...I can't stand you myself."

To which John adroitly responded, "Well f**k off then!" Can't say I blame him.

As we all crowded into the lift to go up to Cilla and Bobby's flat, Mama Cass made a surprise appearance. She had recently been apprehended at Heathrow Airport and accused of stealing a blanket from her hotel.

"Hi there, blanket thief," Paul said, stunning all of us. Fortunately she took it in stride and laughed it off. But my dear husband, Gentleman Jim, was mortified.

Scan this code to see a clip from John's movie (link):

Ray Connolly — Journalist

I remember a very nervous Ray Connolly coming to Rembrandt to interview Mike shortly after Jim and I were married. As Mike was still sleeping, Ray and Jim got chatting. In fact, Jim did most of the talking, as Ray suffered from a bad stammer. Jim did his best to put him at his ease by talking about it and getting it out in the open. He was working for the *Liverpool Daily Post* prior to moving to London to work on *The London Evening Standard*. Mike eventually emerged, and the three boys had a nice chat whilst I made the mandatory pot of tea.

Ray later met Paul in September, 1967, during the filming of *Magical Mystery Tour* when he'd only been at *The Standard* a short while. He'd been told by his editor to follow the coach and file a story. Being new, he didn't know many people and felt very unsure of himself. On the first night in Devon, when Ray was sitting at the bar, Paul came in and sat on the next barstool. Nervously, Ray said to him, "I know your dad." "Dad" was evidently the magic word, and Paul took him under his wing.

On December 26, known as Boxing Day in Britain, *Magical Mystery Tour* was broadcast on BBC Television. Although it was widely panned by the critics in the papers the next day, Ray was asked by *The Standard* to write a follow-up piece. So he tried phoning Paul at his Cavendish Avenue home where Jim, Ruth, and I had been staying over Christmas. He spoke to Jim, who asked him to call back in half an hour as Paul was still asleep (his connections to the McCartneys always seem to involve sleeping!). Ray repeatedly called, and he remembers a memorable gem that came from Jim.

"I tell you what Ray, God loves a trier," Jim said. "I'll go and wake Paul up for you."

So it turned out that Paul chatted to Ray from his bed for about twenty minutes about the disastrous results of *Magical Mystery Tour*. Ray got a front page story out of it, which he says gave his career a real shot in the arm.

Ray and his wife met up with us all at Mike and Angie's wedding reception at Rembrandt. Mike and Angie went off on honeymoon (along with Ruth and I – how romantic was that?), and Paul took Ray and Plum off to Aunty Gin's house in Dinas Lane, Huyton.

Mike often stayed with Plum and Ray at their Campden Hill Road house from 1969 onwards. Jim and I visited him there a couple of times, and Jim always insisted on giving their little 'uns a half a crown each in that old fashioned way of his. That wouldn't go far nowadays, the little 'uns are now big 'uns (Louise, Dominic, and Kieron).

In a very recent email from Ray he said how he has always thought how Jim's phrase, "God loves a trier" helped shape him. He'd never heard it before, but says it still resonates.

He is now perhaps best known for writing screenplays for *That'll Be the Day* and the sequel, *Stardust*, for which he won a Writers Guild of Great Britain best screenplay award, and for his many interviews with The Beatles.

But, going back to our first meeting, it also forged a link between Ray and the McCartney family, which has continued ever since. John Lennon also had great faith and trust in Ray, as do I. As I often say, Ray is one of the only two prominent journalists in whom I have complete and utter trust. The other is Roy Greenslade, who interviewed me about Gary Glitter and kept many confidences.

In later years, some people thought Ray's honesty and loyalty were a disadvantage, especially when it later became known that John Lennon told Ray he'd left The Beatles months before it became public knowledge. John had asked Ray not to divulge it, and he didn't. It meant he missed the scoop of his life as a journalist, but he has never regretted keeping that confidence to himself.

I love reading Ray's blog. He has written some fascinating pieces, ranging from his childhood adventures, to his regrets in life, to his gratitude for the life he has now. His books have kept me enthralled for many an hour on my iPad and Kindle (now considered an antique – the Kindle, not Ray!).

He broke the barrier for many writers when he decided to publish his novel *Sandman* online, downloadable one chapter per day for free! It generated an amazing amount of interest, with 60,000 downloads the first day.

Ray is still married to the same dear wife, whom he affectionately calls "Plum," and of course, their kids are full-blown adults now.

Ray wrote an interesting book, *Sorry Boys, You Failed the Audition*. It tells the tale of what might have happened if The Beatles had not signed a recording contract. It largely features Freda Kelly (with her permission), and is an interesting piece.

There's an interesting YouTube item of him discussing the break up of The Beatles. Scan the code to view it (link):

You should also look him up: www.rayconnolly.com, and you'll find some great reading on his blog. And, November, 2018 saw the release of another new book he penned called, *Being John Lennon: A Restless Life*.

The Magical Mystery Tour Launch Party

Five days before the airing of *Magical Mystery Tour* on Christmas Day, 1967, the Beatles held their annual holiday party. It was a tony affair held at the Royal Lancaster Hotel in London.

Mike was already in London prior to this event and had a suite at the hotel. Jim didn't feel well enough to travel, so Angie McGear and I took the train from Lime Street to Euston, where Mike picked us up and whisked us to the hotel. It was a costume party, and he had rented outfits for us both. Mine was an eastern princess, complete with lots of veily things, voluminous pants, beaded headdress, and curly slippers. The top half was a little snug on me, so I wore it back to front with a blouse underneath.

Upon arrival, we saw various incarnations of Charlie Chaplin, Ringo was a regency gent, Maureen an Indian princess, John was an Elvis-styled teddy boy, with Cynthia as a Quality Street Chocolate Box crinoline lady. Paul and Jane Asher were a matching pair of Pearly King and Pearly Queen. George showed up as an Errol Flynn type character, with Pattie as an eastern princess. Cilla Black's husband, Bobby Willis, was a nun in full habit, but the hit of the night was Derek Taylor as Adolf Hitler. He had rented a perfect SS uniform, right down to the jackboots, and had dyed his hair jet black and slicked it down in the appropriate style. He had, of course, shaved his moustache to the regulation square. A costume like that in today's politically correct culture might cause an uproar, but we Brits thought it was a hoot.

As the night wore on and we all became increasingly hammered, Derek sent over a note inviting me to his room.

"I know I ain't no Robert Taylor, but then you're no f*****g Claudette Colbert. Do you want to get together later?" the note read.

I resolutely declined his invitation, but later he wandered over and said, "Sorry about that. I'll buy you breakfast on the train back tomorrow morning." Angie and I gingerly climbed into a cab and went back to our hotel. Next morning, we caught an early train back to Liverpool, both feeling very much the worse for wear. It was in the days when the waiters would walk up and down the carriages carrying trays of bacon and sausages sliding around in pungent grease. We both refused breakfast and made for the bar carriage to order a hair of the dog that bit us.

I further confused the poor British Rail staff by asking, "Have you seen a man dressed as Adolf Hitler?" They just gave me a puzzled look and said, "No madam, not this morning." Derek never did make that journey. A fun evening indeed, for which we all paid in the next 24 hours. Thank heavens for Alka Seltzer and Bloody Marys!

To see the official trailer of *Magical Mystery Tour*, scan this code with your mobile device (link):

Hey Jude

Way back in the summer of 1968, Paul came home to Rembrandt late one night and roused his dad and me from our sleep. He had brought home the acetate of "Hey Jude," which the Beatles had just cut in London's Trident Studios. He was anxious for us to hear it.

Paul told us of how he came to write it, a story which I am sure is well known to fans everywhere. We listened through, and at the end when he asked us what we thought, Jim was glowing in his praise of his son's latest musical effort. I, on the other hand, promptly inserted foot in mouth, stating that I thought the song was great, particularly knowing his motivation for writing it. However, I couldn't help remarking that I thought the repetitive "nah, nah, nah, nah, nah, nah, nah," could be excluded, as I particularly hate repetition in music or lyrics.

That particular single was No. 1 worldwide (where it stayed on top of the American charts for nine weeks), and went on to become the Beatles best-selling single ever. What the hell did I know?

Paul didn't forget my comment, and further down the line said more than once, "If you want to know what's a hit – ask Ange."

Silence is golden.

Scan to see the Beatles acting silly on "The David Frost Show" just before launching into "Hey Jude (link):"

Blackbird (Singing in the Dead of Night)

My mum Edie was staying with us at Rembrandt, recovering from an illness in early 1968. Paul came home late one night and sat on the end of her bed and asked her if she was sleeping okay. She said "on and off," but always awoke when she heard the blackbird singing outside her bedroom window.

A light bulb must have gone off in Paul's head, because he went downstairs and dug out brother Mike's big old tape recorder, which I believe was a Grundig. He brought it upstairs, and sat with Mum quietly until the bird started his nightly concert.

Paul captured the sounds, took the tape away, and edited it. A little later he went into the studio and recorded "Blackbird." Before he started to sing, he said, "The tune's called 'Blackbird,' and this is dedicated to Edie.'" I still have a copy of the original tape, and whenever I hear the song, I feel very proud that it was dedicated to Mum.

I know there have been other stories over the years where people (including Paul) have tried to say that the "black" in the title was about an African American, and the "bird" was referring to a woman – Liverpool slang – and that it was related to the Civil Rights movement. I'm afraid to pooh pooh everyone's grandiose ideas about the song, but it was in our little back bedroom that Paul originally recorded the sweet singing blackbird (in the dead of night). It is one of the special flowers in my garden of memories.

Ruth & Paul in garden at Rembrandt.

"Blackbird" was eventually finished off, and was one of the highlights of *The Beatles* (aka *The White Album*), which was released in November, 1968.

Watch Paul sing "Blackbird" at Abbey Road Studios (link):

To Malta with Milly

Jim decided that we should take Aunty Milly on a holiday as a thank-you for all the times she had looked after him at Rembrandt. After she lost her husband Bertie, she put her Upton Road home up for sale. She eventually took over a smaller place on Village Road in Bebington, right across the road from Bette and Mike Robbins.

She was such a game girl, our Milly. She had a wealth of comic songs and old ditties from the variety theatres. At parties, we encouraged her to burst into song with such gems as "The Cheese Song" and other items in her repertoire.

Milly, Paul, Angie, Heather, Jimmy, and Linda in the early days of their marriage.

On this occasion, we all flew from Liverpool to Malta. We hadn't realized that it was Easter and that we would be arriving on Good Friday. With Malta being a devoted Catholic country, it was a somber day, with everything closed. Even the maids in the hotel were bowing their heads and praying under their breath as they dusted the banister rails at the Sheraton Hotel.

On our journey, our hostess plied us with far too many cocktails. Before we landed, poor Aunty Milly was feeling nauseous and reached for the little bag in the pouch in front of her and used it copiously.

It was only later, when the message came over the loudspeaker that we should prepare for landing, that poor Milly realized she was minus dentures and rang for the hostess, who obligingly retrieved the missing choppers from one of her bins. What a lovely task that must have been. But she was as cheerful as could be as she brought them back to a very embarrassed Milly, assuring her that they had been sanitized and were all ready for action again.

If only she'd used Fixodent!

Angie, Ruth, Jim, Aunty Mill, and friends at the Sheraton Hotel in Malta, 1967.

Jim wondering how he is going to fit in this adventure with his sister Milly, family friend Nancy Kargol, and Ruth, Malta 1967.

Lady Jane Asher

Before Linda Louise Eastman, whom I adored, there was the lovely Jane Asher.

One day, when Paul and Jane were spending time at Rembrandt, they were all gathered around the kitchen table as I was opening a tin of Nestle's cream to pour over the desert I was about to serve. I was so engrossed listening to Jane's stories from her times at the BBC that I absentmindedly forgot to shake the tin until AFTER I had removed the lid. The cream flew up the wall, in my hair, in my glasses, and all over the dog. See, you don't have to wait until you get old to be absent-minded!

Jane was such a wonderful influence on everyone. Her elegance, beauty, and genuine warmth captivated us all. Yet she was completely adaptable in our more down-to-earth household. She was always happy to cook, and taught Ruth many fun things such as knitting, crocheting, cutting out strings of paper teddy bears, and making a toy theatre from a cardboard box and pipe cleaners. She was extremely artistic and inventive, and gave Ruth a real role model to look up to. She also influenced Ruth with early aspirations to become a good cook. Thank you, Jane.

Jane also fit in perfectly at the family parties, mixing freely with all the rowdies and drinkers who would carouse either at Rembrandt for the traditional family New Year's Eve party, or at Bette and Mike's, Aunty Milly's, or Aunty Ginny's houses, and also cousins Ian and Jackie's home in New Brighton.

Jane had me knit her a full-length jacket one time, which I was happy to do. Shortly thereafter, when she was touring the United States in a Shakespearean play, she sent me a thank you gift of some fabulous Stevens of Utica towels. I kept them for years, until they became threadbare.

When Jane and Paul returned from Rishikesh after their sojourn with the Maharishi in 1968, they visited me in Clatter-

Paul, Jane, Jim, and Angie, in Hispano Suiza, London.

bridge Hospital. I was recovering from a severe asthma attack. Jane was very gracious with all the patients and nurses, who were thrilled to meet her. She brought me a beautiful black velvet embroidered evening bag from her trip, which I still use to this day. More recently I watched her in a hilarious movie called *Death by Accident*, and she still looked radiant and magnificent.

Jane now runs a catering business, specializing in high-end custom-made cakes. I hear that she counts the Royal Family amongst her clients.

What I loved most about Jane was, although her background was very different from ours, she never let it show. I will always have the greatest admiration for her and the many things she taught us all.

I follow her activities online: her catering business, her acting career, and her philanthropic and charity-based interests.

Lady Jane will forever have a special place in my heart.

The Lovely Linda McCartney

The first time I met Linda McCartney was when Paul brought her and her young daughter Heather Louise (by her first marriage to Melville See) to visit us at Rembrandt in the late 1960s. She was such a cool lady; very laid back. I was fascinated to have a first-time exchange with a real live American.

Linda met Paul when she was on assignment photographing The Beatles at a media event for *Sergeant Pepper's Lonely Hearts Club Band*. The event was held at Brian Epstein's house. From an upscale Jewish family, Linda was educated in Scarsdale, New York, and was used to the finer things in life. Her mother was killed in a plane crash when she was sixteen. She was raised by her father, Lee Eastman. Lee's family name was actually Epstein (coincidence you say?), but it was difficult for him at that time as a Jewish attorney to secure the right clients. Wisely, he changed it to Eastman. Thus, Linda grew up as Linda Eastman. She had a brother John (also a lawyer), and two sisters, Laura, born in 1947, and Louise Jr., born in 1950. Lee subsequently remarried a lovely lady named Monique de T. Schless.

Linda's mother, Louise Sara (Lindner) Eastman, was from a German-Jewish family, and was the daughter of Max J. Lindner, the founder of the Lindner Company clothing store in Cleveland, Ohio.

When Linda's association with Paul became public, she was incorrectly identified as heiress to the Eastman Kodak fortune. Another of those tidbits that the press throw out there without verifying their facts.

One of Lee Eastman's clients was songwriter Jack Lawrence, who was unable to pay his bill. To clear the debt, he wrote a song called "Linda," dedicated to Lee's four-year-old daughter.

Paul also wrote a song called "The Lovely Linda," which appeared on his 1970 debut album, *McCartney*. What are the odds of that? Two songs, one girl, one sentiment.

Jim's health was pretty poor by the time Paul brought Linda and Heather to stay with us in the late Sixties. He was losing his mobility, and very anxious that his beloved son's wife like him. We made a

Heather, Ruth, Paul, Mary, Linda with Stella & Jim on the Mull of Kintyre, Scotland June, 1971.

couple of trips to The Mull of Kintyre, but it was Jim's preference to stay at home and have the family visit us.

Her ways were very different from ours, and sometimes difficult to grasp. Her relationship with Heather was vastly different from mine with Ruth. The two little girls approached one another with great caution at first. That changed when Ruth got out her "dressing up box," which was full of lace curtains, feather boas, floppy hats, some of my old long dresses, and lots and lots of beads and baubles. Suddenly, the ice was broken. Heather was very much an outdoorsy kid, loved horses, jumping around, full of nervous energy, as opposed to Ruth's more "I want to be a ballet dancer" attitude. But, somehow, the two of them made it work.

I remember that due to Heather's (and Linda's) love of horses, Paul thought about buying Ruth a pony. As a bossy mum, I made sure Ruth was aware that she would have to take care of it, groom and feed it, and shovel pony poop when all was said and done. She rapidly went off the idea. Paul even talked about the possibility of buying the field behind our back garden to make a stable for it, but this idea eventually fizzled out. Still, it was very generous of him.

Linda was very confident in the kitchen, and could cook up a storm. This was before their vegetarian days, and she showed Ruth how to make a meatloaf, and lots of other family-style dishes, which Ruth still makes to this day.

That first trip was when they were on their way to America, via Manchester Airport. I remember Paul calling from the airport to say that he didn't have his passport. Somehow, officials let him board the flight, knowing who he was. No doubt one of his minions sent a copy of his passport to New York to enable him to get back into England at the end of their trip. It's hard to grasp these days that such a thing could happen. But, hey, fame can open doors and do many strange things for people. Please note that I will be lovely when I'm famous, and will always have my papers in order!

Sometime in the early 1970s, the doorbell rang at Rembrandt. I opened the door to a very big surprise. There stood my daughter-in-law Linda with her daughter sleeping in her arms, dogs around her feet, and not one, but two taxis in the driveway. Paul had been called away, and she was fed up having to stay alone at High Park Farm, near Campbeltown, Scotland. So Linda called a local taxi firm to drive her over 300 miles to Heswall to hang out with Jim and us and the family until they could be together again. The plan for two taxis was to carry the luggage, the animals, and humans, so that if one should break down on this long, arduous journey, there would be backup. I can't imagine the bill on that one, let alone the tip.

My instincts kicked in and I went into the kitchen to put the kettle on to brew a pot of tea. I saw Linda pay these guys from a roll of money in her little multi-coloured "rag" bag, which she always carried. They didn't even want to stop for a 'cuppa,' and we recommended the Victoria Hotel in Lower Heswall to these Scotsmen, where they could get something a little stronger before freshening up for their return journey.

Ruth often reminds us when she's taking pictures that Linda's photography taught her to "look up" when taking photographs.

"There's always another point of view if you just change yours," Linda would say. How right she was.

Sadly, Linda died of breast cancer in 1998. She was 56, and is missed each and every day. There is a breast cancer research wing at the Royal Liverpool Hospital in her name, to which I am pleased to donate a percentage of the sales of my teas, wines, and any other events that generate funds. They do amazing work, and I have a few personal friends who tell me they owe their lives to that amazing facility.

The Lovely Linda is still giving long after she's gone. And August, 2019 will see the re-release of *Wide Prairie*, a record dedicated entirely to Linda.

Watch the *Wingspan* documentary featuring Linda McCartney here (link):

7
All Things Must Pass

The Beatles Break Up

It was a very sad time when The Beatles officially broke up at the start of the Seventies. Surprisingly, we were somewhat out of the loop on Merseyside. I tried to keep as much of the news away from Jim as possible.

Not only were his rheumatoid and osteoarthritis becoming more distressing and painful, but he was suffering from shingles, and his nerves were in a terrible state. But, no matter how we

Paul, Jim, Linda, and Stella.

tried to cushion the blow, the awful awareness was hard to avoid with massive television, radio, and newspaper coverage on the subject. It was akin to a very messy divorce. Publicly, they had split in April, 1970, but the legal stuff dragged on for years.

Paul was greatly concerned that the other three Beatles wanted to appoint Allen Klein as their manager, and rightly so. Paul wanted his father-in-law, Lee Eastman, to take over the running of their affairs. This was cause for dissent amongst them all, and didn't help matters. So, on December 31, 1970, he filed a lawsuit against his fellow band members.

Paul had put on some weight, had grown a beard, and imbibed a little more than usual. He seemed to cling to Linda more than ever for support. They were hounded by the press when they made their appearance in The High Court in London, and it was obviously a very sad and stressful time for them both.

The judge finally agreed to his case on March 12, 1971. How ironic that the Beatles won Grammy for *Let It Be* only four days later. Paul and Linda accepted the awards from movie star John Wayne, and both were dressed very casually at what is normally a black-tie occasion. When they took the stage at the Hollywood Palladium in Los Angeles and took hold of the three Grammy statues, Paul merely said, "Thank you," and then left the stage.

The Beatles were finally dissolved legally in January 1975. A lot of public slanging matches went on, which I know they all regretted later. But words were said in the heat of the moment that caused even more anguish to each of them. Everyone handled it in different ways, but in the end, they all were friends again.

We didn't see much of them around the time of the final split, although Jim and Paul had a couple of phone conversations. Jim never imparted to me what Paul said on the subject, but Jim was always a bit tearful when he hung up the phone. He felt so deeply for his beloved son and what he was going through at the time.

Paul and Linda spent a lot of time at their Scotland farm to reflect on their lives, their future, and Paul's musical career. He decided he didn't want to become a solo artist forever, and thus, the idea of forming Wings began. The rest, as they say…

Wings went on to enjoy great success, and brought in a whole new generation of fans and followers too. In fact, these days, youngsters sometimes say, "Wasn't Paul in a band before Wings?" Watch Paul in 2018 with Howard Stern discussing this whole period (link):

McCartney Family Outing

On one of the occasions when we stayed with Paul, Linda, and Heather at Cavendish Avenue in St. John's Wood, Paul had a wild impulse. He suggested we have afternoon tea. This sounded like a splendid idea, and we all quickly spruced up. Little Heather put on a blue organza frilly party frock, but insisted on wearing her blue wellies. Not the best sartorial choice I will admit, but she was so excited about the whole thing.

We duly drove to the famous Savoy Hotel in London, and were ushered in by an obsequious staff member who was overjoyed to see one of England's most famous faces arriving with a posse of people. We were seated in this hushed restaurant where the waiters seemed as though they were on castors, so smooth were their movements. We were treated to all the usual afternoon tea delights, with white gloved service, cake tongs, three-tier cake stands, cucumber finger sandwiches, strawberries and clotted cream, and of course, ceremonial pots of tea, served to us as though we were royalty.

Little Ruth was just beginning to become aware of her surroundings and was very impressed, although we grownups tried to appear more laid back about it. At one point, Heather insisted on standing up on her chair and causing a bit of a ruckus, much to the consternation of our fellow diners. A nervous maitre d' came over and asked if we might tone it down, which was not very well received by Paul. Poor Jim was mortified. He was very much from the "don't make a fuss" school of thought. Paul and Linda were far more liberated and used to having things their own way.

It was another instance of the difference in attitudes between the older and younger generation, and an example of Linda's self-confidence as opposed to Jim's diffidence. I first noticed it when we headed out of the front door at Rembrandt to get into the car, and Linda automatically sat in the front with Paul. The move left Jim somewhat nonplussed as he got in the back with Ruth and me. Whereas, in other circumstances he, as the older man of the family, would normally expect to sit upfront and have the women ride in the back of the car. How times have changed since then.

These were the little things that would sometimes upset Jim, although he was far too much of a gentleman to mention it. But I could tell from his body language he was uncomfortable and not very happy. And he would always sniff when he was not comfortable with a situation.

He sniffed mightily that day.

To imagine a kid in her wellies in the setting I describe, scan here to see it for yourself (link):

Wings Fun Club

When Paul first had the idea of starting a new post-Beatles band, he came up with the idea of me running a fan club. His new endeavor was called, "The Wings Fun Club."

As my middle name is Lucia, we took the name "Lucy" and made her the secretary. We opened a post office box at Heswall Village Post Office (now no longer in business I hear), and we were off to the races!

It didn't take much time before the word was out and the mail started pouring in. The devoted mailman faithfully delivered the mail, and I would correspond with the fans from my trusty portable Underwood typewriter. I bought it for twenty pounds, which Jim gave me to put on a horse one day at the Chester races. Not being a gambler I pocketed the money and instead sent off for a typewriter, which duly arrived in a lovely little red zippered case.

Following my earlier grooming of Ruth to work with the Beatles fan mail, I once again roped her into opening the mail, paper clipping the envelopes to the letters, checking for enclosures such as postage stamps, membership fees, international reply coupons, and items fans wanted to have autographed and returned. It wasn't anything like the volume of Beatles-related stuff, but it was a steady job.

As time went by and Jim's poor health became more of an issue in our lives, Paul suggested we move the operation to his MPL offices in London. The magazine format later changed to a newspaper type of publication. The Fun Club remained active until after Linda's passing, and people still search Google trying to find copies. They can usually buy them on eBay from time to time. Because they're a collector's item, they can fetch a pretty penny.

It is fun to look back and see yet another venture that began on our dining room table and become a much bigger endeavor, just as it gave Ruth the experience that eventually led to forming our own www.iFanz.com site. She will say that her childhood experience with fan mail sowed the seeds of her realization that it is so important to "know thy customers" to quote her.

James Paul McCartney at the Chelsea Reach Pub

In 1973, ITV decided to shoot an hour-long special called *James Paul McCartney.* This was to highlight Paul's new venture with Wings. One segment was a McCartney family singalong at The Chelsea Reach Pub in Wallasey, where Paul's cousins Ian and Jackie Harris and their brood lived nearby.

A lot of family and friends were invited, and, as the word got out, a huge throng of regulars got wind of it and turned up to enjoy the festivities. People were even climbing in through the toilet windows to sneak in. As you can imagine, the fire marshal was put through his paces trying to limit the capacity crowd.

ITV sent a production crew to Rembrandt earlier in the day to liaise with Paul and Linda, along with hair and make-up artists to ready them for their on-camera appearance. I remember Ruth being terribly disappointed on the day to be told by Paul that she was too young to be part of it, so I guess there must have been some contractual arrangements that had an age limit on participants.

Paul and Linda had already spent a couple of days at Rembrandt with us prior to this day. I recall that Paul was not in a very good mood that day, even being testy with his beloved dog Martha, scolding her for standing in front of the television set.

Early evening saw us all off to the venue, which was already teeming with people when we got there. In those days, everybody smoked in pubs, and we entered the thick atmosphere of beer and ciggies, with everyone vying for Paul's attention.

I recently identified a number of family and friends in attendance, and even spotted a brief shot of myself (a brunette in those days) sitting beside Jim, singing along with the crowd. The camera picked up the moment Paul asked his Dad for money to pay for drinks, which was somewhat odd, but amusing.

This was at a time when Jim's arthritis was really taking hold, and he was nervous about going out amongst crowds, and particularly strangers, but he entered into the spirit of things with his best will.

Of course, all the old family favourites were trotted out. They included songs like "April Showers" and "Carolina Moon," lustily sung by family members such as Aunty Milly, her son Tom

Angie and Wings drummer Denny Seiwell in Las Vegas in 2012.

Kendall, Aunty Ginny, Aunty Dil Mohin, Uncle Joe and wife Joan, and their son Johnny Mac and adopted daughter Carol. There were also Paul's cousins, Bette Robbins and Kath Stapleton, along with husband Reg, and numerous others.

And his Wings bandmates, Denny Seiwell and Denny Lane, were there too. Linda put on a brave face, joining in, although I'm sure it was not her idea of a fun evening out.

The Merseyside pub scene was (and still is) an integral part of the working class get together, where people literally "pack up their troubles in their old kit bag and smile, smile, smile."

This was long before jukeboxes and pinball machines made an appearance – maybe the odd billiard table and dart board, or dominos – but that was about the extent of the provided entertainment in those days. Or, maybe you might find someone playing the spoons or a squeeze box, but it was all pretty simple.

I'm just glad that particular slice of life was captured for posterity (link):

Walking in the Park with Eloise

One afternoon in June, 1974, the phone rang at our Beverly Drive bungalow in Heswall. It was Paul calling from Nashville. I handed Jim the phone. Paul said that he and Linda were in a recording studio with Chet Atkins, the famed guitarist, whom Jim had long admired. Paul and Chet had been chatting about their dads, when suddenly Paul came up with the idea of recording a tune that he had heard Jim play on the piano when he was a lad. Jim had a band in the 1920s called Jim Mac's Band, and they were quite the thing in the Liverpool scene. Jim wrote this ragtime tune when he was in his early '20s and didn't give it much thought, until the day the phone call came in from Tennessee.

Paul couldn't remember the middle eight bars, hence the phone call. Jim went over to the piano in our living room to play the tune for Paul. His hands were badly affected by rheumatoid arthritis by this time, and he rarely touched the keys. But I held the phone to the piano whilst Jim played the song. That's all it took.

Sometime after that call, Paul visited Rembrandt with a copy of the record in hand, distributed on the Apple label. It was called, "Walking in the Park with Eloise," by The Country Hams. The B-side was a Paul and Linda composition called, "Bridge On The River Suite." Jim was more delighted than you can imagine, being a part of this production, and actually holding a vinyl copy in his hands. I still have that record. It has been around the world with me on my various travels.

At that time the public wasn't aware that it was Paul's recording. I believe he played washboard on it too, like the skifflers did back in the day. When I was at a Beatlefest years later, I was asked about it. More specifically, they asked if I wanted to sell my copy. The answer was a firm "no," as it is one of the few possessions I treasure from happier times.

Several years later, we were running Cloth Cap Management in Birkenhead, when one of our people, Chris Mellor, thought that maybe I should be receiving publishing royalties on that song as the sole beneficiary of Jim's will. So, after a lot of digging and delving, this finally came to fruition. Upon seeing a copy of Jim's will, the Performing Rights Society began allocating a percentage of the royalties to me, via MPL Publishing. They are not usually very big payments, but are always most welcome. I have received performance royalties from MPL for this song over the past few years. These trickle through to me twice a year, now, of course, done electronically thanks to all these new-fangled computer systems.

Jim Mac's Band, Liverpool, early 1920s.

Ruth and Angie at the Ethel & Ernest *screening, Santa Monica, CA, 2017.*

The song was featured in a charming Raymond Briggs animated movie titled, *Ethel & Ernest* (featured in a separate section in this tome), which premiered at the Palm Springs Film Festival in 2016. Directed by the late Roger Mainwood, this animated film is a charming look back at WWII.

Watch the trailer here (link):

Four Lads Who Shook the World Statue

Pete Price was working as a deejay in the Seychelle Islands in the early 1970s when he hit upon the idea of Liverpool erecting a monument to The Beatles. He wrote to the City Council and various other bodies who didn't really fancy the idea and nixed it. Go figure. They only put their city on the map and made England untold millions, if not billions, and continue to do so to this day through tourism.

The more Pete thought about it, the more it rankled him. So he did what any good instigator does and wrote to *The Liverpool Echo* about his idea. By the time he got back home from his working trip, the story had exploded and was being featured on the radio shows and other newspapers. It was literally the talk of the town. But still there was no concrete plan to officially do anything about it.

Pete contacted famous Liverpool sculptor Arthur Dooley, and in 1974, together they hatched a plan. They were thinking

Mathew Street, Liverpool, home of The Cavern.

of having a Madonna-like mother figure, with the babes in her arms, and this eventually evolved in the statue that still stands in Mathew Street (adjacent to The Cavern), the famous "Four Lads Who Shook the World."

It wasn't an easy road, as there was a lot of opposition, as well as support for the idea.

Peter took over The Shakespeare Theatre Club and held a fundraiser. The much loved Frankie Vaughan performed, Pete hosted the show, and there was lots of local support from musical acts and comedians. Pete didn't seek any glory for doing this, but was just happy to get it all moving. Jim and I bid on and won a picture in a silent auction, and felt we had at least contributed to the event.

Pete raised about £1,500 that night. He asked Arthur Dooley how much he wanted to create the sculpture and he asked for £1,000, which Peter happily paid him. Pete gave what was left over to Frankie Vaughan for the Boys Clubs Charity that he supported. This created another memorable event in West Kirkby when the streets were blocked off from there to Calday, as crowds excitedly awaited the arrival of Frankie, a hugely popular star in those days.

Then Pete had a scroll made to commemorate the occasion and gave it to the city. The statue has greeted millions of people from all over the world, and is a proud fixture of the city.

You can thank Mr. Pete Price next time you see him.

Joining the Circus

King's Lynn is a little market town in Norfolk, England, where Ruth and I spent a couple of years in the early 1980s.

We had been through a rough time with our business, lost our Merseyside home to the bank, and loaded up what was left in the truck. We moved to King's Lynn, ever hopeful that we would get back on our feet again. How often have we said that? I can't imagine how and why I was so stupid as to fall for the tale that we would be able to pick up the pieces and be helped by a friend of a friend who was said to have the answer to all of our prayers.

I was in business with a guy whose name I do not care to grace in these pages. Suffice it to say, we made some misguided decisions, and finished up in pretty dire straits. Ruth was in a relationship with him, which had already sent us down a path of bewilderment. In retrospect, it's hard to imagine how naive we both were in those days. These days, I rely on my gut instinct to tell me what's what. But not then. Despite my first impression of this person, I was taken in by his solicitous manner, and fell for the story I was being fed. Ah well, we live and we learn.

Originally, we moved into a couple of rooms above a shop on the High Street, where we slept on the floor, salvaged what we could, and, in true British fashion, put a brave face on things. If anyone were to suggest such a move to me now, I'd give them a quick smack upside the head.

But we shambled through and opened a little office, where our one and only management and agency client was rocker Gary Glitter. Need I say more?

Gary Glitter's career had long since moved from big arenas and quality venues to a stage where he was appearing alongside of a circus in the south of England. My business partner was on tour with him, and we rarely saw him in those days. Imagine our surprise to receive a phone call from his wife, asking if we knew where he was.

Wife?

Yes, you heard me right. Having been led to believe that their marriage was well and truly over, and all that remained was to finalize the paperwork, you can imagine the devastation of poor Ruth. This amazingly resilient lady suggested we get together, so Ruth and I drove down to London to meet her, discovering that not only was she still firmly married to her cheating husband, but she was also pregnant by him.

Upon entering her home, we noted that her hairstyle was exactly the same as Ruth's. Not only that, but she was identically clad in a velour tracksuit (he had bought them both the same gear), and hanging on a rail in the hallway was a leather shoulder bag, again, which exactly matched Ruth's recent Christmas gift from the same source. I guess this was his way of not getting mixed up with his women.

This kind lady, it seems, was under the impression that Ruth and I were lesbians, which had obviously been the smoke screen he'd used to allay her anxiety at him spending so much time up north with us.

All that glittered was not gold with this particular client, who was a shining example that when you manage circus acts, life is not all that appears under the big top.

London Town

During our peripatetic times in the late 1970s and early 1980s, Ruth and I moved from King's Lynn to London, where a girlfriend named Julie offered us temporary housing at her new apartment. These were tough times. Ruth and I each had about four or five jobs, shared a beat up old car, and somehow managed to survive, pay the rent, and stay in the game.

The room we stayed in was on the top floor of an older building, with a leaky roof, buckets to catch the rain, and dress rails full of clothes that our friend sold or hired out to photo shoots and videos.

Ruth's main employment was with Roundel Productions, where she was receptionist and general factotum. For some reason, she always carried her passport with her. This proved to be providential when one day, she was asked to fly to Hamburg with some documentation that was needed for one of their productions, the presentation of some new Microsoft technology.

She happily took the offer as she was of the mindset, "anything to get away from the humdrum of daily life." At that time, in addition to my day job with MPC Artists and Management, I had an evening job with a nightly TV show called *Help*. One evening, my phone rang just as we were about to go on air. It was Ruth, spluttering, "You're going to hear something on the news, but don't worry, I'm OK." What's the first thing you do when someone tells you not to worry – you worry! So as our show went live, sure enough, it came through on the wire that there had been a fire at the Hamburg Convention Centre, with notice of injuries or fatalities still awaited.

Imagine my motherly panic! However, it all turned out well in the end. It seemed that her task was to stand behind a curtain, and, on cue, pull the handle that would release a mockup of a huge hairy tarantula, with its tentacles wrapped around a black box onstage, opening to reveal whatever was the newest piece of technology. Something failed, and the bulbs in the box lit up the foam, and the whole damned thing went on fire. The curtains were lowered, and everyone was asked to leave the building in an orderly manner. Denis Norden delivered the statement in his very British BBC voice, hoping nobody would panic.

Ruth remembered that actor Andrew Sachs (Manuel in *Fawlty Towers*) was in an upstairs dressing room. She sprinted up the stairs and banged on his dressing room door to alert him, then made it hot foot (literally) out into the parking lot.

Thankfully, Ruth made it back to London on a late evening flight. But, oh boy, was that a traumatic few hours.

I guess it's no wonder we are so close.

A gentleman she knew, the late Irvin Kershner (who directed *The Empire Strikes Back)*, asked her if she would like to accompany him to dinner to entertain some guests. She happily accepted, as it sounded like a little light relief from her day job, her evening job as bartender at The Admiral Codrington, and our stint as car washers, office cleaners, and laundry girls for two gay guys who ran a restaurant in the city.

As she was going directly from her early evening job, she drove to pick him up at his hotel in her beat up old Mini Cooper. The car had a hole in the floorboard that was covered by a piece of plywood and some old newspapers. He directed her to The Dorchester Hotel on Park Lane to pick up his dinner guests. Lo and behold, when they appeared, it was Sean Connery and his wife and son.

They all crammed into the Cooper and went off to dinner. When they arrived, it was dark and pelting down with rain. So Sean suggested that the others go ahead and get seated, whilst he, the perfect gentleman, would stay with Ruth until she found a parking spot. When this was done, he accompanied her back to the restaurant, on the way, doing a good old Gene Kelly "Singing in The Rain" dance on the pavements of London.

She recalls that at one stage, the wine waiter, whilst charging their glasses, asked, "Shall I fill it for you, sir?" and Ruth commented, "What, from here?" Sean found this highly amusing and said he might steal it. Indeed, it turned up in a James Bond movie some years later.

During the general conversation, Sean asked Ruth, "Who does your hair?" She told him that she did it herself, usually with the bacon scissors in the bathroom or kitchen at home. He found this hilarious and said, "You know, Micheline hires a private plane to fly to Paris to get her hair done, and she comes home still looking like Miss Piggy."

Fun memories. (Well, some of them.)

RIP John Lennon

Like countless other people around the world, I vividly remember the day we heard that John Lennon had been shot.

We were living in King's Lynn in December, 1980, and we had gone into the office early to decorate the reception area. Ruth was up a ladder wielding a roll of wallpaper, and I was on the upper floor doing manual bookkeeping in big blue ledgers for the artists that we managed at that time (the biggest one being Gary Glitter).

One of our young assistants came into the office and asked, "Have you heard the news?" We shook our heads no, then switched on the radio, and there it was.

Unfathomable, unbelievable. Our John was murdered by a deranged fan.

Ray Connolly, our dear journalist friend, had been planning to fly from London to New York that day to interview John. After several rounds of negotiations, he had finally clinched a date with Yoko over the phone.

Ray had a longtime connection with John, as indeed he had with all of the Beatles. The two were really friends and he held many of John's confidences. Does anyone remember when we could trust the media and believe what they told us? Now, the only certainty in a publication are the date and price on the front page.

We were visited that day by Geoff White (of the band Paris 9) and his companion, Carty, who had driven from Liverpool to King's Lynn to spend some time with us. I remember we all went to a local Chinese restaurant that night and sat in stunned silence. Although I had never been very close to John, I felt he was like family because of his closeness with Paul.

Ruth then wrote a reflection of her feelings about the shattering effect on Paul of the sad ending to their amazing musical and emotional partnership (which we included as the first chapter of this book).

Even though almost four decades have passed, John's death is still felt in the McCartney household.

We often wonder, what would his participation in the internet world and digital era have been? And, how would he have dealt with the vagaries of communications, false news, and the slanging matches that now seem to be part of the norm? One can only imagine John's take on it all. Or perhaps, his participation.

The world never forgets John's special days. But weren't they all special? The love that was poured out to him remains.

And he is still missed by all.

Here are some funny moments and how we choose to remember him (link):

Yoko Ono

Yoko Ono was born into an aristocratic Japanese family on February 18, 1933, in Tokyo, Japan, the eldest of Isoko (a concert pianist), and Eisuke Ono's three children. Eisuke, who worked for the Yokohama Specie Bank, was transferred to San Francisco a fortnight before Yoko was born. The rest of the family followed him shortly afterwards. Her father was transferred back to Japan again in 1937, and Yoko subsequently enrolled at the elite Peers School (formerly known as the Gakushuin School) in Tokyo. I remember Paul telling me that in order to have a conversation with her father, Yoko had to make an appointment via his secretary to speak to him. Another tidbit was that when she was a little girl, if she was naughty, he would make her kneel on raw rice.

Once again, the whole family moved to New York in 1940 and then back to Japan in 1941, when her father was transferred to Hanoi on the eve of the Japanese attack on Pearl Harbor.

She stayed in Tokyo throughout the duration of World War II, witnessing the famous firebombing in 1945. Shortly after her eighteenth birthday, Yoko moved with her parents to Scarsdale, New York. She started her studies at Sarah Lawrence College, but left abruptly to elope with her first husband, Toshi Ichiyanagi. Coincidentally, Linda Eastman McCartney also attended the same college, although at a different time.

Eventually settling down in Manhattan's Greenwich Village, she became fascinated with art and also began writing poetry. Considered just plain wacky by many at the time, her work was not well received by the uppity NYC art crowd, but she gained recognition after working with American jazz musician/film producer Anthony Cox, whom she eventually married.

He financed and helped coordinate her "interactive conceptual events" in the early 1960s. The couple had a daughter, Kyoko, born in Tokyo on August 8, 1963. Ono's art often demanded the viewers' tactile participation and forced them to become part of the exhibit. She gave birth to the concept that today we would describe as "experiential." One of her most famous works was the "cut piece" staged in 1964, when members of the audience were invited to cut off pieces of her clothing until she was naked, an abstract commentary on discarding materialism.

Yoko and John met in 1966. The stories of their meeting and subsequent partnership and marriage are now legend.

The couple attracted worldwide attention with their famous bed-ins for peace in Amsterdam and Montreal. They welcomed journalists to their hotels in both locations, but received negative press from people who just didn't understand their cause and how they manifested it.

Yoko has often been blamed for the breakup of The Beatles. In fact, they themselves have often said that it was The Beatles that broke up The Beatles. It was time, they said.

There are some great insights at this page into many of Yoko's installations. Scan with your smartphone to learn more (link).

Yoko conceived and established the Peace Tower (http://imaginepeacetower.com/light-house/).

This is dedicated to the memory of John, and all he strived for in the way of world peace. It is a strong attraction for devotees and tourists in Norway, and as I write this, I am quite aware that several of my friends and relatives have made the trip to visit this exceptional installation, which they tell me is a life changing experience.

Yoko is a supporter of many charities, including Liverpool's Alder Hey Children's Hospital. It's a place very dear to my heart, as they literally saved Ruth's life when she was four years old and had a kidney removed.

It's a small world after all.

May Pang

I met May Pang some years ago at a Beatlefest in Chicago, which also included Cynthia Lennon. Cynthia and I were on a panel together and were answering questions from the fans, when the moderator said he had a surprise for us. We turned around, and there was May.

At first I was shocked, wondering how Cynthia would receive her. After all, May and John were together for some time, which

Ruth and May Pang, 2014.

had been documented over the years. Fortunately, May and Cynthia had a history as well – a good history. It stemmed from the fact that May pushed John to have a relationship with Julian in the mid-1970s when he was separated from Yoko. It was a kindly gesture, and one that immediately bonded the two women.

In Chicago, they embraced, and were very warm and friendly with each other. They continued to stay in contact right up to the day Cynthia died. May often visited Cynthia in Spain.

May was originally personal assistant to John and Yoko, and when they were having marital issues in 1973, Yoko pushed for the two to be together. It's complicated, I know, but then again, so were John and Yoko.

May has emerged as a great photographer, and her book *Instamatic Karma* contains many wonderful pictures. She was

Angie and Julian at The Sunset Marquis, Hollywood in 2014.

quoted as saying, "There were times I was a bit reticent in taking out my camera, like when some old friends stopped by to hang out. I didn't want to intrude on these moments, but John insisted. He felt that I captured him in ways that no one else did because of his comfort level with me ... for years, only my closest friends got to see these photos, which were literally tucked away in a shoebox in my closet. They were surprised that these images did not convey the John that was portrayed in the press during our time together. In fact, they saw a side of John seldom seen." She lovingly portrays pictures of John sailing with young Julian, and even one of John signing the legal papers that officially ended The Beatles partnership.

May is a very active lady – a single mom with two grown children from her former marriage to producer Tony Visconti. She now has a popular radio podcast show and a line of feng shui jewelry. Like a lot of the Beatles' ladies, she has emerged from the shadows and is thriving.

RIP Linda

On a sunny Sunday afternoon in April, 1998, the phone rang at our home in Playa del Rey, California. It was Lyle Gregory, a radio producer who wanted me to go live on the air in a few minutes to talk about Linda McCartney's passing. At this stage, I didn't know anything about it, and her death came as a terrible shock. I called out to Ruth and tried to gather my thoughts. Within seconds Lyle was back on the air, connecting me with radio host Michael Jackson (a South African gentleman, not the other Michael Jackson).

Paul and the children had obviously wanted to keep it all as quiet as possible. The first story out was incorrect, stating that Linda had died in Santa Barbara, California, when in fact it was in Tucson, Arizona. As so often happens when news breaks, the rumour mill goes crazy without accurate and verified information.

Apart from our sadness and shock, I didn't know what to say and I was totally unprepared. Being live on the radio was not an easy way to grieve. I don't remember what I said and I can only hope that I treated Linda with the respect that she deserved.

Paul, Ruth, Linda, and Heather.

Now that I've had more than a decade to think about her, Linda was many things: a world-class photographer, a devoted wife, a wonderful mother, and one of the greatest advocates for the ethical treatment of animals.

As a single mom before she met Paul, she had a strong and loving relationship with her daughter, Heather, and times had not always been easy for them. While living in the States, she would get various trusted people to sit with Heather whilst she went out on photographic assignments. In fact, as is well documented, it was through one of these assignments that she met Paul.

Linda loved to cook, ride horses, be beside her loving husband, and was always happiest with animals around her. I can remember waking up in the middle of the night one time at Rembrandt when she and Paul arrived from the farm in Scotland. In addition to the usual gaggle of dogs, I could hear clucking sounds. Yes, they had stopped somewhere on the journey and bought some hens. She shut them in the downstairs cloakroom until morning. When we awoke, the first thing we did was to clean up the chicken poop. She had lined the floor with newspapers and put down dry food and bowls of water for them, but they still managed to make the place look like Oliver Stone had just shot a war movie there. When daylight came around, she wrangled them back inside of their newly bought cages and prepared them for the drive to London, where heaven only knows what adventures awaited them.

It had never been her ambition to be a music performer, but when Paul wanted her in Wings, she did exactly what he wanted and was the recipient of a lot of grief from both fans and the press. That attitude eased in later years, but the initial reviews were brutal.

But she battled on as usual. Years later, she found her own voice in the McCartney household and established her vegetarian line of frozen foods and cookbooks. I understand she was working on another one when she passed away. I have a couple of beautiful books that she signed and sent to me.

The saddest part of all is that, even with Paul's success and fortunes, in the end there was nothing he could do to prolong her life. He was at her bedside with the kids when she finally closed her eyes and was out of her suffering.

Her name and memory live on in Liverpool where the Linda McCartney Breast Cancer Centre is a dedicated organization working towards not only a cure, but comforting the victims and their families whilst they are undergoing treatment.

Long live the Lovely Linda. You can donate to the Linda McCartney Centre for breast cancer research in the UK here (link):

Pete Price

Pete Price is a well-known Merseyside celebrity and radio show host on Radio City talk. He performs in pantomime, is a standup comedian, charity fundraiser, cabaret artist, Ambassador for Culture to The City of Liverpool, and a longtime friend of the McCartney family.

Angie and Pete Price, Liverpool.

My friendship with Pete Price goes back over a half-century. We first met when my Heswall neighbour Gill Rowlands brought him over to meet Jim, Ruth, and me at Rembrandt in the early 1960s. Our friendship has continued and evolved over decades and continents ever since.

He was working at The Shakespeare Theatre at that time, and would bring various celebrity guests over to have a cup of tea with Jim and me. These visits provided little Ruth with a mind boggling view of stars that she had never previously met. It was all good fun, and Jim enjoyed it. So did I.

It was around this time that Pete "came out." It was an assumption on our part that he was gay, and we were both fine with it. We had already experienced the friendship of Brian Epstein, whom we both liked and respected immensely.

As I write this in late 2019, Pete and I are still doing live weekly radio chats between Hollywood and Radio City in Liverpool. We've been doing these shows for about a decade. We just chit-chat about showbiz gossip, world news, fun stuff, and it has helped us keep connections alive all around the world. He recently scaled back from five nights a week to just one show on Sundays.

His book, *Pete Price, Name Dropper*, has covered all aspects of his life and work. He threatens that a second book will be published after his demise that will have all the nitty gritty details of his love life. That should be a best seller. I'll be the first in line. (If I outlive him.) Hmmm … How long is the life of a lizard?

Lizard, you ask? Pete has been deemed by one of his radio fans as a shape-shifting lizard. This story has grown worldwide, and Pete has had a splendid green lizard costume made for events, fundraisers, and general fun-filled activities. There are "Pete Price is a lizard" banners regularly flown at International Football games and other events. I wonder if he sheds any scales in the bathtub?

When I launched *My Long and Winding Road*, Pete introduced the two-night show at The Royal Liverpool Philharmonic Hall, and a rollicking good time was had by all. We were welcomed by old friends and family. I am so glad we did this, as I have lots of great memories and photographs for my garden of memories.

Over the years, he has won numerous awards in the field of broadcasting. In January 2019, The City of Liverpool recognised him as Citizen of Honor for his charitable work and other efforts to raise the profile of the great city, which he holds so close to his heart.

He also pops up and down to London occasionally to review the daily newspapers with *Sky News*, which I am pleased to be able to see in California. It brings us just that much closer on days I can't be with him. Here is a QR code to his website (link):

Down Under

When things got really tough for us in the United Kingdom in the autumn of 1982, we had the most wonderful invitation to join our dear friends, the Crawfords, in Sydney, Australia. We had known them since Bette and Mike Robbins had asked us to give them shelter when they sailed to Liverpool for Ted Robbins' 21st birthday in August 1976. Their docking in England was well-timed. Babs had been entertaining on the cruise ship, and son Rory was her accompanist. Husband Willy and daughter Shayne were also travelling with them.

It was one of those moments when you know the second you lay eyes on one another that there is a terrific spark. Babs and Will, parents of Shayne and Rory, stayed with Ruth and me at our bungalow in Gayton, Wirral, for a few days, and the dye was set.

Some years later, we took them up on their invitation to go stay with them for a while in North Curl Curl, a borough of Sydney, when most of our luck seemed to have run out.

We had lost our home on Merseyside to the bank due to a bad business deal, which I won't dwell on here. As luck would have it (both good and bad), we experienced a robbery in our Hammersmith Bridge Road apartment in London. Additionally, we were both working a variety of jobs when Ruth was invited to dinner by the late Tony Barrow.

Wanting to appear very grown up, she asked if she could borrow my mink coat. Imagine our shock and horror as she was on the way out to dinner to find that the hall cupboard contained only the belt and a coat hanger!

The next day, I discovered that I had five days remaining on an insurance policy which covered the missing coat. So, to cut a long story sideways, we claimed on the insurance, bought two one-way tickets to Sydney, and off we went.

Ruth had been working as a barmaid at The Admiral Codrington, located behind Harrods, in London. One of her clients was a travel agent. When she told him our tale of woe, he advised her that we would never get into Australia with one-way tickets since they would need evidence of our financial situation. So this marvellous man loaned her two ongoing airline tickets from Sydney to New Zealand, and onwards back to London. He had her promise to mail them back to him as soon as we had safely landed in Sydney, which we did.

Mind you, because of the nature of our tickets, we went the "pretty" way from Heathrow to Paris, Paris to Bahrain, Bahrain to Singapore, Singapore to Jakarta, Jakarta to Darwin. and Darwin to Sydney. We left on a Tuesday morning and arrived on a Friday night, utterly exhausted and jetlagged. Once we landed,

Rory Crawford, Martin and Aussie music legend Dr. Brian Cadd after a "liquid lunch" in Sydney.

Willy and Rory Crawford were awaiting us in their old Peugeot, telling us with great excitement that they had arranged a private tour of backstage at the Sydney Opera House. After a four-day flight! Splendid. I'm not sure how we staggered through that, and when we arrived at their home in North Curl Curl, we were greeted with cries of "surprise, surprise" as the lights were flicked on. There we discovered a party of happy, somewhat inebriated friends and neighbours of the Crawfords. They were all in fine fettle, ready to meet us and celebrate.

Bless them, the Crawfords, with the help of neighbours, had actually built an extra room for us. The room contained our foldout bed, lots of cozy stuff, and of course, a bar in the corner (it was Australia, after all).

We partied till we almost puked and eventually tottered into our beds, only to be awoken shortly afterwards by the most horrendous downpour the area had seen in years. The place was flooded. Rory and his Dad, Willy, got out ladders, buckets, flashlights, and all the paraphernalia they could muster. I tell you, that sobered us up quick smart. We were all bailing out with anything we could lay our hands on: pans, pressure cookers, anything, until it subsided enough for us to try to get a little more sleep before their bloody cuckoo clocks began to greet the new day.

That was an amazing time in our lives. After living on a knife edge for so long, it was literally a breath of fresh air to be enveloped in the warmth, love, sunshine, and laughter that these good people brought into our lives. We will never forget them for their kindness. We often chat on the phone and laugh about those times.

Very close to their house is Curly Pool (proper name North Curl Curl rock pool), which is like many Aussie beaches, a three-sided brick structure built at the edge of the ocean. This allows one to swim in the ocean water without actually being in the ocean. Here is where the locals bask in the salty, splashing water, and enjoying the spectacular views of the surf. Ruth and Martin spent their honeymoon there in 1998, and she could hardly drag him out of the water. He has a picture of Curly Pool on his office wall. Forget about leaving your heart in San Francisco.

To get to Sydney proper from the Northern Beaches, you either have to drive over bridges or through tunnels, or, more pleasantly, you can opt to take the Manly Ferry across the famed Sydney Harbor. That is another adventure filled with salt air, seagulls, waves, and the most spectacular view you can imagine. Many people travel that way to work every day, and yet somehow, there is always a feeling that a holiday is just around the corner.

On Fridays around lunch time, most Aussies start packing up and getting ready for the beach. Their attitude is that they work to live, whereas we live to work. They have drive throughs called "grog shops." They are like boozy bank ATMs. You drive in, pop the trunk of your car, and speak into the unit (a bit like McDonalds, only different), give them your order for beer, wine, ice, booze, etc., whereupon a guy muffled up as though he is about to climb Everest comes out into the frozen drive through; you crack your window a smidge, and give him your credit card. He then takes your money, loads your grog, and off you go. Party time!

Off indeed, to Bondi Beach or Curly Pool, or whatever sun drenched beach or bay tickles your fancy. And so the weekend kicks in. It's a wonderfully relaxed way of doing things. Of course, the women folks usually turn up with the grub, and in many areas there are barbeques, which the guys usually tend to, and a good family time is had by all.

It's hard to remember all that on Friday afternoons on the 405 Freeway in Los Angeles, struggling to get out of town, when you're bumper to bumper surrounded by people staring at their text messages and glaring at you when you eyeball them.

I know everyone is familiar with pictures of The Sydney Opera House, the Sydney Harbor Bridge, and the main tourist attractions. Just a few miles outside of the centre of town, you are soon in lovely lush areas that are so peaceful and quiet that you might even take a nap on one of the picnic benches in the parks and gardens.

A truly wondrous country is Australia. And the people are unique, not to mention the marsupials.

Have a look at sunrise at "Curly" Pool here (link):

Ruth's Music Trivia

```
    I am willing to bet that you didn't know that
if you sing "How Much Is That Doggy In The Window?"
backwards, the lyrics will still fit the melody!

    TRY IT

    Window the in doggy that is much how?
    Tail waggly the with one the
    Window the in doggy that is much how?
    Sale for doggy's that hope do I

    See? Now didn't that just make you a whole lot
more scintillating at dinner parties?
```

8
Here, There and Everywhere

My niece, Beryl Kendall (who was at that time married to Aunty Milly's son, Tom), graciously offered Ruth and I our first home in the States in March of 1983. It was a kind thing to do, but she didn't know what she was letting herself in for. Her son-in-law, Van Cline, picked us up at LAX from our dateline-crossing trip from Sydney and our last temporary home with the Crawfords. As we left the airport, we pulled onto the 405 Freeway, which to us was the craziest thing we had ever seen and experienced. Four lanes each way. People driving like bats out of hell. No signals, and as for hand signals – I have yet to see one in all my years in California.

Convertibles like we had only seen in the movies, and such a cacophony of noise and activity, it was just too much for our little jetlagged minds.

We had some wonderful times at Beryl's lovely home in Laguna Niguel when she and her kids helped us acclimate to our new and very different way of life. Laguna is a very laid back area. They have a yearly art festival and lots of community events, which are well supported by the local residents. Property is all high end; no slums. ("What's a slum?" a local Orange County resident was heard to ask.)

Monarch Bank, where Beryl took us to open our first American account, was like Disneyland to us, with its piped-in music, greeters, colouring books for the kids, and balloons. We were offered tea or coffee on arrival. I began to wonder which McCartney they had been expecting. But we were treated royally, even with our small account to place in their coffers.

Beryl loaned us her car, and in doing so, gave us a stern warning to be careful when we filled up with gas. This was because, in the not too distant past, she had driven away from a gas station with the pump still attached to the car and only when she was pulled to a frightening stop a few feet away, and seeing the startled staff in her rearview mirror, did she realize what she had done.

Another of Beryl's lovely stories was that, on a visit to her local Monarch Bank, she used the drive through, which in those days had one of those tubes that you put your money in, and it was swallowed down a mysterious tunnel into the actual bank building. Then it was returned to you with your receipt. She decided to put the whole thing into her bag and drove home with not only her receipt, but the tube as well. She only discovered this the next morning, and when she approached the bank, she saw workmen with pneumatic drills, opening up the drive-through. She rolled down her window and asked what was going on. She was told that they were missing one of their tubes, and it must be stuck underground. She then swiftly drove home and threw the tube into a neighbour's trash bin.

But this was not her finest hour. I think that was when she was preparing to entertain her husband's boss for Christmas dinner and nervously made the necessary steps to get the turkey and the trimmings ready to serve.

Imagine her distress when she asked husband Tom to carve the turkey. The first thing he pulled out, when looking for the stuffing, was a well roasted tea towel. Beryl had used it to wipe out the bird, and left it there when placing the stuffing inside.

I may have even topped her: I found myself plus bathtub liner rapidly descending through the floor and into the living room below whilst taking a shower upstairs. Fortunately, she and Ruth were on hand to rescue me. They switched off the water main, called for a disaster service, followed by a quick trip to the liquor store to purchase a very large bottle of Bacardi. We promptly consumed it to steady our nerves. Poor Beryl then had a lengthy saga with the insurance company and the homeowners association to get this remedied.

But what to do with those damn lodgers, The McCartneys?

We will never forget the kindness and hospitality of the Kendalls, who helped us get established in America.

Here's a peek at Laguna Beach (link):

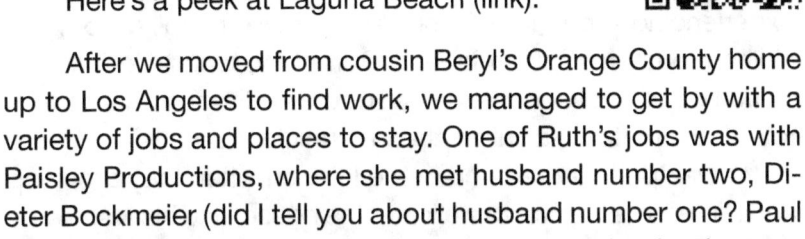

After we moved from cousin Beryl's Orange County home up to Los Angeles to find work, we managed to get by with a variety of jobs and places to stay. One of Ruth's jobs was with Paisley Productions, where she met husband number two, Dieter Bockmeier (did I tell you about husband number one? Paul Antonelli, a wonderful musician and arranger, who, by the way, has just received his fifth Emmy Award).

Dieter the Running Meter (aka Dieter Bockmeier)

In early 1988, Ruth was working as a production assistant and prop truck driver on a film crew, shooting a Mentadent toothpaste commercial for a German company in Baker, California, a no-horse town on the side of the 15 Freeway, 90 miles east of Las Vegas. She was footloose and fancy free at the time, and happened to spot a handsome looking chappie, the gaffer on the German film crew.

It was her job to check everyone into the hotel, make sure everything was in place, and ready for them all when they arrived at the end of the first hot day's location scouting in the desert. Being the little schemer that she was, when she checked out Dieter's room, she placed the customary half dozen beers in the fridge, and then promptly unplugged the fridge.

She finagled a room next door for herself, and sat back and awaited results. Needless to say, when the tired, dusty, thirsty, and jet lagged Dieter got to his room early evening, she could hear a number of cuss words being bandied about on the next-door balcony. So she knocked on his door to enquire if she could be of any assistance.

She gladly complied by getting the maintenance man to examine the fridge, and lo and behold, he switched it on, and voila! In no time, the beer was chilling, as was Dieter, who finished up inviting her to dine with him that evening. At the swankiest restaurant in town at the time – Denny's.

Need I tell you the rest of the story?

She and the rest of the crew returned to Los Angeles area, and I will never forget my first meeting with Dieter. We had been experiencing a gas leak in our area of North Hollywood, so I called Southern California Gas Company, who said I was to switch off all appliances, open all doors and windows, and NOT to strike a match. I awaited their technician anxiously.

I was puttering around in the kitchen when they drove up, and Dieter was the first to walk into the house, and his first words, in his cute Bavarian accent were: "Hmmm ... I think I smell gas." Without missing a beat, and without a thought, I responded, "Of course you do, you're a bloody German." Thank heavens he saw the funny side of it and laughed. Maybe that's what got him to "pass the audition" in Ruth's eyes...

Ruth broke it to me that they were planning to elope to Las Vegas to be married at the infamous Little White Wedding Chapel (which boasted a sign over the door saying "Joan Collins was Married Here").

She planned to wear an off-white coat dress, black high heels (as if she didn't already tower over Dieter, who was all of 5 feet 7 inches tall), and had a large lavender raffia hat that she proceeded to spray with black paint to complete her outfit.

Off they went, and their Nevada nuptials took place, in POURING RAIN, on April 20, 1988. Hitler's birthday, I might add, so at least Dieter might not forget his wedding anniversary.

The registrar asked if they would like the musical acompaniment of a wedding march, and when they accepted, she said "that will be an extra five dollars please." And, on seeing the colour of their money, pressed the "play" button on the boombox on the altar.

They were duly pronounced man and wife, but only after Dieter (whose English was not too good at that time) interrupted to ask, "vot is this DOOUSS part?" (Until Death Do Us Part.)

The mandatory photos were taken, and when Ruth took off her hat, she had a lovely black paint ring on her forehead. The paint had not had time to dry properly on her chapeau in the rare humidity that day.

When the music video shoot for Dieter Bohlen and his band Modern Talking ended, Dieter went back to Munich, and soon after, sent for Ruth to join him, staying at his parents' home on the outskirts of the city in Neuhausen.

Not one to hide her light under a bushel, she combed the yellow pages (which were of course in German, which she didn't speak at the time), looking for record companies, so that she might see what she could do about getting herself a record deal. Little did she know that "Record Company" is not under "R" - it is under "S" for "Schallplattenfirma." Damn clever zee Germans.

She eventually hooked up with Virgin Records, had an interview, and was told enthusiastically by the A & R guy that if she was only able to be a resident in Germany, they would definitely offer a deal. At that point, she called me and said, "Hand in your notice, get your ass over here, it's all gonna be great."

The ever dutiful little mother did as she was asked, and got moving to ready things to join them in Germany.

Needless to say, by the time she had come home to North Hollywood, ordered and packed crates, given notice on the rented house and her job, and then flown back to Germany and got Dieter to direct a video clip made to match her demos, that guy had been fired from Virgin Records, and the hunt started afresh. She eventually landed a deal with a lovely chap by the name of Ralph Siegel who owned Jupiter Records, part of the BMG group, which, after negotiating the contract, Ruth now describes the acronym as "Big Mean Germans."

The day after I arrived, Dieter was off to spend three weeks filming on a location in northern Germany, leaving us to stay with his bewildered parents, Fanny & Fonzie, in their very small flat, but who did their very best to make us welcome and cope with these two crazy foreigners. Thank heavens for Berlitz.

After the stress of travelling for his job, and Ruth being on the road with the music career for a couple of years, sadly the marriage fell apart, and Ruth moved back to the U.S., where she eventually married Martin (another German – hey what is up with that?). Dieter stayed in Europe, where he is a director of photography and concept / script writer at his Munich-based production company Electric Avenue Films, but they remain great friends to this day, and he still signs off every call and Skype with "I love you honey." A healthy way to move on, I'd say.

Living in Germany

Back to the plot. We lived with Dieter's parents, who were wonderful people. I got a job at the McGraw Kaserne Army Base. My three years in Munich was a varied and interesting time.

Dieter's parents, Fanny and Fonzie Bockmeier, lived in an apartment in Siegrunnerstrasse, on the outskirts of the city. They were so hospitable and made us very welcome. Neither of us spoke a word of German, and the parents didn't speak English. So we invested in a phrase book, which paid instant dividends. The phrase: "Wo is dach buch?" was frequently heard in that household. It led to some hilarious exchanges, with lots of drawings and partial explanations as we all explored our need to communicate.

I had hawked a Brother word processor with me that I had just bought with the intention of writing a book. The first one I wrote (but never published) was a secretarial handbook, containing many of the tips and tricks I had learned over the years. When I read it today, it seems so utterly irrelevant in this computerized age.

The day after we arrived, Ruth's husband Dieter was called away on location to Cologne, and our only other English speaking inmate was gone for a couple of months. He was a gaffer in the German film industry.

One of the first things we had to do (which one must in Germany) was go to the "Amt" and register our location. An Amt is a government department that deals with registrations of all kinds. It must be done every time there's a move. In our case, as incoming foreigners, it was even more complicated.

It is necessary to disclose your religion on your paperwork, as all churches deduct an automatic donation/tithe from your paychecks (imagine the outcry in America if they tried to pull that). It seems that, unless you are registered as a Catholic, at least in Bavaria, you cannot be married or buried on consecrated ground. A pox on all you sinners. I never did find out what they do with the remains of non-believers.

Ruth and I duly presented ourselves at this forbidding building where people sat meekly in rows awaiting their turn at the questioning. I was called first and handed over my paperwork, passport, confirmation of my current residence etc., and was asked the first question.

"Religion?" she spat the question at me, having decided that as I was a dreaded English person, I was to be treated with the utmost suspicion (after all, we won the bloody war you know). Nobody had warned me of this situation, so I naturally reacted in shock and horror.

"Religion?" I asked. "Why on earth do you want to know?" The hissed response was "because it is necessary." In a moment of panic, I blurted out "Calithumpian." It was, as far as I was concerned, a made up word, although I later learned that there is such a word. When Grunhilde questioned me further, I said that it was an ancient Scottish sect. She accepted this and duly noted it on my papers. We completed the forms, which were vigorously stamped and returned to me.

Next, it was Ruth's turn. Ruth said she was a "pedestrian." The steely middle-aged lady with bad feet duly made a notation on the form. How did I know she had bad feet when she was behind a counter? Because she got up and waddled over to the old metal file cabinet to replenish her desktop paperwork.

The same procedure ensued, and eventually, she applied her stempel vigorously to each sheet and thrashed on a poor unsuspecting stapling machine. Then off we went on our merry way.

Another adventure awaited us. Just up the street was one of those sunbed places, and Ruth decided to go in and have a treatment. I opted for sitting in reception and staring glassy eyed at the German magazines, which of course, made no sense whatsoever to me.

It turned out that when Ruth got off the tanning bed and was leaning across the cubicle to get a towel, she was aware of someone peeping through a little crack in the wood panelling.

She got dressed as quickly as she could, joined me, and tried to explain to the receptionist what had transpired. After much gesticulating, this flustered woman said she should file a police report.

This we did, which was another exercise in frustration. Nevertheless, Ruth filled out some more paperwork and left it in their good hands.

It seemed that Ruth was not the first person to file a complaint, and a couple of days later, she was visited by Herr Plod (zee police officer), who said she needed to go to an identity parade. Lo and behold, this was not one where the victim stood behind glass and looked over the line up, but she was actually in the same room. Imagine her stress when she pointed out the guy she thought was the one, although she didn't have much to go on, having only seen his eye and a small portion of his face. We never did hear what the outcome of that episode was. But it sure was scary.

The next time we were visited by the police was when we moved into our own flat a little while later. On moving day, Ruth was barbecuing sausages on the balcony. We had cousins visiting from Australia, and were also about to watch a documentary on TV about Ruth and Dieter, how they met on location in California, their subsequent marriage in Las Vegas, and transplanting to Munich.

When Ruth opened the front door and was confronted by two young policemen, she assumed it was about the peeping Tom. No, it was the sausage police. They informed her that it was against the law to barbeque on a Saturday. Furthermore, the smell of the food was disturbing to the neighbours. I promise you, I'm not making this up.

I got a job at the American Army base in Kaiserslautern. That was fun and very interesting. One of the fellow workers who lived on the base said that she too had been visited by the cops for washing her car outside the house on a Sunday. Oops! It was Bavaria, after all, when the only thing you were supposed to do on a Sunday was to go to church.

Dieter's sister, Christa, ran a beer garden nearby, which belonged to the railway authorities. She and her Mum were fantastic bakers, which is where Ruth picked up a lot of her cooking skills. Most of the people who patronized the little social club were retired railway workers, usually accompanied by their wives. They mostly viewed Ruth and I as somewhat odd (I can't imagine why). However, in due time, they took us into their circles and made us welcome.

It was a charming, old fashioned place, where they played dominoes, cards, and the children ran around in the gardens outside, playing hopscotch, riding on the swings. It was like stepping back in time.

The night before May Day, the men would stay up all night guarding the Maypole, as it was customary for warring villages to steal one another's Maypoles where possible. It was a custom that went way back.

I think Ruth shocked them all to the core when one day she turned up with an African-American man with whom she was writing songs. They had been introduced by her record company. He had landed in the area as a G.I., and after getting out of the service, continued to live there with his German-born wife. You could hear a pin drop when the two of them walked in. Then after a little pause, people recovered their composure and resumed their talking and drinking. But you could tell they were not used to seeing anyone who didn't quite fit the mold.

Take a look at Ruth on German TV sporting hair extensions and falling through a hole in the stage (link):

Kim Cooper (The Original Malibu Barbie)

I got a job as Kim Cooper's assistant in the late 1980s. She was then a freelance producer and post production supervisor on a movie called *Earth Girls Are Easy*. It was a fun and action-packed romp about aliens who landed their spaceship in the San Fernando Valley backyard swimming pool of a hairdresser gal who ran a salon called Curl up and Dye. The cast included a bunch of unknowns such as Jim Carrey, Geena Davis, Julie Brown, Jeff Goldblum, Charles Rocket, Damon Wayans, Angelyne, and many more.

Kim also hired Ruth to work with me on the credits of the movie, and we did our work on an early model IBM computer out of her apartment on Kraft Avenue in Studio City. We learned not only about computers, but got a first-hand glimpse of the film business.

When we were not busy, Ruth would also take on the mantle of house cleaner for Kim, and even rearranged her nail varnishes alphabetically by colour. Those were the days. We knew how to enjoy ourselves.

Kim and I decided to join Weight Watchers together. Because of her grueling schedule on the movie, I would frequently have to call them to explain her absence from the weekly meetings. It was quite an experience dealing with their overzealous telephone operators, who demanded proof of why she was not turning up. It was far from the softer approach that I am sure they have to take these days. They seemed more like probation officers than a support group.

My first introduction to Kim was at RKO Home Video on Radford Avenue in Studio City, in the early days of this relatively new aftermarket. I worked for a boss who was a stickler for protocol. Once, when I popped my head around his door to say goodnight, he noted that I had a pencil stuck behind my ear. He reminded me that it would be stealing if I took it home! This from a man who would have me spend hours typing up drafts of sermons for his church services. I guess he hadn't figured that we were stealing my employer's time by doing this.

Within the first few days of working there (I was not using my real name for reasons that I will divulge on deposit of your signed check), Kim celebrated her birthday and invited us all into her office for birthday cake and champagne. When introducing me as a newbie to my fellow workers, she asked where I was from. When I told her Liverpool, she said she'd once run away from home to travel to Liverpool to marry Paul McCartney. I managed to keep a straight face and didn't say a word. She and a couple of school friends had been systematically purloining their fathers' pocket change to buy Greyhound bus tickets to New York, where they planned to stow away on a ship to Liverpool, get jobs as chambermaids at the Adelphi Hotel, meet the

Beatles, and plan their weddings. When it came down to it, the others chickened out, and Kim sallied forth alone.

The school called her mom to check on her absenteeism, and the plot was uncovered. She remembers the cops hauling her off the bus in Arizona, where she spent a scary night in jail, until her father came next morning to pick her up and drive her home in silence. You've got to admire the tenacity of those early Beatles fans. To think if she had pulled it off, I'd have been her mother-in-law. We have laughed about this many times.

My friendship with Kim lasts to this day. She employed me again some time later at 20th Century-Fox when I returned from the three-year stint in Munich. This time the movie was *Alien III*. I remember sitting with my eyes shut tight at the premiere because I couldn't bear to watch this slimy creature dripping all over the screen.

Kim subsequently worked on *Speed*, *Mrs. Doubtfire*, *Life of Pi*, *Titanic*, and *Avatar*. Despite her hectic schedule and location travels to Australia and Europe, she has remained a constant influence in my life, even attending my recent Doctorate ceremony, and supporting me at book signings and other activities.

Her drive as a woman in the film business has been an inspiration to me. Her generosity and warmth are legend. And that's not counting the after parties, celebrations, fun times, and sleep overs in Malibu – memories too vast to relate.

Bless you, Kimmy. I hope now you understand how much you mean to me.

San Fernando Valley

Over the years, we have lived in several areas of the San Fernando Valley, providing us with lots of happy memories.

I can remember a day when Ruth called me at *USA Today*, where I was working in advertising sales on Santa Monica Boulevard in West Los Angeles. Her words were brief and to the point.

"When you finish work today, don't go home," she said. "You don't live there anymore." Just like that. But by now, I guess I had learned to live with these odd changes of plans in our lives with Ruth at the helm.

Friends from Germany, Arno Gmeinwieser and his wife Sherey, were in California on a trip. Over a boozy lunch, they all decided that if we found an apartment where we could all stay when they were over here and share the expenses, it would work out well. Firstly, they combed the local ads and located a place in Randi Avenue in North Hollywood. They whizzed over, saw it, completed the paperwork, paid the deposit, and that was that.

Then they were off to Ikea, bought all kinds of furniture and stuff (Arno's credit card must have been limitless), and arranged for it to be delivered.

The next few days passed by in a whirlwind of U-Haul rental trucks and friends to help with the heavy lifting. It all came to pass without much contribution from moi. I just had to turn up at night, after work, have dinner, tumble into bed, and start again the next morning.

We developed a liking for many of the local watering holes and music venues. We would think nothing of working a full day, and then setting out at about 9:30 p.m. to hear a favourite band or catch a movie. With hindsight, I can't imagine how we did it and still functioned. Or maybe we didn't function all that well, but we lived to tell the tale.

We used to frequent a bar called Josephina's on Ventura Boulevard to hear Preston Smith & The Crocodiles and Billy Vera and the Beaters. One of our best bars was Stanley's, which was next door to Record One Studios, owned by Val Garay. A lot of iconic records were recorded there by Steve Perry, Don Henley, and Toto. Don Shane ran a lovely restaurant called, funnily enough, Shane's. We spent many a night carousing there. Ventura Boulevard seemed to be a never-ending street of music, food, camaraderie, and goodwill.

Ruth became friendly with many of the locals, musicians, engineers, and behind-the-scenes people who hung out in our preferred bars. Around this time, several of our friends and relatives from around the globe began making the pilgrimage to the shrine of Hollywood. Many of them stayed with us and expected us to be able to drive them places, pick them up, drop them off, and it became something of a chore at times.

One particular visitor, who we thought was coming solo, got off the plane at LAX with her precocious 9-year-old son. This "child" wanted to rule the roost, watch porn on TV ("my Dad lets me watch it at home"), and protested when he was banned from watching. That was when we decided to put the blocks on visitors. After that, when people would get in touch and say they were coming to LA, we would ask for their fax number, and say we would send them some yellow pages of hotels and car rental companies. It never ceases to amaze me how people think, when you live in an area such as ours, you have all the time and resources in the world to pander to their needs.

And, some would be too young to rent a car and would be quite offended when we didn't offer a suitable alternative. I guess some folks have to learn the hard way. I even remember one lady guest calling me at RKO Home Video office asking me to drive home in my lunch hour and pick up some cigarettes for her. She was quite miffed when I refused.

But we are not really cruel people, just a little pissed off at finding we had become an unpaid vacationers' service. Next time – get an Airbnb!

Nashville Here We Come

After the shake, rattle, and roll of the 1994 Northridge earthquake, we felt it was time to move to somewhere a little more peaceful. Since I was working for *USA Today* in Los Angeles at that time, I asked my boss, the lovely Eric Belcher, if he could get me a transfer to somewhere a little less stressful.

Our newspaper was part of Gannett, which had publications all over the States. Eric came up with a suggestion for me to move to *The Tennessean*, based in Nashville. I interviewed over the phone, got the job, and was up, up, and away.

Ruth and Martin packed up the truck and the cat and hit the road. Another Willie Nelson moment in our lives. And believe me, there have been many.

We rented a small apartment on the edge of a golf course called Deerfield, and we three happy wanderers settled in and looked forward to some peaceful nights.

I drove into town each morning in sizzling heat, clad in suitable office attire, including stockings, heels, silk dresses, or a business suit. I was overjoyed to find that my assigned parking place was a few hundred yards from the office entrance, across the railway tracks, over a bridge, down numerous rickety steps, and into the snake pit.

By the time I got inside the building, my carefully coiffed hair was sticky and flat. The humidity was like nothing I'd ever experienced before, and my silk dress was clinging to my back. But I took it like the brave little secretary that I was, and got into the swing of things.

I needed a little time to adjust to the Nashville accent, which, while charming, was a bit hard for me to grasp sometimes. Like every area, they had their own slang and ways of stringing words together. I was amused and unnerved to be constantly addressed as "Miss Angie," which is evidently a mark of respect for people of a certain age.

We had a young receptionist who I once heard answer a phone call from Al Gore, who was friends with our publisher, Craig Moon. When she asked, "Who is calling him?" and he said his name, she responded, "You're shittin' me!" and promptly hung up on him.

We had some really happy times there. Life was much slower than in Los Angeles, and was filled with music and hospitality. We started our multimedia business there, and opened up a mailbox where the owner slept on a cot at the back of the property. Division Street, it was called, and one of our current famous clients actually still uses that same address for their mail. Small world, huh?

There were so many places to go to listen to live music, including a retail boot store. Inside this store, they also had live bands playing in the shop window. And how could you ever forget Tootsie's Orchid Lounge? Oh, and those magnificent places that featured line dancing, fun for all the family. And places where they did the chicken dance and wore lampshades on their heads. It was so refreshing and such a relief after the earthquake. We quickly settled into the South and made lots of lovely friends, with whom we are in touch to this day.

Martin laid down his first U.S. recordings there in a studio run by Bob Krusen, aided by his lovely wife Ann.

The music was still mainly country and western at that time, but, of course, lots of changes were to come over the next few years.

Some of the eateries were fascinating. There was a little dive bar close to the office where most of us would go for lunch. I remember being there the day the O.J. Simpson trial judge Lance Ito announced the verdict. The place was in an uproar. Their boast was that their waiters and waitresses were the rudest you could possibly find in any establishment. You went there expressly to be insulted. It was hilarious.

In the ladies room there was a huge chalkboard on which people would write the most unbelievable things, including a constant stream of "for a good time, call ..." that many would use to post their friends' and frenemies' phone numbers.

After three years, we got antsy for Los Angeles, and moved back.

Nashville has grown a great deal since we were there, and has lots more hotels, restaurants, arenas, and sports venues. The march of time.

Here's a sneak peek at a project Ruth and cameraman Ed Heffelfinger shot for Australian TV in 1995 at The Grand Ole Opry, Harlan Howard's Birthday Bash, around Music City, Tennessee. If you listen closely, you will hear Martin singing a song he and Ruth wrote called, "The Firefly Song" (link):

The Birth of McCartney Multimedia

As just described, I was able to transfer from my job with *USA TODAY* in Los Angeles to *The Tennessean* in Nashville, where we launched into our next adventure. And what an adventure it turned out to be! Ruth and Martin made inroads into getting jobs locally. Martin worked for Nippon Airlines at the airport using his skills as a forwarding agent.

The timing was good, as Martin planned to record his first musical tracks in Nashville, which were at least a diversion for him

Backyard photo in Playa del Rey, 2018.

during this transition. I remember going with him and Louise Harrison, who was visiting town, to record "Rain Dance." Ironically, we had the most torrential downpour I have ever experienced and we literally did our own rain dance, bailing out water from the studio throughout the session.

Ruth got various jobs temping, writing songs, and generally became acclimated to the different pace of life in the Deep South. She did catering on music video and movie sets. One notable experience was working on the Sharon Stone movie *Last Dance* as personal assistant to Peter Gallagher. This stark movie about a prisoner took them on location to an actual Death Row prison in Kentucky, which was a harrowing experience for the cast and crew.

When Ruth and I had to go out of town to appear at a Beatlefest, Peter kindly agreed to have Martin fill in for Ruth. This, in turn, led to Martin being re-hired in various positions as the movie progressed, from which he learned a lot about movie production, which proved beneficial to him throughout the coming years.

We were fortunate enough to make many friends in Nashville, including Bob Mather of EMI Music Publishing, Bob Krusen and his wife Ann Stokes and their music production business. It was in their studio that Martin made his first demos, grafting away at his craft.

If you landed a job with a publishing company, the norm then was for songwriters to report for duty daily and sit locked away in their little caves. Once there, they were expected to grind out songs for a weekly pittance and sign over all their writer's and publishing rights to their employer.

One of our former Australian friends said Ruth should meet up with Brian Cadd, a prominent Aussie rocker, who was staying in Franklin (near Nashville). So off she went, accompanied by my sister Joan, who was visiting from Liverpool.

Caddo was (and still is) a wonderful, colourful character, and he took them for shepherd's pie to the Bung-a-Nut Pig pub, where they cemented their friendship in grand style. During their time together, Caddo asked Ruth if she had ever heard about "a Yahoo." She had not, but he whetted her appetite about this new-fangled technology that was emerging. This led her to ask the local library if they had any books about the internet. The lady there was bewildered at the question and thumbed through her cardboard box of rolodex cards. Not coming up with any answers, she said she would send away to the Knoxville Branch Library to see what she could find.

The librarian called a few days later, saying she had some information, so Ruth trotted off to the library and came home armed with a stack of books about this mystical new "hypertext markup language," or HTML. She and Martin hunkered down, ordered pizza, and settled in to learn the wonders of this emerging technology, which started developing through the auspices of Al Gore's father in the Advanced Research Projects Agency (ARPA), which I believe created the first available-to-the-masses computer networking system. Previously, it had only been used by the military, academia, and in relation to space-related technology. Everyone said it was a flash in the pan and would never last. Ha!

Incidentally, Caddo's wife, Amanda Pelman, recently informed me that he is about to embark on a new tour in Australia. I have seen lots of great press about him to this end.

I was busy integrating into my new job at the newspaper and made friends with several of our advertising clients, one of whom was Robert Hendrick. He headed up a company called EdgeNet Media, a tech company that brought computer users into the 20th century. I didn't understand much of it at first, but I certainly learned a lot.

A little while later, Rob offered me a job to move over to his nearby Brentwood offices to be the general office assistant, keeper of the timesheets, and nightly shredder of unwanted documents. From there, I learned more about computers, the Internet, email, even scanners. I was so impressed with this incredible machine that could take a picture of your document and send it to your computer, or some other one. Robert was kind enough to let Martin come into the office in the evenings to learn a little more about this new-fangled technology, which proved invaluable to him.

I withdrew the princely sum of $100 from my savings, and we formed McCartney Multimedia, Inc., a Nashville Corporation (later to become a California corporation). Still crazy after all these years. Who'da thunk it?

Rob Hendrick helped us land our first website clients, as I recall, a pair of Australian brothers, the LeGarde Twins, who had their own little theatre on Music Row. Martin built them a website. Ruth decided to get in touch with one or two old friends and convince them that they needed a website, and we were off and running. The first to come forward was David Cassidy, who was our first celebrity client. This association helped beyond measure.

Those beginnings helped us gain entry into a world that is still expanding. I recently looked at our client list, which numbers in the hundreds. We have had a colourful and varied roster of clients. They range from musicians, writers, actors, photographers, cosmetics creators, restaurants, the U.S. Navy, government departments, film commissions, small businesses, the MGM Grand and related Las Vegas hotels, lawyers, winemakers, entertainment managers and agents, automobile giants, authors, celebrities, magicians, medical researchers, event coordinators; you name it, we've worked on it. Even Weight Watchers (although we don't practice what we preach and treat them better than they treated my old employer when she missed meetings). Oh, and yes, we had a miniature horse that had his own website and was a member of iFanz. He was a darling, and we met him when he did *The Chelsea Handler Show* in Hollywood.

We eventually became a woman minority-owned business, which enabled us to pitch for government jobs, public utility projects, and large publicly-traded companies who have a diversity vendor program. From sole proprietors and entrepreneurs to multinational corporations, no project is ever dull!

And two days are ever alike. Scan here to visit our website (link):

Playa del Rey, You Say?

Playa del Rey, where we currently live, is an old-fashioned beachside town. It has lots of neighbourhood watering holes, flower shops, second hand stores, and real estate agents who offer rental properties, ranging from posh to downright scruffy. It has a great atmosphere. Bars where you can take your dog, sit inside or outside in the sun, read your newspaper, and menus written on chalkboards. It even boasts what is said to be LA's smallest bar. It only has eight stools. There's a chalkboard in the doorway that says: "We're open, but don't expect much."

It is called, "The Harbor Room."

The locals patronize it, do their crossword puzzles, place their bets on the gee gees, and bring their used books to leave on the shelves for others to enjoy.

When I first moved here, I went in one Saturday afternoon with my friend Lora Colvard, a substantial lady. The bartender asked,

"What do YOU want? We don't usually serve obese people in here in case they sweat on the wallpaper." We felt truly welcome.

Indeed, a splendid atmosphere. They have an old fashioned cash register, where everything is rung up at $11, no matter what you are drinking. Even if you order two drinks, it is still $11. They are open until 1:59 am, and they are packed to the rafters after midnight when people are looking for somewhere to go for a last call. Despite the California "no smoking" ban, patrons are puffing away at their pipes and ciggies, and maybe something even a little more exotic. It really is the bar where everybody knows your name. It makes Cheers look like a state penitentiary.

The Harbor Room is just steps from the actual beach, where you can kick off your shoes and wiggle your toes in the sand, breathe in the air from the Pacific Ocean, and watch the planes taking off from LAX bound for who knows where. At this place one can feel a sense of well-being.

Its history is fascinating and there is a great website with lots of historical photos here (link):

We enjoy living here, with good neighbours being a real bonus. We have keys to each other's homes, a neighbourhood watch group, a local newsletter, and a great community attitude. Many grow fruits and veggies and often pass them on to Ruth, who cooks up a storm most Saturdays, and doles out food parcels to all and sundry. It's a win-win situation for us all.

John Cleese

Our working relationship and friendship with John Cleese dates back to 2004, when McCartney Multimedia was hired to create his first online presence.

This was our biggest project at the time, and we were all very excited to work with the talented man.

Initially, we spent time at his ranch in Montecito and at our Playa del Rey offices, discussing the whys and wherefores of how he should be presented to the world online.

Whenever he needed to stay in our area overnight, he favored The Inn at Playa del Rey, who had a specially long bed installed for him. (He is 6 feet, 7 inches tall.)

He also favored Tandoor-a-India on Pershing Drive in Playa, and we all spent many long hours on our project over food and drink. John said it was the best Indian food he had found outside of London, which is the Mecca for Indian food.

John always wanted everyone present at meetings to each have a freshly sharpened pencil and a fresh yellow legal pad. I ordered scads of them from our local office supply people. We assembled a great team of programmers, graphic designers, copywriters, and photographers. He had us build a green screen in one of his barns so that he could record any random thoughts as they came to him, sometimes in the middle of the night.

After many long hours of exchanges of ideas, we finally arrived at an outline for this most entertaining website. John had huge scrap books of old postcards and family photographs shipped to us. Newspaper clippings and video footage were sent over from the BBC in England, which were a treasure.

We spent weekends at his ranch, which was home to llamas, peacocks, horses, chickens, and all manner of birds, both caged and free. He had more books than we had ever seen in one house, even in the kitchen drawers, every available nook and cranny (does anyone know what a cranny is please?) and

Martin and John Cleese, Montecito, hard at work.

bookshelf. His thirst for knowledge was insatiable. He had an impressive collection of first editions, and could quote from them at the drop of a hat. He would even quote the page and paragraph number. Fascinating.

For a man so acclaimed for his wit and humour, he was surprisingly serious. Ruth analyzed this as being due to the fact that he was not that experienced at working solo, but had always been a part of a group, be it the Pythons, the cast of *Fawlty Towers*, or a movie cast and crew.

When we launched the website, John suggested a little get together at our offices in Playa to bring all the creative team together. This was a great success.

Angie and John Cleese (one of the funniest men alive) outside Playa del Rey Offices. He is holding two of his favourite things: me and a bottle of fortification.

The official photographer informed me that he was running to a tight schedule and needed to leave soon. He wanted a picture of John and me together. I tugged at John's sleeve. He was deep in discussion with one of our designers. He finally looked down, and boomed at me, "Woman, if you don't stop it, I'll have to put the cover back on your cage." As if I were a budgie. Indeed.

He wanted his beautiful daughter Camilla to learn the ropes by interning at McCartney Multimedia. She was friends with Paris Hilton at the time, and they would go out clubbing in Hollywood and Beverly Hills until the wee small hours. We had asked her to present herself at 10 a.m. each morning, and some days she would turn up on what we called "CST" – Camilla Standard Time. That was maybe 11 to 11:30 a.m., possibly wearing one shoe ("I think I lost my other Louboutin at a club last night"), or missing her cellphone, which was one of many. She had a tendency to leave them scattered around West Hollywood at various places of entertainment.

On days when she was scheduled to come to the office, we laid out an extra supply of cold drinks and ice. It was essential to keep the males in the office calm and cool, as Camilla is extremely beautiful and her wardrobe was always very fetching.

Camilla was a talented horsewoman, and John was happy to buy her a new horse to further her championship Gymkhana career. That is, until Ruth suggested to him that he might want to consider leasing horses instead of owning them. He thought this a capital idea.

Camilla told us some hilarious stories about her childhood. One in particular was about being asked to bring something to school for a "show and tell" with the subject "what I did on my summer holidays." She turned up with an Annie Liebovitz portrait of her dad in full drag, including wig, lipstick, eye liner, the full monty, swinging the young Camilla round like an airplane. He also sported a substantial moustache at the time. This evidently went down like a lead balloon with her teacher.

When she asked, "Daddy, where did I come from?" The response was, "Harrods." (And she believed him.)

On another occasion, at their London home, a celebrity dinner party was in the works and the caterers evidently turned up with live lobsters in a tank. Camilla was apparently rather horrified as a young'un to see these spiny creatures bobbing about and asked her daddy if she could "take them for a walk around the garden before we kill them." The request was granted, dog leashes were found for the lobsters, and off they went on their perp walk before being plunged into hot water, murdered, and served presumably with a warm drawn unsalted Danish butter and a crisp, chilled Verdicchio!

Camilla called Ruth one day and said bluntly, "You know this 10 a.m. thing is not gonna work for me." Thankfully for her (our loss entirely), her office desk days were short lived. She is now a successful touring stand-up comedian and has also been on tour with her equally hilarious, and equally tall, father.

The very first time Ruth, Martin and I traveled up to Montecito, John wined and dined us all evening, and then decided it was far too late for us to drive back to L.A., so he just threw

A confused John Cleese with Angie at Playa office.

us the keys to the ranch and said we should stay overnight, and he went off to sleep at the beach house close by. Imagine trusting anyone like that.

I was particularly pleased to find a room with a big table for jigsaw puzzles, which is where you could find me if the discussions didn't really concern me.

As I write this, John is still making appearances all around the world and lives on an island in the Caribbean with his present wife.

Those were truly some fascinating days (and nights).

Watch some of the best *Fawlty Towers* moments here (link):

Wedding Facts from the Reverend Dr. Angie

As an ordained minister, I am available to officiate at weddings. I always find it most helpful to have a few facts at my fingertips.

For example, do you know why June is considered the most popular month for weddings?

In the olden days (when Adam was a lad), most people got married in June because they took their yearly bath in May and still smelled pretty good by June. However, by the next month they were starting to pong a bit, so brides carried a bouquet of flowers to hide the smell. Hence, the custom today of carrying a bouquet.

There are lots of interesting wedding traditions worldwide. For example, in Italy, wedding festivities usually kick off in the morning, ideally on a Sunday. According to regional Italian folklore, you should never marry (or leave for your honeymoon) on a Friday or Tuesday, or you're bound to have loads of bad luck, whilst Saturdays are reserved for widows getting hitched to husband number two (or three, or four).

Fathers once used their daughters as currency to a) pay off a debt to a wealthier landowner, b) symbolize a sacrificial, monetary peace offering to an opposing tribe, or c) buy their way into a higher social strata. So when you feel all sappy and sentimental about daddy walking his little girl down the aisle, remember that it's just a tiny hangover tradition from the days when daughters were nothing but financial investments to dear papa.

And as for wearing a veil over her face – that was so the groom wouldn't know if he was stuck with an ugly one until it was time to kiss the bride (and too late to back out). There is also some superstition about warding off evil spirits. Personally, I prefer the first option.

And as for the best man? I have read that he was like the second shotgun to stand guard over the proceedings, in case anyone tried to kidnap the bride, or some even worse fate that might rear its ugly head. Now it has merely become a symbol (or the guy who goes out with the groom the night before and gets hammered and finishes up with the strippers). All he has to do is not lose the wedding rings.

Something old ... This dates back to Victorian times in England. The something old was meant to tie the bride to her family and her past, while the something new represented her new life as the property (yes, property!) of a new family. The something borrowed was supposed to be taken from someone who was already a successfully married wife, so as to pass on a bit of her good luck to the new bride. The colour blue (Virgin Mary-approved) stood for all sorts of super fun things like faithfulness, loyalty, and purity. My, my, how times have changed.

The first ceremony at which I officiated was when my dear friends, Tim Arendt and Donald Dale, exchanged nuptials. Same sex partnerships first became legal in California in October, 2008, and I was delighted to unite them in marriage. They were married on the porch of their beautiful Playa del Rey home and surrounded by friends and family. A beautiful reception at The Ritz Carlton in nearby Marina del Rey followed. It was a truly memorable occasion. And, I got to marry two wonderful people who care for one another.

Who'da thunk when I was a little 'un growing up in Liverpool that in my late eighties, I would be in a position to officiate at such an important occasion in the lives of two loving people?

Ruth and I LOVE weddings – in fact, see us narrate (link) Prince William and Ms. Kate Middleton's nuptials from bed (with big 'ats on).

Rikki Klieman and Bill Bratton

I had the privilege of getting to know Rikki Klieman, firstly as a website client at our McCartney Multimedia company in Los Angeles, which she continues to be. I also came to know her as an author, a criminal defense lawyer, a legal analyst, actress, filmmaker, and wife of Bill Bratton, who at that time was the chief of the LAPD.

They would occasionally come down to our little patch of heaven in Playa del Rey on Saturday afternoons, and we'd go for a low key lunch, usually a burger. I remember one time when we all went to Outlaws (appropriately named?) and, after, being seated, there was a long delay. On checking with the kitchen, it appeared that half of the busboys and cooks had made a run for it when they saw who was sitting in the back room, reading the menu with items on it like "Bandit Burgers," and "Bonnie &

Rikki Klieman, Bill Bratton, Angie, and Ruth at a screening.

Clyde Burgers." We hastened to assure the good folks that Bill was just visiting as a private citizen, and was not investigating their immigration status.

They later moved to New York City, where Bill served as its police commissioner until moving on in September, 2016. A man more dedicated to his work would be hard to find (and he likes cats, too).

Originally from Boston, his skills in law enforcement are legendary, and he is ably supported by Rikki. Theirs is a far from easy life, which they both tackle with amazing energy and vigor.

He re-entered the private sector, where he continues his forthright endeavours in law enforcement and security.

On September 11, 2009, Bill was awarded the honorary title of Commander of the Most Excellent Order of the British Empire by Queen Elizabeth II, "in recognition of his work to promote cooperation between the United States and United Kingdom police throughout his distinguished career." Then Prime Minister David Cameron wanted to invite him to become Commissioner of Police for the Metropolis of London, but it was found that to hold this position, he had to have been British born.

Angie with Bill Bratton and Rikki Klieman at a British Consulate gathering in Los Angeles.

In late 2016, Rikki invited us to a screening in Los Angeles of *In The Line of Fire*, a documentary that she had produced and narrated relating to many of the heroic events carried out by our men and women in blue. It was a very moving occasion, and we met a lot of the current law enforcement people, many of them youngsters who are dedicated to protecting and serving us all.

I was so jazzed when Rikki agreed to write the foreword for this, my second book. And after reading it, I think we should form a Mutual Admiration Society.

Check out her *CBS This Morning* legal analysis on such high profile cases as Bill Cosby, Jussie Smollet, and more, here (link):

Tribute Bands

It's not only The Beatles who have a legion of tribute bands, but also many other performers from the early days of pop music, rock and roll, and even punk and new wave.

When we first began planning stage appearances, the scope was utterly bewildering. Many of them are brilliant and some even get plastic surgery to look like their heroes. I wonder how they will feel about that when they get really old.

We were fortunate to work with the Cavern Club Beatles when we did appearances to celebrate the 50th anniversary of the filming of *HELP!* in Obertauern, Austria. These boys were, and are, amazing, and helped us have the most wonderful trip. Some of the locals told us that, although somewhat advanced in years, they felt that our shows transported them back to the magical days when the filming of this movie changed their lives.

Two of these boys are brothers, Tony and Jimmy Coburn. They play Paul and John, and do it with uncanny similarity. They are such lovely-natured guys, too. They were managed by Jon Keats, one of the directors and owners of The Cavern, who himself is quite a performer. We never wanted that trip to end.

It should be noted that, due to our aftershow gatherings at our hotel, they actually ran out of wine and had to get a special delivery one morning, way up there in the Alps. They had never experienced anything like it before, but maybe they hadn't had too many Scousers as guests until then.

And we have worked several times with The Moptops, whose John Lennon is played by Joe Stefanelli. He has been a friend since our earliest days in Los Angeles. His portrayal of John once stunned Cynthia Lennon and brought her to tears, so uncanny his performance seemed to her. Now that's saying something.

In more recent times, when we needed to scale down our accompaniment for a smaller show at a Staten Island Arts College, we worked with a Lennon and McCartney team named Tom Raider and Morgan Cates, who enchanted Ruth and me with their performances. It always seems that when we are seeking performers to play Beatles music, we meet up with so many very talented and dedicated people. The circle expands.

QR Codes

A few years ago, Ruth was approached by Paul Reitz, a Texas businessman whom she had met as a client when he co-owned Two Bunch Palms hotel in Desert Hot Springs.

Fast forward to the time when he had become interested in QR codes, the square things that look like a bathroom tile. They were well established in Europe and Japan, and were just beginning to make their mark in America when she met Paul.

They formed a company called "Connect Codes" to introduce this technology to our part of the world. Unfortunately, they were well ahead of their time, and it didn't gain the mass acceptance that they hoped it would. The public was just not yet quite ready to embrace them, and sadly, the scheme didn't reach its full potential.

Fast forward to today, when we have adopted the use of QR in order to introduce you, dear reader, to numerous links to many of the items referred to in this book, thus helping you step further into today's and tomorrow's technology and let yourself be one of the "in" crowd. You, of course, have already found many of them scattered throughout this book. So go on, click and see what is behind that magical tile. You'll be glad you did.

9
Number 9, Number 9

Celebrity Cookbook

Many moons ago, Ruth and I hit upon the idea of a celebrity cookbook. It was in the olden days before the internet, when we actually telephoned people and wrote letters to ask for their submissions.

I still have all of their responses, including one or two from folks who are no longer with us, but are hopefully cooking their delectable recipes at that big drive-through in the sky.

I was reminded of this today, when a Facebook friend published a recipe for gin pancakes. It was a replica of one that Dudley Moore sent us in a letter, and it went like this:

Gin Pancakes

Ingredients:
- Eggs
- Flour
- Salt and Pepper
- Milk
- Gin

Method:
- Mix all ingredients except the gin in a large mixing bowl
- Chuck it into the trash
- Drink the gin
- Send out for food to be delivered

Here endeth today's lesson.

Mrs. McCartney's Teas & Mrs McCartney's Wines

For the past few years, I have been selling my organic teas online and have been able to make donations from the sales to the Linda McCartney Breast Cancer Research Centre at the Royal Liverpool Hospital.

We visited Houston, Texas, in 2015, and were there to attend my friend Barry Coffing's annual music bash, Springboard South, for his Music Supervisor organization.

Whilst there, we nipped across the road to sample the delights of the Discover Wine Festival. After a chat with vintner David Skinner of Clear Creek Winery, we decided to create some wines in similar ("Beatley" named) flavours, and presto! Mrs. McCartney's Wines was born. The fruits are grown in Texas, and the juice comes from various award-winning sources in Napa and Sonoma in California. David waves his magic wand, blends it all together, bottles it, and so … after a long and winding road from California to Texas, said wines were finally launched at the Discover Wine Festival at David's Clear Creek Winery on June 26, 2016. And what a great success it turned out to be.

Angie having afternoon tea at home in Playa del Rey. (Photo courtesy DawnBoweryPhotography.com.)

There was live music provided by several of the talented youngsters who were appearing at the Springboard South event. It was such a fun day, with some lovely food prepared by David Skinner's "eculent" restaurant [*no capitalization in the name*].

Lots of enthusiastic volunteers helped Ruth, Martin, and I dispense samples of the fruity flavours to the crowds of wine tasters. The "happy snaps" of me behind the counter do not note the fact that I was standing in a bowl of cold water to keep me cool for several hours in the steamy hot Texas weather. I can see why the local ladies have such great complexions, with all that humidity.

Ruth has created some thirst quenching cocktails to slake your thirst, and in Texas, there's never a shortage of thirsts.

I'll spare you the details here, but if you log on to www.mrsmccartneyswines.com you can learn all about the flavours, the cocktails, and how to order.

At Rock 'n Brews, El Segundo, sampling their new White Album Sangria from Mrs. McCartney's Wines collection.

Currently we like the "White Album Sangria," featuring Mrs. McCartney's Maharishi Peach that is served at the El Segundo flagship of the Gene Simmons and Paul Stanley chain of restaurants called Rock and Brews. If you happen to go there, please ask for it by name.

Likewise, on www.mrsmccartneysteas.com, you can find out about how the teas are sourced from all over the world, brought into the United States, delivered to my trusty suppliers, and shipped to me to dispense to my many friends and avid tea drinkers. Now get the kettle on!

Dinner with the McCartneys

Once we teamed up with Chef David Skinner, we began holding gourmet dining events at his Kemah, Texas restaurant,

David Skinner and Angie at USA TODAY*'s Food & Wine Event in Scottsdale, AZ.*

eculent. Eculent is a fabulous farm-to-table intimate restaurant about 35 miles south of Houston. We have held several of these dinners over the past few years, with Ruth and David working together to devise menu items that relate to Beatles-themed ingredients.

David and his wonderful crew, including Chef Nancy Manlove, have all contributed and created these memorable meals. The evening consists of a welcome cocktail (by Mrs. McCartney's Wines, of course), appetizers, and a main course, or should I say, courses. At the beginning of each course, David tells diners how the food was prepared and what they can expect. He has some amazing items, and pairs each with a suitable wine accompaniment. There are also several screens around the restaurant that display many of Martin's media pieces, some Beatles related, others depicting nostalgic commercials and other entertaining items. Plus, there is a soundtrack of songs by The Beatles being performed by diverse performers, from Willie Nelson to Anne Murray to Nancy Sinatra.

Then, whilst the tables are being cleared and prepared for the next course, Ruth and I mingle with the guests, tell Fab Four stories, answer questions, and generally create an atmosphere of family style warmth and goodwill.

Prior to dessert being served, David takes the guests upstairs to tour the winery and then to his incredible food laboratory where he creates the magic.

We constantly hear from people who have attended these events, asking when they can expect a repeat. David is not only the master chef and vintner, but is a world traveler in search of more ideas for his gastronomic creations. We don't do these as often as we might like, but we certainly keep it top of mind.

Here is a promo for the Dinner with the McCartneys events (link):

NASA's Dental Magician

During one of our trips to Kemah, Texas to host a "Dinner with the McCartneys," we became friends with Dr. David Gordon and his lovely family. They offered us great hospitality, even a dental implant. I told him that I had received an exorbitant quote for such treatment in Los Angeles.

He suggested that I visit his office the next day for a consultation. He ordered X-rays and impressions of my mouth taken in preparation for our next visit.

This duly came to pass (I sounded a bit Biblical then, didn't I?) and during our next trip, I went to have the implant fitted on our final day, en route for the airport.

I was worked on by various members of his very capable staff, and when the deed was done, I asked for my bill. I was surprised and delighted to find that all they needed was autographed copies of my book, *My Long and Winding Road*.

In response to my questions about the procedure, David explained that the implant was held in place by a fiber optic post, which would dissolve once the tooth was firmly settled. He said it was a procedure he had perfected to use on NASA astronauts who needed special attention when they returned from outer space, where their gums receded due to the lack of gravity. As it turns out, I was the only non-astronaut person to receive this innovative procedure.

So much for the benefits of being related to a former Beatle. You see, it does have its perks.

At the end of the session, he invited us into his private office where he performed card tricks and other forms of "magic" (another of his skills) and entertained us. Ruth, Martin, and David Skinner, my partner in mrsmccartneyswines.com, were all highly entertained. It put us all in a good mood before setting off for the airport on our journey back to Los Angeles.

I wonder if I can get Netflix on my bionic tooth?

Springboard South

Our old friend and music colleague, Barry Coffing, invited us as guests at his annual Springboard South Music Festival in Houston, Texas in June, 2015. It was an amazing lineup of talent and a great weekend of music.

We made a quick visit to the Deborah Duncan Great Day Houston Show. During the preamble, she admitted that she was a diehard Beatles fan. Surprise, surprise! And she had some great footage of their early days to show viewers.

The audience was very welcoming, as was Deborah, and it helped publicize the upcoming event.

The festival ran for three days, and there were performers from morning until late evening, every day, with other outside activities, like get-togethers at bars and local music venues. The overall effect was one of great warmth and spirit.

Ruth and I appeared on one of the mentor panels and tried to give some sound advice to these enthusiastic youngsters.

As has been proven all too often in the past, these young folks are so keen to get ahead they are usually willing to sign just about anything that is put in front of them. We urged them to proceed with lots of caution, and if offered contracts, to seek the best legal advice possible. Then, when they do achieve success, they have a far better chance of controlling their own destiny, both financially and artistically.

Two years later, in early 2017, we attended another of these events in San Diego, with even bigger crowds of young hopefuls. It was a real joy to hear some of their success stories, and even more inspiring to hear tales of their tenacity in hanging in there. They all need a little encouragement, and we were happy to supply lots of that.

Barry Coffing runs www.musicsupervisor.com, an organization based in Texas. They supply copyright-cleared music clips and beds to film, television, music videos, commercials, corporate events, and wherever they may be needed. It is a great resource for people who may be looking for music for their products without having to go through all the hassle of licensing and the other necessities. Contact Barry if you need anything. He will be happy to guide you.

And tell him I sent you. He's a lovely fella, with four talented kids. His wife Megan often works with and for us on various design projects for logos, packaging, etc.

Scan the code to see our appearance on Deborah Duncan's KHOU show Great Day Houston (link):

HELP! In Obertauern, Austria

On the 50th anniversary of the Beatles filming *HELP!* In Obertauern, we were invited to do a celebratory show at a couple of different venues in this charming little Alpine town.

We were delighted to bring The Cavern Club Beatles over, together with their manager, Cavern Club co-owner, Jon Keats, and more than a great time was had by all.

On the day that the boys arrived, they went swimming in the lake in the afternoon before sound check. As the sun was waning, we were watching from our hotel balconies, seeing three of the lads waving their arms about wildly. It was only later that we found out that Tony Coburn (aka Paul McCartney) was having issues. Tired and emotional, I believe they call it. So someone swam out, rescued him from his floating mattress, and hauled him ashore. We were all holding our breath when it came time to get to the venue for sound check, but he came through like the trouper that he is.

Their performances were terrific, and audiences loved them. And no wonder. Each night, after the show, we would all meet in the hotel bar and swap stories, sing, laugh, drink copious amounts of wine, gather round the piano, and totter off to bed as the sun was coming up. It was one heck of a trip.

We even used to get Jon Keats to do his lovely Ken Dodd impression, which was always hilarious.

As I mentioned earlier, the hotel actually ran out of red wine (not my fault, I drink white). They had to send a truck to the brewery in a nearby town for additional supplies. They had never experienced such a thing before, even in the height of tourist season. But, they were reckoning without Scousers.

Ruth crocheted a huge red and white scarf (like the Beatles wore in the original movie) for our fearless Cavern Club Beatles. We took some great photos of them in it, and we sent it back

Freda Kelly, Angie, and Ruth with Mag. Raimund Carl, who heads our McCartney Sports division in Vienna.

to Liverpool in the care of Jon Keats for future events. I wonder where it is now? Not on Ebay, I trust?

Freda Kelly joined us on that trip, too, for part of the time. Then off she went to do appearances in support of her award-winning documentary *Good Ol' Freda* in nearby towns.

One of the locations was at the hotel where the boys stayed. They even had the original menu that they had all signed. It was just stuck in a drawer under the cash register. Not even laminated, would you believe?

Herbert Lürtzer, the owner of the hotel and other establishments in the town, told us that he was Paul's stunt double in the skiing scenes, and invited us to go up to his lodge at the top of the mountains on the coming Friday afternoon. He said he would send a "schnee taxi" for me. I thought that meant a vehicle. When we arrived at the appointed meeting place, they had me sit on a motorcycle, which I thought was merely a photo op. But no! This was, in fact, said schnee taxi, which would ultimately whisk us away up the mountains. Fortunately, I was held in place by Raimund Carl, our partner who runs our Vienna office (McCartney Sports), and up, up, and away we went.

If you scan the code (link) with your mobile device, you will see the high speed surprise they pulled on little old me! Who knew that was going on in broad daylight at the top of a mountain?! *(Note: we presented this code in Chapter 5. We just want to make sure that you watch it!)*

Imagine our surprise upon reaching our destination, when we came upon this massive ski lodge with literally hundreds of pairs of skis stacked up outside. When we got inside, with the aid of some security guards, we were plied with various adult beverages until we felt less anxiety, and were invited to stand up top, overlooking the throngs below, who were literally dancing on the tables. Hr. Lürtzer told us that he had had the tables reinforced for that purpose. It also meant that the waiters and waitresses could pass by more easily with their heavily loaded trays of drinks and snacks for the carousing clientele.

We had to leave early evening for another appearance. The thought of the return journey was a little hair raising, but as before, I was bungee corded to the driver, who eventually got me to the bottom of the hill without mishap.

Lined up at the bottom of the slopes were an array of doctors and lawyers, crutches, stretchers, and business cards at the ready, preparing for new business in the broken arms and legs department. They probably did a roaring trade in mending limbs.

That evening, we also attended a screening of Klaus Voormann's interesting documentary *All You Need is Klaus*. This was a fascinating event and Klaus was very gracious during the Q & A session which followed.

I remembered a story where The Beatles had said how impressed they were, when they were first driven into Obertauern, at the number of young people lining the route on both sides, and they took it as a mark of their respect and welcome. Not so. It seems that there had previously been an avalanche that wiped out numerous people and properties, and these youngsters were there on watch, to be able to give the warning immediately if they thought there might be another such event. This small tourist-driven town didn't want to go down in history for burying The Beatles in snow!

Turkey for Beginners

After our Obertauern trip, due to some very complicated ticketing arrangements with our travel agent, we ended up flying back via Turkey to Munich, Germany.

Our arrival in Turkey was after dark, and the taxi ride from the airport to our Airbnb was like something out of a *Speed* movie. There didn't appear to be any lane markings on many of the streets, and it was just one big happy free for all. By some miracle, we arrived safe and sound.

Ruth had booked an Airbnb on the outskirts of town, asking the owners to please provide easy access for me. (We use wheelchairs at airports so I can avoid long walks, and we also get to board first, which is always helpful.) The guy must have thought I was completely disabled and placed a piece of plywood from the curb to the entrance, where a wheelchair awaiting us. When Ruth asked about it, he said he had borrowed it from his grandfather for the evening, putting him to bed before leaving for the night shift.

Imagine our pleasure at finding the fridge already loaded with bread, cheese, fruit, whiskey, Coke, wine, beer, and water. So thoughtful of him, and he even offered at that late hour to go to a nearby shop if we needed anything else. They couldn't have been more hospitable and friendly. And the cost of these goods was amazingly low. No ripping off tourists here.

After a good night's sleep (we awoke the next morning by calls to prayer from the nearby mosque), Ruth and Martin went out in search of early morning coffee, which was plentiful, plus local pastries, giving them full benefit of the local atmosphere. There were building sites around us, and the men got started on their day's work very early, before the sun got too high.

Our first day of touring took us to the Blue Mosque, an incredible experience. Even the locals were impressed to see that Ruth had come prepared with head covering, as they offer free ones to women tourists before entering these hallowed walls.

The use of cameras was limited, but we were permitted to photograph certain areas, including the row of sinks where worshippers are required to wash their feet before entering. There were separate areas for men and women.

We spent time in a local restaurant, which, again, was so completely Turkish, with all the little knick-knacks and pictures adorning the walls, amazing soups and salads, red wine, and great coffee (but not a drop of Mrs. McCartney's Teas in sight). Martin started chatting with one of the local businessmen, who took him off to see his carpet shop, and up on to the roof to watch the amazing sunset.

That night, when we got back to our apartment, there were more fresh breakfast rolls and milk, again, thoughtfully put there by our apartment manager.

The weather the following day was not good, so I elected to stay in and read, rest, watch television, and catch up, whilst the kids went out sightseeing again. (Television in Turkish was a challenge.)

Then it was time to move on.

I can honestly say that I have never experienced an airport like Istanbul, both from a security standpoint, and from its grandeur. I could have happily abandoned all future travel trips and stayed there forever.

When our taxi dropped us off, we had to go through three checkpoints, with our tickets and passports, before we were even allowed to access the entry hall of the airport. So rigorous was their security system.

We had previously purchased the necessary transit visas online (or so we thought), having paid $50 each for them. But, when we went to the check-in desk, we were told that what we had was not valid for exit for Ruth and me, but Martin's was. So we had to go to another area and pay another $50 each in order to be processed. Meanwhile, time was ticking away, and we were becoming more than a little anxious.

I got a strong feeling that this was some kind of a scam, but in a country where you don't speak the native language, it's not a good idea to protest. So we paid up, and eventually were on our way.

When we got to the transit lounge, it was like a wonderland. In all my travels, I've never seen such an elaborate display of foods from all nations, even a honeycomb, from which you could hack a fresh piece of honey for your tea or coffee.

There were pool tables, pinball machines, a cinema with luxurious reclining seats, a spa, a beauty parlour, prayer areas for the Muslims, and a non-denominational chapel. Upstairs and outside was a smoking area.

Of course, there were the usual international newspapers and magazines, colouring books for the children, and a play area. It was all just too much to take in. We each had our fill of nourishment, and were more than comfortable when we boarded our Turkish Airlines flight to our next destination.

Once we took off, we were treated to even more luxury, being handed menus by chefs, fully attired in the traditional uniforms and tall hats. The pre-meal cocktails were served on trolleys bearing illuminatis, beautiful linen and silver table settings, cut glass tumblers, water and wine glasses. I have seldom seen such luxury, even in the finest European hotels.

The in-house entertainment was vast and did not disappoint. I can remember we watched an amazing documentary about bees, which held us fast until our main course was served. The appointment of the cabin was so comfortable and inviting and the service was near perfect. It was the one and only flight I have ever been on that I didn't want to end.

Scan the code to see Ruth and Martin's video account of three days in Istanbul made on their smart phones (link):

A Most Ebullient Gentleman

I was introduced to the ebullient Dr. Simon Mills, an Australian gentlemen of many talents, in early 2015. We met via our old friend, musician Brian Cadd. Simon, who now lives in New York City, asked if I'd be interested in receiving an Honorary Doctorate of Business Studies from City University in Los Angeles (CULA). After following various protocols and finding that I met the requisite conditions, I was accepted and received this honor in September, 2015.

Also being awarded a Doctorate in Music was our friend Brian Cadd, who flew in from Australia along with his wife, Amanda Pelman. Ruth offered to hold the ceremony at our house, which made for a lovely and warm gathering, not to mention a good excuse for a party.

We gathered a select few special friends for the ceremony, and Martin and Ruth "produced" the affair and taped it for my future grandchildren. No, strike that ... just kidding!

The honors were presented by Dr. Henry Anderson. Caddo and I were pronounced graduates at our somewhat "mature" ages. I was fortunate enough to receive some great letters of recommendation from people I have worked with over the past twenty or so years in Los Angeles. I did my best Sally Field impression: "They like me. They really, really like me."

You can only imagine what a delight this was for me, whose formal schooling ceased in 1941 when I was eleven years old.

Not that I minded much at that age, when any excuse not to go to school was good enough for me.

Amongst my esteemed sorority sisters from CULA are the late Coretta Scott-King and Aretha Franklin, so I am in good company.

When I told my friends on Facebook about this new development, a few wags asked me if I am now able to write prescriptions. Err, I don't think so. I'm not THAT kind of a doctor.

But I am a pill!

Around The World in 10,000 Bites

August of 2019 saw the fearless McCartney Studios mob valiantly belly up to the ticket counter at LAX for a Southwest flight to Houston, Texas. Oh, and by the way, did you know they can no longer call themselves "peanut airlines" due to a complaint by a passenger that she was allergic to peanuts? So they had to cancel that entire deal, and substitute pretzels. (Couldn't that passenger have flown any other airline? Nah!)

However, I digress. We were off to film a Chef David Skinner extravaganza entitled "Around The World in 10,000 Bites," an international foodie event held at The Houston Museum of Natural Science. It was attended by 120 guests, and produced by 40+ chefs from around the globe, presenting food from their 10 respective countries.

We stayed at the ZaZa Hotel, whose staff were most accommodating, and even greeted us at reception and check in with glasses of chilled rosé. They loaned Team 10,000 their entire kitchen space for a week to prep, as we learned a few weeks before that the Museum doesn't have a commercial kitchen.

We left Los Angeles Wednesday morning at zero dark hundred to prep and get set up. On the first evening, David invited all who had arrived to dinner at an amazing restaurant nearby, which was a great way for folks to get to know one another before they all plunged into their work. It is called Himalaya and is run by a lovely man named Kaiser Lashkari. He told some wonderful stories about the time that Anthony Bourdain filmed an episode there. After a long day of travel, not to mention the Texas heat and humidity, I decided to do the sensible thing and give it a miss and settle for room service. However, at about midnight,

Ruth came in with scads of samples of Kaiser's dishes that he kindly sent. In fact, he was so disappointed that I had not turned up that he came to the hotel the following day with plates of vindaloo and other delights.

The kitchen staff of Hotel ZaZa, where our 40 chefs and their assistants prepped all the food, were obviously so used to the in-house menu that they were delighted to have Indian and Pakistani food for a change.

The next morning, Ruth and I peeled away to the tony River Oaks Country Club, with its six kitchens, pools, tennis courts, golf links, ballrooms, and restaurants, for lunch with Executive Chef Charles Carroll and a discussion regarding a future "Dinner with The McCartney's" event, featuring my teas and wines, which I am very excited about. As I write, it's in the planning stages for the end of 2019.

Everyone on our film crew was up bright and early each morning, filming the arrivals from around the world, food prepping, and interviews with many of the chefs (plus interpreters in some cases). In the evening, David Skinner again invited everyone to an informal and fun evening at Chef Brandon Silva's Wooster's Garden Restaurant. The lovely hotel sent us all there in their limos, duly decked out with Texas longhorns, and picked us up at the end of the meal.

When we got back to the hotel, it was rumored that I suggested, "Why don't we go to the hotel bar for a nightcap?" Wrong!!! We finally wound up the evening (technically the morning) around 3 a.m., with many of us teetering off to bed ready for the land of nod.

Friday morning was meant to be a strict working day; our McCartney Studios film crew ready for action by 6 a.m. Just as the action started, the power went off, plunging the entire hotel into darkness, lifts and all. We were instructed to evacuate to the swimming pool area, which presented its own set of problems. Because of the sweltering humidity, our camera lenses fogged up and made it impossible to film. Ruth and Martin, however, were able to shoot some stuff on their iPhones.

Angie and Ruth with hotel limo (plus horns) at Zaza Hotel, Houston, TX, August, 2019.

I decided to do the British thing, and stayed put in my seventh floor room and slugged down a couple more cups of tea. I didn't fancy tackling 14 flights of stairs in the dark!

After a while, the power came back. I texted the kids and said I'd meet them in the restaurant, took the elevator down, and lo and behold, as we reached the lobby, there were the screeching sounds of fire alarms, people running hither and thither (I did neither). However, I was asked to exit the building and wait outside in the lovely heat. In no time at all, a slew of fire engines, ambulances, and police cars turned up. It was like a scene from a movie. It was eventually discovered that the power outage had triggered the alarm system. Phew!

So even before the two-night event (Friday and Saturday), we'd already had our fill of excitement. Despite the drama, the whole thing was a terrific success, and we are hopeful that it may extend to other countries next year. We shall see. The Friday night champagne reception (dubbed "Bubbles & Baubles") was held in the McFerrin Fabergé Collection amidst 600+ collectibles, from crystals and mineral gems, to the family's actual Fabergé eggs. 'Twas quite the swanky affair. The other fabulous part is that it benefitted not only the James Beard Foundation Women's Leadership Program, but also, in honor of Chef Dominique Crenn, who was slated to take part but had to cancel due to a breast-cancer diagnosis, Chef David Skinner is also making a donation to the Linda McCartney research fund at Liverpool's Royal Hospital.

To learn more about the event, you can view it online at AroundtheWorldin10000Bites.com, and when Martin has finished the mammoth job of editing all the 27 hours of footage, we will have a documentary to show you as well.

I was pleased that, at the end of the proceedings, David Skinner raised a toast (with Mrs. McCartney's Blackbird Blackberry Wines in his glass) and bid everyone a fond farewell. If you're interested to see what cocktails you can make with our wines, scan this code and download the recipe booklet (link):

After his toast, we were toast. But it sure was a memorable experience.

Scan the code to visit the 10,000 Bites website (link).

Ruth's Life Hacks

When adding up a tip and totalling out a check in a restaurant, always do the math so the final amount comes out to an even number. That way, when you check your credit card bills online, the ones with the odd pennies will stand out so that you can check them faster!

Before you travel overseas, call your credit card company and pre-negotiate the fees - sometimes they charge you a "foreign transaction currency conversion fee" of 2% on every single transaction, PLUS the interest on that. If you have to, threaten to use a competitor bank's card. That usually does it.

If you're going abroad, call your wireless carrier ahead of time and make sure your plan is not going to put you in the poor house for "roaming changes."

If you have a credit card that gets "compromised," don't throw it in the trash when you get the replacement. As long as the expiry date is still good, use the "hacked" card in restaurants where they ask you for a card to run a tab. That way, when you come to pay the bill, you can either cash out, or use your valid card and keep an eye on it while they run it through.

If you put your purse in the grocery cart, add a layer of security by fastening the handle or strap to the child safety seat belt in the top part, so that if someone tries to make off with it, they will have a surprise and a struggle!

When you can't quite reach the wick of a candle that has burned low, light up the end of a piece of spaghetti. You'll then be able to bring the flame to the wick with ease, and without burning your hand on an upside down match.

Don't want to wait for an entire bottle of wine to chill in the fridge, but can't stand the thought of watering down a glass with ice cubes? Plop in a few frozen grapes and you're all set. If you don't have frozen grapes on hand, other frozen fruit, such as strawberries or blueberries, will work just as well.

Never throw out perfectly good eggs again. Just place them in a bowl of water and notice how they behave. Very fresh eggs will lie on the bottom, fully on their sides. One-week old eggs will sit at an angle on the bottom of the bowl. Stale eggs that are two or three weeks old will rest on the bottom of the bowl with their rounded ends towards the surface. Very old eggs will float.

Never waste a single squirt of toothpaste. When your tube is almost empty and you are struggling with the contents, roll up the end of the tube and secure the rolled portion with a bobby pin or heavy paperclip (a hair clip if you're British). You can then slide the clip along the length of the tube to move the toothpaste up to the top of the tube.

10
With a Little Help from My Friends

Art and The Beatles

Recently, Ruth assembled a presentation aimed at inner city youth and high schools that are attended by mainly underprivileged students. The presentation demonstrates the influence The Beatles have had over music, fashion, food, humour, attitudes, social matters, cars, and lifestyles, amongst other things.

Martin created one of his usual colourful media presentations, which simplifies the approach to all of these subjects, and it is usually avidly embraced by both students and faculty alike.

Ruth interacts with them, asking who has seen a Beatles movie or cartoon, or been to a show, or read a book on them. The kids are encouraged to stand up and relate their own awareness of the phenomena. I remember a Latino boy in downtown Los Angeles who said his parents had asked him the night before to ask Ruth certain questions. This in turn sparked a discussion with other kids. It was good to see such interest and enthusiasm in the topic.

One interesting question: "Was John Lennon assassinated or murdered?" Hmm… challenging question, which led to a great deal of discussion and clarification.

When Ruth asks them questions, they jostle for position to get their hands up in the air. "Miss, Miss" they yell, craving her attention, until she singles each one of them out to tell her of their observations and opinions.

Many of them have said, "My grandma took me to see Cirque du Soleil in Las Vegas," or "My parents took me to see *Yellow Submarine* at a movie theatre, and we really enjoyed it."

One image that is shown to them is one of just four hairpieces. And they all know who's who without fail. So it proves how much this is all embedded in their minds.

Throughout Ruth's PowerPoint presentation, she addresses the class in easy to understand terms, never talking down to them or stressing the show biz aspect of The Beatles.

At the conclusion, every student is given a blank white card and a packet of crayons and asked to create a CD cover, focusing on a particular song title. The results are really interesting, and the teachers particularly appreciate this part of the event.

Without a doubt, the main ones that the children like to create are "Yellow Submarine" and "Lucy in The Sky with Diamonds."

Then, at the end, we take group photos with the kids holding up their artwork, and it always ends with a great feeling of goodwill and enthusiasm.

Citizen Martin

On July 20, 2016, my son-in-law, Martin Nethercut, proudly became a U.S. citizen. Having been a Green Card holder for several years, he felt it was time to come to grips with his paperwork. When he found out how easy it was to do online, he was off and running.

He had a few bumps in the road when he found that his previous renewal Green Card had been sent to a female in Cologne named Martina who had a different last name (don't ask me how they managed to screw that up). Martin had help from a wonderful friend connected to Homeland Security who got that matter moving, and eventually it all fell into place. So somewhere in Germany is a lady named Martina with an out of date Green Card.

The day dawned, and we set off to the Los Angeles Convention Center bright and early to make sure that we could get a parking place without any problems. The crowds were huge, and there was traffic control for a few miles before we reached our destination. Then, we were directed to a "gimp" parking spot (I have a blue sticker for disabled parking, which is always useful for a senior citizen). We discovered that the $25 payment was by cash only, so that was another performance to find an ATM machine. I mean, who carries cash these days?

Then we set off, walking, walking, walking … it took us ages to get to the first checkpoint. Handbags and purses were searched, wands wafted over us, and a lot of the non-English speaking folks were utterly bewildered by all of this. Eventually, Martin was shuttled off to a separate area, whilst Ruth and I took our places in the roped off audience part.

It was a cavernous room, with a big screen and a podium. The process of getting almost 4,600 people seated took over an hour, and by the time they were ready to begin, many already needed a bathroom break.

Martin would tell us later that, during the presentations, including a filmed message from President Obama, a guy sitting next to him dressed in flip flops, shorts and a Hawaiian shirt, was noisily chewing gum and playing a video game on his phone. So much for the seriousness of the occasion.

We were shown a video of the countries that were represented that day, and the people sitting around us were totally uninterested, chatting, slurping from water bottles, eating, with kids slithering around on the floor. It was really shocking to us to see how little this meant to many of them.

I got the impression that many of them didn't have a clue where most of the countries were, although they were shown clearly on a map above us. Only when their own country was mentioned did they show a glimmer of interest, before resuming their other pastimes.

There were words of congratulations and wisdom spoken by various dignitaries, largely falling on deaf ears. The noise in the area was unbelievable, and one might have thought they were at a pop concert or a boxing match.

In due time, participants were invited to stand and move forward to receive their Certificate of Citizenship, accompanied by a package of information, including how to register to vote.

Much to Martin's surprise, on the way out he was approached several times by volunteers from various parties asking him to register to vote right there on the spot. He declined,

Angie and Martin working in the studio.

as he wanted to study the paperwork, and know what he was signing. Smart boy.

Of course, this being Los Angeles, there was plenty of merchandise for sale, including baseball caps, tote bags, photo albums, bumper stickers, and badges. What a country!

Having been separated in the melée, we subsequently texted, and then toasted one another and met for a celebratory drink at a local hotel in downtown's L.A. Live district. That evening, good friends Carol and Tony Busching threw a dinner party for Martin to mark the occasion. They had red, white, and blue napkins, plates, bunting hanging, and busted out some amazing cheeseburgers – it was indeed a day – and night – to remember.

Martin is such a big part of my life. He and Ruth met in Munich, when they both worked on projects for Ralph Siegel's Jupiter Records. Their first meeting was at a funeral! A young American girl, Hannah Grace, was also under contract to Ralph, and the three of them became friends. Sadly, Hannah came to a sad end when she evidently wandered into the woods at the back of her temporary German home, and was found days later

Ruth with Martin, Dieter, and Paul in Playa del Rey.

lying face down, having been covered by a heavy snowfall. It was only when it thawed that she was found.

The kind-hearted Ralph Siegel made funeral arrangements, and flew her parents in from Cincinnati for the service. He assigned Ruth and Martin to take care of them, as they did not speak German, thus this was their first meeting. Ironic, eh? When people ask where they met, she tells them that she "picked him up graveside – not curbside." Ruth's marriage to Dieter Bockmeier was winding up, and she and Martin eventually got together, returned to Los Angeles, and were ultimately married on the beach at Playa del Rey.

I am happy to relate that all three of Ruth's husbands are the best of friends. All are artists: Paul and Martin specifically in the music field, and Dieter in the film business in Germany. In fact, at a subsequent house party, we took a photo of Ruth with all three of them, bearing labels # 1, #2 and #3. We reckon Martin is a keeper, as he has stood the test of time for about 20 years.

Martin and Dieter on location at Aikens Lake in Canada.

For Martin, music was always his passion, writing and singing since his teenage years, belonging to several bands in his home country, and even performing in a Eurovision Song Contest one year. Not one of his proudest achievements, he will tell you, but we all thought it was a big deal when he was selected by famed producer Harold Faltermeyer to represent Germany.

He spends as much time as he can on his trilogy, a work in progress called "Geist Musik," for which he wrote all the music, recorded literally hundreds of tracks, laid down vocals, included various guest artists, and designed the graphics and artwork for the covers – it is his labour of love.

Of course, as president of McCartney Multimedia and McCartney Studios, his time there takes him away from his music due to our intensive and varying workload. He is also very much in demand for German and English speaking voice overs, with requests from all over the globe. Thanks to technology (and an amazing Neumann mic), he is able to carry out many of these jobs from his own studio.

In more recent times, he has become my "Direktor" for our various stage shows, such as Behind The Beatles, Dinner With The McCartneys, etc. Then came his brainchild: just over a year ago, we launched a weekly live show on Facebook, *TEAFLIX Tuesdays*, which has enabled us to have many fascinating guests.

We all live and work together in Playa del Rey, and he is often heard to remark that, when he married Ruth, he didn't read the fine print, which said "buy one, get one free." My last words to him each night as I totter off to bed are, "Good Night, John Boy," to which he always responds, "Good job, Ange." We are also known as the Unholy Trinity.

And he is still friends with Dieter.

Ellen DeGeneres

Our friend Bill Miller, of Virgin Australia, invited us to accompany him to a taping of *The Ellen Show* in Burbank in late December, 2016.

It was a show in which she gave away lots of gifts and prizes for the twelve days of Christmas. During the warmup, one of the greeters invited anyone to come on stage and dance. So our shrinking violet Ruth readily volunteered and did her thing. It was all good fun.

The show was most enjoyable, and it finished with Ellen giving everyone in the audience a wonderful selection of goodies. They included two pieces of Samsonite luggage, Oliver Peoples shades, Visa cards, cosmetics, and the usual chotchkies such as pens, luggage label holders, and vouchers for a free holiday at the Disney Aulani Hotel in Hawaii. This had to be taken within the following twelve months.

After much "oohing" and "ahhing" and gasping by the delighted and almost hysterical audience, we were taken to an areas after the show, where we filled out paperwork and were informed that we would be contacted shortly after with the details of the trip.

It turned out that, as Ruth and I each had separate invitations, she was able to include Martin as her guest. We discovered

Angie in Christmas (Ho Ho Ho) mode in Playa del Rey.

the trip did not include flights, but did include accommodation plus a $500 room credit for each of our two rooms. This would be sent to us in the form of a voucher to present at check in.

We would each ultimately receive a 1099 tax document from the resort in the sum of $2,396, considered the value of the trip, which we paid good old Uncle Sam tax on at 15%. We purchased our three airline tickets separately, and by the time we added up the flights, ground transportation, gratuities, baggage extras, it was far from a free holiday. Regardless, we decided to go for it and made the trip to coincide with my 87th birthday in November, 2017.

Because I am not too nimble or quick on my feet some mornings, Ruth called the hotel well in advance to make sure that our rooms would be adjoining or adjacent, and that I would have a walk-in shower. She was assured not once, but twice, that this would be taken care of upon our arrival.

When we checked in, we were asked to lodge a credit card for additional charges, as is the norm these days. Ruth left them an American Express card.

It turned out that I had a regular bathtub and when Ruth asked if this could be remedied, she was told that this could

Our unholy trinity in Christmas mode.

only be done if I moved to a different tower on the property. Obviously, that was out of the question.

Unfortunately, as soon as I got there, I was overcome with a severe asthma attack, which curtailed my activities. Ruth contacted the front of house staff again who, it seems, were not able to assist. The only solution they could come up with was that I might want to try using the shower in the departure area, where people could remain after normal check out if their flights were not until hours later. This facility was, again, in a separate tower, and we would need a wheelchair if I was to choose that option. Poor Ruth went through hoops before finally obtaining a wheelchair (after being told she could "rent" one for $35 a day). She and Martin wheeled me to and from meals on a couple of occasions, and down and across the area where people leave their luggage after checkout and prior to departure to shower each morning. I felt dreadful at messing up their trip, but as always, they were both wonderfully kind and attentive. I didn't want to call a doctor, because I feared being admitted to the hospital and left behind on the Island.

On the morning of our departure, we got an electronic itemized bill on our screen, indicating that we had been charged for various meals and beverages on our American Express card.

Once more, Ruth went downstairs to figure out what went awry. They pointed out that because I was not always personally present at mealtimes with my resort credit card (due to my asthma and inability to get around), those meals were to be charged to our Amex card. After much ado, they finally assured her that the charges would be removed.

When we got home and did my daily check of our credit cards, sure enough, they had charged over $600 to our personal Amex. So off we went again, contacting Amex, and getting them to reverse those charges. This was eventually done, but only after considerable inconvenience.

Upon reflection, I can only wonder if the onset of such a severe and unexpected asthma attack, the likes of which I had not experienced in years, might have had anything to do with the fact that Aulani Hotel sits just a mile south of the Waimanalo Gulch Refuse Landfill on Farrington Highway, which burns refuse in the breezes blowing on to the north side of the resort where our rooms were situated. Being unable to get about much, I spent much of the trip sitting out on my balcony, breathing I knew not what. Ah well, I guess you can believe the saying that there are "no free lunches" in this world.

So it sure as heck wasn't my "happiest place on Earth."

I am sure that, knowing of the generosity of Ellen DeGeneres, she would not be too pleased if she knew that this was how her guests could be treated. But hey, we had a nice afternoon when we went to her show. And we did get to see a rerun of Ruth dancing on television, so it wasn't all bad.

Oh, and on the way home from the original show in Burbank, Bill Miller's car broke down. Thanks Bill – no good deed goes unpunished.

Farrah Fawcett Foundation

Not that long ago, we were invited to become "Angels" on the Farrah Fawcett Foundation, a charity created in her memory. It is headed by former model and actress Alana Stewart, ably assisted by the tireless Christine Romeo. The purpose of this registered foundation is to provide funds and comfort for cancer patients and their families during their treatment.

The Foundation hosted a Christmas 2016 party for children suffering from cancer, which was held at The Museum of Flying at Santa Monica Airport.

We provided Mrs. McCartney's Teas and hot chocolate, sandwiches and cookies, and obtained donations of pizzas (four separate deliveries, no less) from Nando Stefano of The Good Pizza. To make things interesting, we recruited a fire engine, and its crew brought it along for the kids to ride and experience. Then there was a wonderful vintage police car brought to the event by Fireball Tim, and the children also loved clambering in and out of that vehicle. There were many great photo opportunities for them and their parents.

Ruth had Diana Maiman arrange to bring her son, DJ Astrojaxx, to set up his disco equipment and play holiday songs in the airport lobby to help set the mood, although it was a blazing, hot sunny day. But nobody was complaining.

Our neighbours, Fred and Mitra Nourpour, who run a children's clothing manufacturing business, donated six huge boxes of brand new clothing. There were some delightful things, like party dresses, jeans, pretty blouses, and nice shirts for the boys.

Our friends who were connected with Mattel brought us a couple of hundred toys and games. Nick Marechal, our client, also donated a bunch of money so that gift vouchers could be bought for the goody bags.

The late Mary Willard ("Angel in Chief") was on the upper level, entertaining the guests and giving out some great gift bags to everyone. Sherry Kinison and her husband Bill (who played Santa Claus) were on hand taking photographs.

There was also a flight simulator on the upper level, which was another great adventure for the kids. There were lots of other fun activities, such as face painting and cookie decorating to keep the youngsters occupied. The late, great Mary Willard's daughter, Hope Mulbarger, took care of all this.

That event was a very thought provoking day, watching all these brave families getting on with their lives, despite their difficulties. It really made us reflect on how fortunate we are.

It also made me realize that Farrah Fawcett was a much-loved lady who handled her health issues with great dignity and bravery. It is an honor to help keep her legacy alive.

You can watch the smiles on the kids' faces here (link):

The Marriage of the Trans

I recently had the privilege of performing a wedding ceremony for Kennon Holton and retired Staff Sergeant Thom Tran. It took place in the sunny garden of their home in the Hollywood area. It was attended by Kennon's family and friends and Thom's fellow performers in his "The GIs of Comedy Tour" act. They are all veterans whose byline is "Still Serving, One Joke at a Time." It was a mixed and wonderful group of people from all walks of life, and from all parts of the world.

Thom's father, himself a military veteran, was very proud to see his son in his full dress uniform. He joined in this lovely ceremony, and was surrounded by lots of love and warmth. We also had the company of several of Thom's radio buddies from KNX 1070 news radio, where Thom is in charge of traffic information.

The Holton family are all-American, and the Tran family came to the United States from Vietnam when Thom was just a toddler.

I was delighted when they asked if I would marry them. Our trinity swung into action: Ruth stage managed the event, Martin took care of the music and oversaw the filming of the wedding, and I presided over the wedding vows. After they had exchanged their nuptials and I pronounced them husband and wife, I finished by saying, "You may now update your Facebook pages."

Thom is not only our traffic guru, but is the leader of "The GIs of Comedy Tour," comprising former members of the armed services who entertain veterans and active service men and women at home and abroad, and raise funds for the Veterans' various charities. Thom, a holder of a Purple Heart and other noble acknowledgements, was shot in the head whilst serving in Afghanistan. He was honorably discharged.

In fact, when we make trips, Ruth will text Thom at the radio station and say, we are on our way to Palm Springs, San Diego, San Bernardino, or wherever. In no time at all, Thom will punch up any road hazards we might need to be aware of, such as flying mattresses and other debris that tend to make their way on to the California freeways.

His boss has become wise to this, and when Thom strays from the normal reports, he'll chip in with "so the McCartneys are on the road today, eh?" But he is cool with it. Ruth, in turn, texts Thom to alert him to anything odd she sees whilst Martin is driving us to our destination.

I remember when Raimund Carl, our business partner from the McCartney Sports office in Vienna, was here visiting and met Thom at one of our Sunday afternoon get-togethers. The next day, he was going to the Austrian consulate with Ruth, and was impressed when Thom piped up on the radio that there was a traffic snarl up in that area. He couldn't get over the fact that we seemed to have our own private traffic reports coming to us over the air.

Just one of the perks of having friends in high frequencies.

James McCartney

Ruth, Martin, and I had the pleasure of seeing and visiting James McCartney at an intimate Hollywood gig in May, 2017, where we experienced firsthand his creative talents. He played selections from his most recent album, *Marshmallow Maiden*. Ruth proudly wears the T-shirt he gave her that night. He is one very talented songwriter (I wonder where he gets that from?), and still is a little reticent about interacting with his audience. This, in fact, adds to his charm, as he is not at all brash or overconfident.

Ruth had called the venue to find out about parking, reservations, and ticket availability. They were somewhat vague, but said that under the circumstances, they would make sure that we had a table close to the stage.

Someone must have told James, because after the show, we got in line at the very end of the stream of people going forward to buy merchandise and get autographs and take selfies. James and his companion were inside the box office, and when Ruth stuck her head through the window, he looked up and said, "Ruth? Angie?"

Angie and Ruth with young James McCartney in Los Angeles.

He had never met Ruth before, and my only time with him was when I held him in my arms at a couple of days old in The Avenue Nursing Home in London. This was after Paul had called to tell me that he and Linda were the proud parents of a son named Jim, after "me Dad."

It was a very emotional moment for us all. After James wound up his merch business, we went into the dressing room and chatted and had drinks, and caught up with each other. It was a memorable night for me, particularly when he held my hand and called me "Grandma." That's something I have only heard from Benna (Mike McGear's eldest daughter) in the past. I know I'm not their biological grandmother, but it felt good to be addressed that way.

He and his friends were driving on to their next gig, in the Bay Area, after the show. While we waited outside for our Lyft, he stayed behind and watched until we were safely on our way.

We exchanged updated contact information and assured him that the kettle is always on when he passes through Los Angeles.

Minerva Perez

Minerva Perez was one of the earliest female anchors in Los Angeles, starting when she worked at KTLA TV-5. She spent three decades in TV news, and covered many big stories.

She told us of the many trials and tribulations she endured in those early days. Minerva was not accepted by most of the good old boys in the industry, and had to work very hard to make her mark. She would drive home at night with tears streaming down her face after facing many put downs and insults.

The fact that she was a Latina made it a double whammy for her. She received hate mail with people writing for her to go back to Mexico, even though she was born and bred in Texas. She was the one who always got all the crappy assignments and didn't dare to breathe a sound of dissatisfaction, lest she be fired or assigned to something even worse. She started out in radio, and transitioned to TV with high hopes, which were quickly dashed by some (but not all) of her colleagues.

She was at her desk in LA on the night the Rodney King beating occurred. George Holliday, the man who shot the footage, took it to CBS, who wouldn't even let him through the gates to pitch it. Next, he tried KTLA, where the security guard took the tape from him and brought it to Minerva and her partner. After viewing the first few minutes of the footage, they realized what they had, and took it upstairs to her bosses.

The folks at KTLA realized the significance of the material, and arranged for TV reporter Stan Chambers to take it to the LAPD. Minerva said the short clip released to the media was only a fraction of the entire film. I wonder whose archives hold the original tape? It went on to be syndicated and shown around the world, and is still to this day used over and over in documentaries and news anniversaries.

During her tenure in California and Texas, Minerva covered many high-profile stories, including the visit of Pope John Paul II in 1987, the 1994 Northridge Earthquake, hurricanes Rita and Katrina, and the David Koresh siege in Waco. She briefly met Fidel Castro in Cuba. She covered the death of Tejano Queen Selena, and did an exclusive interview with Selena's father after her tragic death.

She also worked on the Christian Brando murder trial in Santa Monica. She has a lot of behind-the-scenes stories about that time. And to her ultimate delight, Marlon Brando even acknowledged her outside the courthouse, where throngs of journalists were milling around him. She values that moment greatly.

She now runs her own production company in Houston, called Minerva Perez Media.

And of course, she has a thriving Facebook page. Oh, and by the way, she is a Beatles fan just for good measure.

She graciously agreed to be interviewed for my planned documentary about strong women, *Here's A Story*.

Minerva has chronicled all of these stories and more in her book, *I Gotta Story*, which you can find on Amazon. It's a great read.

It's a true story of perseverance, grit, and determination; see also www.minervaperez.com.

Watch our *Here's A Story* series interview with Minerva here (link):

Pamela Des Barres

Ruth, Martin, and I have had the pleasure of knowing Pamela des Barres for a number of years. She first came to prominence when her book, *I'm With the Band*, entered *The New York Times* best-seller list, and has since gone on to write several other successful ones. In addition, she shares her talent for writing with a group of folks in various parts of the United States, and is now even moving into England.

Her talents are many. She is a clothing designer and jewelry designer. She paints, acts, sings – oh my goodness, what a gifted lady she is. And she is a warm friend, too.

She has happily attended many of our events and vice versa. She holds musical events from time to time at her home to showcase various up and coming musicians, writers, and poets. These occasions are always great fun and are a terrific place to meet people.

And it's not unusual for some of her celebrity friends to look in also. We have, on more than one occasion, taken out of town visitors to these soirees, and they are always absolutely enchanted with the great variety of entertainment and hospitality.

Pamela has a big heart. In early 2018, she decided to relocate from Marina del Rey to her original home town of Reseda.

Ruth and I volunteered to help her pack up many of her treasures, and what a mammoth project that turned out to be. She had been collecting knick-knacks, crucifixes, rosaries, hair adornments, cat ornaments, belts, buckles, jewelry, vintage clothing, feather boas; you name it, for years. It was like Pandora's box, big time. She periodically has yard sales to thin out the mass of "stuff" that she has accumulated over the years.

She was gracious enough to allow us to interview her for our planned documentary, *Here's a Story*, which is in pre-production. And, when I began my new *TEAFLIX Tuesdays* shows on Facebook, she came to our Playa del Rey Office and regaled us with some of her celebrity stories, including some very funny stuff about Keith Moon. You can find all of her books on Amazon. I urge you to take a look. It is a wonderful peep into her past and present.

She currently lives with her son in the San Fernando Valley and runs www.pameladesbarres.net

To see her *Here's A Story* series interview, scan the code (link):

Beit T'Shuvah

In early 2017, one of my long time Facebook friends, musician Glenn Goss, asked if we would consider coming to their synagogue and recovery center in Culver City to one of their Friday night Shabbat gatherings. These always feature music, food, prayers, dedications, and other social activities.

We duly planned to visit on the evening of Friday, February 17, but due to a massive storm that blew the roof of our house completely off, we had to spend the evening desperately trying to find a local handyman to accompany us to Home Depot to buy tarpaulins and slabs of stone to anchor it down to keep the rain out of the upstairs rooms.

After various trials and tribulations, it was rearranged for the month of May. The plan was for Ruth and me to just say a few words here and there about how our lives had been impacted by The Beatles. The actual main event was to celebrate the anniversaries of several of their residents achieving milestones in their sobriety, and it was a very moving occasion.

The in-house band (made of up residents) played and sang Beatles songs. We were given song sheets with all the words in Hebrew, which was hilarious for us, but de rigueur for the rest of the attendees. I was astonished when I looked at the row behind me and saw the great Annie Lennox singing along with her husband and daughter.

The young lady cantor said that, when she arrived for rehearsals, she was horrified to see the front row seat placement "RESERVED FOR MCCARTNEY" on three seats. She was terrified that it would be "HIM." She was much relieved to find out it was only "US."

Rabbi Mark Borowitz and his wife Harriet Rossetto were warm and welcoming, and we felt at ease and at home amongst so many wonderful people. Not only were the residents there, but many of their families and general supporters of the center.

Angie and Annie Lennox at Beit T'Shuvah, Los Angeles.

I might add that they are completely non-denominational, totally non-judgemental about people's creed, colour, addictions, gender, and they all work together for the common good.

A few months later, Martin worked closely with Glenn Goss and the musicians and technical people to arrange another event. He produced media, to display on their jumbotron, of family photos, archived newsreels of the times, and other stuff of interest. This was interspersed with performances of much loved Beatles songs and chat sessions with Ruth and me, doing our usual stuff about our family background, and some of the stories behind the songs.

Again, it was well received, and at the end of the evening during the playing of "All You Need is Love," the entire audience was on its feet singing and dancing. It was a terrific feeling. There was a lot of love in the room that night.

Their amazing catering in-house staff served up a terrific meal afterwards, which was a fitting end to a memorable evening. It had British goodies too, which pleased one of our audience, the iconic Annie Lennox!

Even though, tragically, we lost our dear Glenn in July 2019, we are considering more in the same vein in the future. These good people also have a thrift shop in Culver City, and are always happy to accept donations, so I have been encouraging my friends and neighbours to pass on their good stuff, so that the residents at the centre may benefit from other people's generosity.

Even our local chiropractic surgeon, the gentleman who fitted me with two titanium knees and a plastic hip, donated his entire office furniture and kitchen units to them when he had to move offices recently, and they were really delighted with that. They maintain dozens of residential rooms attached to the synagogue for their people to stay whilst undergoing their treatment and counselling. Check them out. Mazel Tov!

Sweet Alice

Alice Harris is one amazing lady, and I am proud to call her my friend.

"Sweet Alice" was born in 1934 in Gadsden, Alabama to a poor family. She lived a tough life, was arrested at the age of twelve, and had a baby at the age of 14. She moved from pillar to post through her earlier years, eventually married, and had a total of nine children.

She studied cosmetology, and later ran her own business in Detroit, Michigan. She moved to Los Angeles to take care of her elderly, ailing mother in the late 1950s. In 1976, she obtained a Bachelors of Arts Degree in Sociology at California State University.

Today, she lives near downtown Los Angeles. She came to prominence during the 1965 Watts Riots, when she took to the streets and got a group of volunteers together to work with the youth and their families. She gave up her house and allowed it to be transformed into a community center, concentrating on helping children stay in school. She also formed Parents of Watts, which is still thriving today. It includes fifteen houses, and they work tirelessly to help children with their education and how to have a hopeful outlook to improve their lives and the lives of those around them.

She has also instigated immunization shots for every child that needs and wants them. Their main focus is to keep kids off drugs and in school. They run summer school classes to help the young with English and math.

Martin, Sweet Alice, and Angie on set of Here's a Story.

Alice and her wonderful band of helpers work constantly to obtain donations, both financial and in-kind, to provide food, toys, bicycles, clothing, medical help, and above all, hope. Her Thanksgiving and Christmas celebrations are well-documented online. It would do your heart good to search for her on the internet to see many of the amazing events she has organised. You will find several YouTube videos.

I was privileged to interview her in 2017. She regaled us with stories of her passionate course to make Watts a place to be proud of and to shed its former reputation, which rose from the ashes of the devastating events during the civil unrest.

Alice has received countless awards and acknowledgements. She was honored by President George H. Bush when she was named as one of his "Points of Light." This honor is bestowed on people who have made a significant impact on communities because of their volunteer work.

Then, in 2002, when her house was badly damaged by rain and flooding, she was the subject of an edition of *Extreme Makeover Home Edition*. You can see a video of it on YouTube.com.

Now in her mid-eighties, Alice still works tirelessly to improve the lives of those less fortunate, and she is succeeding big time.

She personally intervened in a domestic property situation for me, which took place over the course of three years. With a couple of phone calls, Alice was able to find a resolution to our problem. Before she left my house that day, we all prayed together in our doorway, and now those prayers have been answered. I have a new roof.

She is an inspiration to all who come into contact with her and she encourages people to be tolerant, and above all, to talk to one another. Every community needs a Sweet Alice, especially in these troubled times. See Alice's story here (link):

Long may she continue to reign.

Val Camilletti

Val Camilletti was an inside promotions person for Capitol Records when The Beatles broke it big in America in 1964. She was assigned to pick them up from a Chicago airport, which was a saga in itself, and take them to their hotel. But it seems that, due to the extreme fan pressure, their flight kept being diverted from one airport to another. She had to rely on phone calls from her boss as to where and when she needed to meet them. But, as always, the fans were always one step ahead. She spent many hours flitting from one airport to another. And remember, there were no cellphones in those days, so she had to keep getting out of her car and finding a phone booth to keep ahead of the game.

Eventually, it all came to pass, and she safely delivered them to their hotel in the dead of night (like a Blackbird singing).

Naturally, it was expected that Val would be at their shows and have an all-access backstage pass. When her boss checked in with her, she said, "You couldn't pay me enough to go to the venue and listen to all these screaming little girls having their first orgasm, whilst our boys were playing their hearts out and not being heard."

I bet she regretted that decision in retrospect.

We met with Val, who ran Val's Halla Vinyl Record Store in Oak Park, near Chicago. We were there to do a show for Ron Onesti at his delightful Arcada Theatre and Speakeasy in St. Charles with Liverpool Legends, Lou Harrison's boys. We came out in between their sets and told stories of old. And I mean OLD.

We spent a lovely (if rainy) afternoon with Val at the record store, which is a veritable cornucopia of memories from the 12-inch vinyl days. Val also permitted and encouraged local bands and budding artists to perform in her shop window. You can not only browse the records and memorabilia, but have a musical experience too.

Oh, and if you go there, be sure to ask to use the bathroom. It is a monument to Elvis, and something not to be missed.

Val passed away in late 2018 after a short illness. The record store still carries on in her memory, one that is worth keeping alive.

Watch Val's "Here's A Story" series interview here (link):

Arise Sir Richard Starkey

We were delighted to learn that Ringo Starr had been honored by Her Majesty for the 2018 New Year's Honors List. He finally became "Sir Richard" in the early part of the year.

I celebrated the event by sending him some Mrs. McCartney's English Breakfast Tea, which I trust was duly quaffed.

Ringo fans around the world were also happy that he has finally been acknowledged as a vital member of The Beatles, and part of the most historical musical act of the 20th century. After all, they helped to open up awareness around the world of the power of music, and the power of peace and love.

I know his mum Elsie would have been so proud of her boy. She and I spent many happy afternoons poring over her photo albums and press cuttings of her "Ritchie."

By then they had come a long way from the days when, if there was a knock at the door, she would get Ritchie to kneel on the hall floor and look under the gap in the door to see if there was a pair of boots on the step, in which case she wouldn't open it because in all likelihood it was the rent man! How could she possibly have dreamed that her lovely son would go on to reach such heights of fame, wealth, and affection?

She once proudly showed me a little blue Post Office savings account book, where she would put away five Great British pounds at a time for him when she received her monthly allowance. Her feeling was that, "When this music thing dies down, which should be in a couple of years, I will have a bit put away for him to open a hair salon like he has always dreamed of." Bless her heart.

She and Harry Graves, Ringo's step-dad, were a wonderful warm and stable influence during his childhood and early years when he suffered several illnesses and setbacks. But he achieved his dream, and is still fulfilling it, recording and playing live throughout the world.

And I think he would agree with me, it's a better gig than owning a hair salon.

See Sir Ringo's big moment here (link):

David Cassidy

David Cassidy first burst upon the British entertainment scene in the early 1970s, having already well established his career in his native America.

The son of famous showbiz parents, Jack Cassidy and Evelyn Ward, David had very early exposure to the world of music and film.

It was fate that threw him together with his stepmother, the beautiful Shirley Jones, with whom he was cast (as her real son) in *The Partridge Family*.

His career was booming when he made his first tour in England. Our good friend Tony Barrow, who had been doing PR for The Beatles, knowing Ruth had a massive crush on David, arranged for us to get tickets to a concert in Manchester. Once tickets were in hand, Ruth and I set off in a state of great anticipation.

It was a wild night indeed, with fans going crazy. It felt like Beatlemania all over again. David needed a police escort to get on and

Ruth and David Cassidy, Sunset Marquis, Los Angeles.

off the field. It was an open air venue, and, like a Beatles concert, it was almost impossible to hear David above the shrieks of the girls.

One time when Paul was staying with us, Ruth told him about her fondness for David. After a bit of sleuthing by his people, Paul got the phone number to David's hotel in London, and decided to call him. When David haltingly answered the phone, Paul announced himself, saying simply: "Hi there, this is Paul McCartney." To which, David promptly answered, "Yeah, and I'm the Duke of Edinburgh" and slammed the phone down.

Ruth with some of her David Cassidy treasures.

Undaunted, Paul made another attempt a few minutes later, and this time, David paused, took a deep breath, and realized that he really was talking to one of HIS idols. So they had a nice conversation, and Paul gave him the address of his dad's house to send an autograph for Ruth. Not only did an autographed photograph arrive a few days later, but a stack of LP's, which we still have to this day. And the signed photograph is framed and hangs on our living room wall.

In case you're wondering, the autograph reads: "Be happy, stay free." Ruth took the first piece of advice, but not the second. She's always been a gal with a mind of her own. Oh, and by the way, those albums have travelled all over the world with us.

Much later, after we had moved to Los Angeles and my little girl was all grown up, she stepped into a lift (elevator) in a Beverly Hills shop one afternoon, and there was David in living colour. She did the mandatory double take, and he was friendly and started a conversation. She pointed to her one sticky out tooth and said it was dedicated to him. She used to surreptitiously prod at it with a nail file to make it lunge forward to try to look like him. That was quite a conversation opener, and they struck up a friendship that lasted throughout the years, up until his sad passing in November, 2017.

As the years rolled on, and we moved to Nashville after the Northridge earthquake of 1994 had pretty much wiped us out, we became interested in this new fangled internet thingy. Ruth got in touch with David and suggested that he should have a website. Although he had no idea what that meant, he said she should go ahead, keep him posted, and let his people know what it cost. A good business relationship started then, and continued for many, many years.

We still treasure a big collection of David's music, photographs, press clippings, programmes, and posters. Yes, we are still hardcore fans deep down inside, despite our ages.

We had the good fortune to become friends with Sue Shifrin, David's wife, and mother of his lovely son, Beau. Sadly, their marriage eventually went the way many showbusiness couplings do, but we all stayed in touch. We still hear from Sue, who is now a successful businesswoman, and even pilots her own plane.

Beau is a talented actor, and has inherited the family's good looks. He has appeared in numerous movies, and seems to be a young man who is going places.

David's career took him in several directions, from Las Vegas stage shows, to television work, to studio work, and we faithfully attended his shows, including a fun one at the CBS studios on Radford Avenue, Studio City, at a taping of *Ruby and The Rockits*.

Upon reflection, I'm not really sure David knew how much he was loved. He spent most of his life trying to make his father, Jack Cassidy, proud of him. I am sure he must have been, but it's funny how often families don't always manage to convey what they feel for one another until it's too late. So remember, hug your loved ones, and tell them you love them. They'll never forget it. I don't, and I am blessed to be told this every night as I am going to bed.

Watch this touching, candid interview with Piers, from 2014 (link):

Geoff Emerick

In the early part of 2018, we ran into Geoff Emerick at East West Studios in Hollywood. Geoff was once the assistant engineer to George Martin on many classic Beatles sessions at Abbey Road Studios in London. His innovative techniques are all over Revolver and Sergeant Pepper's Lonely Hearts Club Band. He had some fascinating stories to tell of those days and nights.

Geoff eventually moved from England to Los Angeles, and worked with many of the top musicians at some of the great studios, like Capitol Records and East West Studios. Throughout his life, he was very much in demand. I hadn't seen him since the Abbey Road days, but we chinwagged during a recent recording session and let the time roll away.

The young technical crew we had working for us that day were so impressed to meet him. Several of them told me that they looked upon Geoff's book, *Here, There and Everywhere,* as a Bible to which they frequently refer, looking up some of his pointers and advice. He is a legend in his own lunchtime, as he once put it! He was really great with them all, and they were blown away to be talking one-on-one with someone who was really in on the music scene from the early Beatle days.

Long after he had left the EMI stable, Paul asked Geoff if he would work with Wings, which he was very happy to do. He formed a good bond with Paul, Linda, and the rest of Wings. His work on Band On the Run was essential in bringing Paul back to mainstream success.

We spent a good while with Geoff in 2018, catching up and remembering many of the wild and crazy things that used to happen in the good old/bad old days. We chatted about how much technology has changed over the years, and how much simpler things were back then.

We were working with one of our recording artist clients, Nick Marechal, who had booked the Beach Boys room at the studio. That's where they recorded *Pet Sounds*, amongst others.

Some of these great Hollywood studios have a feel about them that almost transports you back to the days when they housed The Rolling Stones, CSNY, Quincy Jones, Michael Buble, Barry Manilow, Maroon 5, Ziggy Marley, and vast orchestras creating the soundtracks for many of the blockbuster movies.

There really seems to be something in the air.

Geoff passed away of a sudden heart attack in Los Angeles on October 2, 2018, whilst preparing for an upcoming show with Denny Laine and others in Arizona the following weekend.

We went to a touching memorial service to Geoff at Capitol Studios on January 21, 2019, attended by over a hundred former colleagues and friends. They were mostly studio engineers and filmmakers who had benefited from Geoff's advice and expertise over the years and around the globe. He was greatly loved, and will be sorely missed. Rest in peace dear Geoff.

His good friend, engineer Bill Smith, has created a beautiful resting place from him in Los Angeles. Learn more about paying Geoff a visit here (link):

Angie with Geoff Emerick at East West Studios in Hollywood.

Geoff Emerick's marker. He is greatly missed.

Anthony Bourdain

The sad and sudden passing of Anthony Bourdain in 2018 was a shock to us all. He was one of those people that everyone felt they knew, even if they had only seen him on TV.

Ruth and I had the pleasure of meeting him at a food and wine event in Los Angeles a few years back, hosted by Madge Claybion for the UCLA Culinary School. Anthony was utterly charming and surprisingly shy on a one-to-one basis.

At that time, he was doing his utmost to help his friend Roy Choi get established in the food truck game. Part of his contract for the event was a proviso that Roy's newly launched Kogi BBQ trucks should be available outside of the venue for the guests to sample. This was a pretty revolutionary idea at the time. The attendees made a swoop on the trucks when the main event was over. Since then, Choi has gone on to great things in the food world (as the foodies amongst us know).

Here is their CNN episode of Koreatown (link):

During his presentation, Anthony made a couple of snarky but humourous cracks about the Olive Garden chain. He didn't know that, seated at our table, were several people from that company. Unfortunately, they didn't have a sense of humour about his tongue-in-cheek remarks. They got up and left in the middle of the meal.

When he reached the end of his talk, he asked if there were any questions. Needless to say, the ever NOT so shy Ruth was up on her feet with a good question, asking him about how he got away with taking the notoriously stinky fruit, dourian, in a New York City taxi! This prompted another entertaining story and helped him to relax, thus ending the presentation on a light and funny note.

Ruth, Anthony Bourdain, and Angie at a UCLA Food & Wine event in Westwood, CA.

We were sampling Mrs. McCartney's Teas that day, and the atmosphere in the general area after his talk was very convivial. Ruth, being such a big foodie, was more than pleased to be able to have a chat with him when he was free of his duties. He also signed a couple of his cookbooks, which she treasures in her collection. Our time with him was brief but memorable.

To share some of the moments Anthony and Roy spent together, scan this code with your smartphone or tablet (link):

Mike Portnoy

Amanda Cagan, of ABC-PR, who represents several prominent musicians, got in touch with us, asking if we would like to feature some of her clients on *TEAFLIX Tuesday*. We immediately said yes.

The first person Amanda sent us to grace our space was Mike Portnoy, the award-winning drummer from Sons of Apollo, Dream Theatre, and Carpe Diem to name a few. We beamed him in from his home in New York State, and he was a huge success. Of course, when a guest has a following of their own, it helps tremendously when they circulate the information about their upcoming appearance. Mike went on to tour Europe shortly after our get together, and I arranged for him to meet up with my step-granddaughter, Benna McCartney (Mike McGear/McCartney's eldest daughter) in the south of England. They enjoyed a nice visit after the show.

Mike is not only a fantastic drummer and personality, but he gives advice to many young up and coming devotees of the skill, and to date, has won at least 30 awards from *Drummer* magazine. Oh, and he is, of course, a huge Beatles fan. He even has a *Yellow Submarine* tattoo all down one leg. Yes, and he showed it to us on camera.

Mike plays a hilarious game of "Name That Beatle Tune" with rock legend Neal Morse – scan to view (link):

All of the TEAFLIX guests can be seen at our MrsMcCartneysTeas.com website or by scanning the code here (link):

Lawrence Gowan

Another of Amanda's clients is Lawrence Gowan of STYX. Scottish by birth, he has been in Canada for many moons. He was another lively guest. STYX is a band of great renown, with more hits under their belts than you can shake a stick at (and why on earth would you ever want to shake a stick at a band, I ask myself?).

They launched a new tour and their triumphant new album *The Mission* in 2019. Their sixteenth album is a 43-minute thrill ride that chronicles the trials, tribulations, and ultimate triumph of the first manned mission to Mars in the year 2033. If that doesn't get you tingling, I don't know what will. Everywhere they play, their audiences go wild.

With these people, I have made new friends. It's also great for my regulars, who tune in to get to know more about folks they might otherwise not know too much about. The circle widens.

Here (link) is our TEAFLIX episode on Facebook:

Melissa Manchester

And once more, Amanda hooked us up with a very famous guest, Melissa Manchester, who also happens to be her aunt.

Our session with Melissa was fabulous. She is such a talented and very active lady, who works tirelessly to help people. She devotes a lot of time to women prisoners and has spent time with these ladies, giving them support and encouragement, which they so badly need. Many of them are separated from their children and feel that the world doesn't care about them anymore, and a visit from Melissa can be a tremendous lift for them. I was so jazzed when she consented to be on our little homespun programme.

See www.melissamanchester.com and here is our TEAFLIX episode on Facebook (link):

Strummer Hollis

My youngest guest was the lovely Strummer Hollis. She is the daughter of Jason Hollis of the Punk Aristocrats. Strummer was just one day short of her fourteenth birthday when she came over to tell us about her many ventures.

Her first venture, Slime, really put her on the map. Yes, the green gooey stuff that kids like to hurl on the young people's award shows. She built up quite a reputation (and a healthy bank balance) with that venture, and is truly a wiz on the computer.

She has a real head for business. And it was a joy to find out how well mannered she is. Her parents have certainly raised her well. She is too young to have a Facebook page, but you can find several videos on YouTube, showing what a range of talents this young lady has.

Here (link) is our TEAFLIX episode on Facebook:

The Nelsons

We were pleased to welcome Matthew and Gunnar Nelson to the show in early 2019. I know their many fans were delighted to see them talking to us live from their homes in Tennessee.

They tirelessly tour all over the country, and even made a quick trip to England not long ago. Not only do they have their own touring rock show called Nelson, but another one dedicated to the memory of their father, the late Ricky Nelson.

Ruth has been directing their social media strategy and content for them, and they are such a pleasure to work with. Unfortunately, on the day they did TEAFLIX, we experienced some technical difficulties (Martin explained that it was connected to bandwidth on Facebook, but that's all a bit beyond my pay grade).

We hook up from time to time when they speed through LAX enroute for various locations, and their armies of fans follow their every move. They have an infectious sense of humour, and take the tribulations of being on the road in good spirits, which they manage to convey to their audiences.

See them sing one of their father Ricky Nelson's biggest hits, "Garden Party," by scanning the code (and check out all their tour dates at www.matthewandgunnarnelson.com) (link):

Gavin Scott

Prolific author, fellow Brit, and filmmaker, Gavin Scott, recently visited and told us about his new book in the trilogy, *The Age of Exodus*. It's the third Duncan Forrester mystery, which was published in September 2018.

These three books are masterfully presented, and I particularly like his mix of fact and fiction, which makes the characters all the more identifiable. Look him up on Amazon.com. And I recommend that you read the "About Gavin Scott" section for a full list of his amazing input.

Gavin has produced over 200 documentaries for the BBC (this fellow Brit now lives in Santa Monica), and his many other artistic creations are a feast for the eyes and ears. He is on Facebook, and his website is: www.gavinscott.com.

And scan the code to see us all being tew-wibly Bwitish on TEAFLIX (link):

Ivor Davis

Ivor has been around The Beatles world since their first tour of the States, when he was assigned to cover them for his UK-based newspaper. He had some great fun and frolics on the road with them, much of which you can find in his very entertaining book, *The Beatles and Me On Tour*. It is on Amazon and is a smashing read.

Angie with author Ivor Davis, guesting on TEAFLIX Tuesdays *in Casa McCartney in August 2019.*

I first met him at one of Mark Lapidos's Fests for Beatles Fans in Los Angeles a few years ago, and we hit it off immediately, sharing a similar wacky sense of humour.

More recently, my editor, Marshall Terrill, told me he had been working with Ivor on a book about the Manson murders, and this turned out to be one of the most compelling books I have read in years. I was delighted when Ivor arranged to be my guest on *TEAFLIX Tuesdays*, and we could have gone on for hours. It turns out that we had several other interests in common, such as relating to my working at Littlewoods Pools in Liverpool and his connections there, and also to him being a PR person for Butlins holiday camps when I was a regular "inmate" there. So we plan to do another session together when we can fit it into our dance cards, which are pretty full at the moment.

The publication of *Manson Exposed* coincided with the release of Quentin Tarantino's epic movie, *Once Upon a Time in Hollywood*. Although they had very different endings, each of them was tremendously entertaining. Fortunately, Ivor lives in Ventura, so we are almost neighbours and can tackle more of our adventures in the not too distant future.

So I urge you to wander over to amazon.com/books and check out Ivor Davis. Here is our TEAFLIX episode on Facebook (link):

Christine Romeo

Christine joined us to talk about her involvement with Alana Stewart and The Farrah Fawcett Foundation, a wonderful LA-based organization dedicated to the memory of Farrah and finding a prevention (yes – prevention!) and cure for cancer.

McCartney Multimedia is working with them on the business and social media side of their fund raising events, and you can find more about this aspect of their work by clicking on the code.

Here is our TEAFLIX episode on Facebook (link):

Jim O'Heir

Recently we had a visit from Jim O'Heir and his manager, Lynda Bensky. Jim originally hails from Chicago (as so much talent does), and has carved out a great career in acting. McCartney Multimedia created his website, which is how we met. Go check it out: www.jimoheir.com.

This being the 10th anniversary of the very successful *Parks and Recreation* TV series, there has been a lot of publicity about the show and the very talented cast. It includes Rob Lowe, Amy Poehler, Rashida Jones, and a host of others. I had several requests from Facebook friends to repeat the episode, which we did, and thus gained another whole lot of new followers. You can find it archived on: www.mrsmccartneysteas.com/videos. It's a bit naughty in parts, but lots of fun.

Angie with Jim O'Heir and Lynda Bensky guesting on TEAFLIX *Tuesdays.*

Here is our TEAFLIX episode on Facebook (link):

Xavier Burgin

This chapter wouldn't be complete without telling you about Xavier Burgin, a young and certainly up-and-coming filmmaker, whom I met when we both did an improv stint with National Lampoon's Lemmings in Hollywood. I urge you to check him out. His insight and dedication is tremendous, and he gives it his all. Check him out on Facebook or on his website: www.cuethelights.com.

A few very high-up folks in the film industry are beginning to take notice of this young man. I have every confidence that he will be around for a long time.

Xavier Burgin, Angie, and Ruth, guesting on TEAFLIX *Tuesdays.*

Here is our TEAFLIX episode on Facebook (link):

All Worn Out...

Finally, our cats, Butch Cassidy and Sundance, always try to get their closeup, and have to be shifted off the couches right before showtime every week. So, if you see little tails floating past, here is what they look like! I say "our" cats, but we all really know that dogs have owners; cats have staff.

Butch and Sunny, exhausted after the weekly TV appearance.

Ruth's Life Hacks, Continued

If you burn yourself cooking, slather yellow mustard over it, wait a few minutes, then rinse with cold water. It will be well on its way to healing.

Next time you have a splitting headache, try eating a mint. It has been scientifically proven to reduce the tension in your head, and mint can also often reduce your overall stress levels.

Having trouble getting those annoying price tag stickers off something? Slowly move a hair dryer over the area, and it will warm the glue, making it super easy to peel off.

Salt stains on your shoes in snowy areas? Wipe with a cloth dipped in a solution of one tablespoon of white vinegar to one cup of water. Boom! Stains be gone!

Spill nail varnish? Pour a large amount of white sugar on top of it. This will make the polish clump so you can easily sweep it up.

If you feel compelled to take flowers to your hostess for a dinner party or other occasion, make sure it is a plant in a pot, and not a bunch of flowers that will make her have to drop what she is doing, find a vase, dispense of the wrapping, et cetera. While she may smile sweetly and thank you prettily, it's a pain in the neck for her when she is putting the finishing touches to the meal or buffet. And a plant will probably last longer.

11
In My Life

Big Data and Cryptocurrency

Ruth is an expert on Big Data, and is often invited to speak on the subject. It is usually to groups of educational types and academics at colleges and establishments around the United States.

Over the years, this approach to information has rapidly changed, and she keeps up with research on an almost daily basis. She's also up on the emergence of cryptocurrency and the Bitcoin revolution. She and Martin are wizards at all of this, whilst I have to take it a slower pace. But I am beginning to get the hang of it. Me – I'm still reeling from pounds, shillings, and pence. And as for Euros ...

To see some of our Crypto funnies, scan this code with your mobile (link):

Of course, the brick and mortar banks and other financial institutions poo-poo the whole idea, because they obviously don't want the peasants to become too aware of what is out there.

But I have to say, with guidance from our friend Dr. Simon Mills, we have not put a foot wrong yet. I usually view it all with cautious optimism. Ruth and Martin did invest a small amount (that they could afford to lose), and up to now, they have not lost their initial investment. Martin is a genius at this type of thing, and early mornings are devoted on checking the currency markets worldwide. He has graphs on his computer that look like something from a sci-fi movie to me, but I guess they all make sense to him.

If nothing else, it is good exercise for the brain, and the international markets and political pundits have much to say on the subject. One can only wonder where this is all leading. I can remember the days when the only money was cash. You know, that stuff that you kept under the mattress for a rainy day?

Then we advanced to a stage where the working class actually had postal savings accounts, and then bank accounts. Why, that was thought to be world shattering. I was the first one in my family to be progressive enough to open a bank account. They all thought I was a bit nuts, and they were probably right.

Then, in the 1970s, came those magical things called ATM machines. We have a good friend in Arizona who was instrumental in the invention of those. It occurred to him that if people had to drive to a bank, park, get out (often in inclement weather), and go into a bank and stand in line to withdraw cash, then why not devise a machine where they could drive through and do the deed? Wow, did they think HE was nuts?

But here we are today, and still moving forward.

To see one of Ruth's speeches on Big Data, scan this code with your mobile device (link):

Artificial Intelligence

I began addressing the subject of artificial intelligence (AI) in the middle of August 2018, as it's becoming more and more relevant to the age in which we live.

AI seemed like something that only happened in the movies, but as we progress and advance as a society, it has become more of a reality and a part of our daily lives.

In my own small way, I have seen my body take on two titanium knees, a plastic hip replacement, microchips behind both eyes, and a tooth fitted in place with a fiber optic connection. Martin laughingly refers to me as the "bionic woman."

As my life has become more and more fulfilled in recent years, I have every reason to want to prolong it as long as I can, and remain active and mentally alert. To date, I have managed to do so. As I approach my 90th birthday in November, 2019,

I am not always as steady or as mobile as I would like to be. That's partially due to my own laziness and lack of discipline to exercise. At least I have a couple of two-pound barbells on my desk now, which I use in between bursts on my computer, or if I am on hold on the phone, in hopes of strengthening my upper arms.

Added to this regimen is a yoga strap, which I keep on my bed, and yank my sorry old legs up and down before I start my day.

I recently had the good fortune to meet a lady who is working closely with an AI research organization, and she has encouraged me to make myself more familiar with the concept.

As I noted in "Back in the Saddle Again" at the very beginning of the book, I have already made a pledge to myself to live to be 104. I laughingly attribute that to the fact that I want to receive a telegram on my 100th birthday from the Monarch, be it Queen Elizabeth II, or King Charles III, or whoever.

Growing up in England, it was a big feature of one's centenary to receive (what was then) a telegram from the King or Queen, which would be delivered to your front door by the postman. In the digital age, I understand it comes in the form of a Tweet.

I have a friend whose mother attained the age of 100 a few months ago, and she said that the process is now very different, as indeed it must be. It seems wonderful to me to think that our gracious Queen has embraced the entire medium of communication, no doubt with the encouragement of her grandsons, and even has a Twitter account. Time marches on.

This being my second book, I am now of the mindset that there may even be a third, maybe published from another planet.

National Lampoon Lemmings Improv

In April 2016, I was invited by Alan Donnes, president of National Lampoon, to join their Lemmings Improv class at The Complex Hollywood for eight weeks.

It was run by Allison Bills, a very accomplished coach and actress. My companions were a dozen up-and-coming young filmmakers, stand-up comedians, writers, actors, and actresses.

Angie with her fellow Lemmings on the Hollywood Improv *series in 2018.*

It was one scary but very fulfilling experience for me to trot off to the The Complex Hollywood every week for two months. They all treated me like a queen. It helped my self-confidence no end, and I have made lasting friendships with these very talented young people. They are from all over the States, and have made Los Angeles their base in order to hone their skills and dive in the deep end of theatre, comedy clubs, film, and television. They are all so dedicated. Obviously, my skills could in no way match theirs, but they were so supportive and affectionate, and this made for a great experience for me at this late stage in the game.

I don't care much for driving in the city after dark these days, so each week I took either an Uber or a Lyft, which in itself proved to be an adventure. I met some of the most interesting drivers – male and female – who had their own fascinating stories. Ruth was comfortable with the fact that, as the rides were ordered via her account, she could track my progress online and know when to expect me home. That way she could make sure I was not sneaking off to some den of iniquity to carouse with the youngsters.

Angie and Ruth with Lemmings coach, actress Allison Bills, in Hollywood.

The final week was a showcase with an invited audience, who were very responsive. And it was all captured on film by Martin for posterity.

I even roped in Henry Drayton, one of my fellow Lemmings, to stay at our house for a week when we went off to Texas to launch Mrs. McCartney's Wines at the Discover Wine Festival in Houston at the end of June, 2016. All of our cats gave him two paws up when we returned home. Henry has proved to be such a talented cameraman, too. Martin has hired him to work on other music-related projects.

Another offshoot of this was that National Lampoon put me forward to read for a part in an upcoming sci-fi movie starring Vanessa Williams. It was just a few lines, calling for an old gal in her mid-eighties to be filmed making a telephone call to an unknown authority offering some vital information about a missing person. I got down to the last two candidates, and then received a call from the producer saying that, although they loved my audition tape (which Martin had filmed), the director felt that I didn't look old enough! After the initial disappointment wore off, that really made my day!

Women and Credit in England

This passage was inspired by a story that appeared in a British newspaper that was published in July, 2016.

When the first British credit card launched almost fifty years prior, it was mostly used by men. Women not so much. They were viewed as a riskier investment by banks and stores, and usually had to get their father or husband to sign for most loans, even if they earned more than them.

This was Britain in 1970 – a world away in its attitude toward women.

"There was still this mindset that a woman got certain rights through the relevant man in her life," said Cambridge University Professor Lucy Delap. "Women had long been in charge of household budgets, but it was the husband who gave his wife the housekeeping money and held the financial power."

But, over time, women had an increasing amount of purchasing power. In 1951, about 36 percent of women aged 20 to 64 were part of the workforce. By 1971, this had risen to 52 percent. However, women were still considered second-class citizens by lenders.

Susan Woolley, from Chester, earned a third more than her husband, and ran into problems.

"I wanted to buy a three-piece suite on hire purchase soon after I got married," Wooley said. "But I had to get my husband's signature, even though I earned £13 per week whilst he earned £10 a week. I was extremely annoyed."

How times have changed.

Swannies

Recently, Dr. Simon Mills introduced me to Swannies, a type of blue light blocking, non-prescription glasses. They were marketed by his old friend, James Swanwick, a fellow Aussie entrepreneur with whom he has worked over the years on many projects.

Initially, I was a bit skeptical. I kept thinking that this might be another online scam to part us from our money. However, after James sent us a couple of pairs, I tentatively tried them out, and was astonished at the difference they made in my life.

Ruth and Angie displaying their "Swannies" blue blocker protective glasses at home in Playa.

My eyesight has been a problem since I was about two years old. Pneumonia left me with a turn in one eye (a "lazy eye" it was called in those days) and diminished eyesight. I wore little round gold wire framed specs from that tender age, and went through my school years being known as "specky four eyes," which did my self-esteem no good. Even my brother Bob, whom I looked up to, addressed me that way. Sadly, it influenced my lack of self-worth all through my childhood and adult years.

I began to suffer with macular degeneration in the early 2000s, and Rikki Klieman, the TV analyst and wife of Bill Bratton (former New York City Police Commissioner), suggested that I consult with Dr. Kevin Miller at the Jules Stein Institute, in Westwood, California. He in turn operated on me, one eye at a time, with amazing results. I was finally able to throw away the bifocal glasses that I had worn throughout life up to that point. I now only need to use dime store reading glasses for extra small print, or when using the computer.

I had hitherto usually only slept in about three-hour increments, but once I started using my Swannies, I was sleeping seven to eight hours a night. Boy, did this make a difference to my energy, attitude, and overall well-being.

All humans are subjected to the damaging ultraviolet rays that invade our lives, not only from the sun, but from all the devices that we are slaves to these days, from cell phones, to computers, to television sets.

Now I wouldn't go anywhere without them. You can see them advertised on TV, and there are many videos online to extol their virtues, as do I. Obviously, they may not suit everyone, but they have helped me immensely. I even wear them in bed if I watch television (which I know is not advised), and they make the screen less glaring. They do change the appearance of colours, though, and it's quite interesting to see the differences when you remove them.

But they've got my vote. I was even prompted to burst into song and video a little clip for James, singing "Swannies, Swannies, how I love you, how I love you, my dear old Swannies." It didn't result in a record deal, I'm sad to say.

Dang, there goes my chance at a Grammy for another year.

But maybe after my sex tape propels me into the public eye, the offers will come pouring in.

To learn more about the effects of blue light on eyesight (link), scan this code with your smartphone:

Men Are Just Happier People!

Men. What do you expect from such simple creatures? Your last name stays put. The garage is all yours. Wedding plans take care of themselves. Chocolate is just another snack. You can never be pregnant. You can wear a white T-shirt to a water park. You can wear NO shirt to a water park.

Car mechanics tell you the truth. The world is your urinal. You never have to drive to another gas station restroom because this one is just too icky. You don't have to stop and think of which way to turn a nut on a bolt. Wrinkles add character. Wedding dress: $5,000. Tux rental: $100. People never stare at your chest when you're talking to them. New shoes don't cut, blister, or mangle your feet. One mood all the time. Phone conversations are over in 30 seconds flat. You know stuff about tanks.

A five-day vacation requires only one suitcase. You can open all your own jars. You get extra credit for the slightest act of thoughtfulness. If someone forgets to invite you, he or she can still be your friend. Your underwear is $8.95 for a three-pack. Two pairs of shoes are more than enough. You almost never have strap problems in public. You are unable to see wrinkles in your clothes. Everything on your face stays its original colour. The same hairstyle lasts for years, maybe decades. You only have to shave your face and neck.

You can play with toys all your life. One wallet and one pair of shoes – one colour for all seasons. You can wear shorts, no matter how your legs look. You can do your nails with a pocket knife. You have freedom of choice concerning growing a mustache. You can do Christmas shopping for 25 relatives on December 24 in 25 minutes.

No wonder men are happier!

Charity Begins at Home

We formed a long-time habit of donating clothing and other stuff to various charities who collect from your home. They regularly call or send postcards, inviting you to make use of their services, telling you what days they will be in your neck of the woods.

They leave you a blank charity receipt, trusting you to fill in the true value of the donation to use with your next tax return.

However, in September, 2018, we changed our minds about this practice. Why the sudden 180-degree turn? We watched an episode of *Anthony Bourdain: Parts Unknown*, filmed just before his untimely suicide in France. (Or was it?)

He made us alert to the fact that many of the clothing donations we make to the well-known charity stores and house-to-house collectors finish up being sold to third world countries. This practice puts their own already unstable clothing industry out of business. People in the Far East prefer to be seen sporting a T-shirt with Mick Jagger's face on it, or some other rock star. I'm sure they don't know how much wheeling and dealing has taken place for the charity organizations in the United States to sell and ship all this stuff.

Knowing this new practice, we are now bagging up clothing, particularly socks (which is one of the biggest needs of the homeless), and dropping them off in some of the areas where people are living on the streets in downtown Los Angeles, Silverlake, and other areas where there is great need.

Recently, we were in Silverlake where Martin was doing some voiceover work in a local studio. Ruth dropped off a bag of socks, undies, and toiletries to a lady living on the sidewalk in a tiny tent. After voicing her thanks, she walked outside and asked the man in the next tent if he would like to share in her bounty. And this, only yards from a big Goodwill Store.

It's enough to make you weep.

The Man on the Moon

In June of 1969, Ruth and I were on a little holiday in Malta, and staying at The Sheraton Hotel. Jim had decided it was time for me to get a little R and R, and we two set off on our adventure, a little anxious, but glad to know that Jim would be well taken care of at home in Heswall. Not only was his sister Milly staying with him, but Cynthia Lennon promised to swing by regularly.

That was when we met friends Barbara and Jack Sambrook and their kids, Jane and Nigel. Their daughter Helen was but a baby and remained back in Yorkshire being ably taken care of. Ruth and Janey Sambrook (now Jane Webster) chummed up immediately, and we had many memories of the two of them playing "Over The Sea to Skye" on Ruth's rather wavery recorder.

It was during that trip that I also met Nancy and Franck Kargol. Nancy was another Yorkshire lass, like Barbara, and he, a Polish meteorological expert who was stationed on the Island. They were great music lovers, and we had many a musical evening clustered around the piano, either in the hotel, or at Nancy and Franck's apartment in Sliema. We would hammer songs like "Some Enchanted Evening" and "You Can Roll a Silver Dollar." All high class stuff.

Nancy also introduced us to her friend, Michael Barratt, who was at that time a well-known BBC TV broadcaster. He was featured on Nationwide, Panorama, and other current affairs programmes.

Angie chats with Buzz Aldrin at an event at the British Consulate in Los Angeles.

This was in the days when hotel rooms didn't have the luxury of a television set. The room just had one communal area off the lobby with a little black and white telly. Certainly nothing as grand as we have today.

The never-to-be-forgotten day came when Neil Armstrong took his first giant step for mankind. We all crowded into the little TV room. I remember seeing famous actress Connie Stevens, along with the cast and crew of *The Avengers*, who were filming on the island. So I got young Ruth out of bed and brought her down to witness this mammoth event. The TV was not blessed with very good reception, but we were all excited to be witnessing this historical occasion, which Ruth tells me she can still remember. She was nine years old at the time.

Little did we think that many years later we would be privileged to meet Buzz Aldrin at an event at the British Consul's residence in Los Angeles.

When we saw the reruns of the moon launch recently, memories came flooding back. I remember getting a dig in the ribs from Ruth when I had the nerve to ask Mr. Aldrin, "So who took the pictures of Neil climbing down the ladder on to the surface of the moon?" To give him credit, he adroitly avoided answering the question, and asked me a question in return. He asked something trivial like, "So what brings you here tonight?"

Ruth, Martin, and I recently went through our photo archives and found photographs of each of the three of us speaking with this great man. We also saw film of him at a reception at The White House recently, when the only two living astronauts from Apollo 11, Buzz and Michael Collins, were standing. I was a little shocked to think that nobody thought to afford these elderly heroes a seat. But I guess that's life today. It saddens me to think that these two men were not afforded more respect.

Young Janey is all grown up now, and is an international businesswoman, travelling the world, but based in Los Angeles. We frequently meet over a 'cuppa' and exchange yarns about our ongoing adventures. I recently saw a picture of her on horseback in the ocean off Turks and Caicos, where one of her daughters lives.

It really IS a small world, after all.

Liverpool

I'm sometimes asked what Liverpool means to me. For starters, it's a place that is indelibly stamped in my DNA. I don't think you realize it until you move away and become aware that a part of you is missing. It's the laughter, the kinship, the feeling of belonging, like you never seem to achieve anywhere else in the world.

My childhood was overshadowed by World War II. We spent most of our nights in an air raid shelter by candlelight, listening to the bombs falling and the shouts of air raid wardens: "put that light out" and "take cover." Phrases that became part of our every day and night lives.

Upon reflection, I now look back and realize that the phenomenon that became The Beatles was obviously partly due to the fact that they were all the product of wartime Liverpool. This, combined with their working class background, was no doubt a part of their inner strength. The grit, tenacity, and get-up-and-go spirit that held them together in the early days helped them have the staying power that they needed to develop when the fame and frantic lifestyles were upon them.

From my own perspective, I didn't think I was having a hard time. We just took every day as it came. I guess that's the British attitude, and especially the Liverpool attitude, where you just make the best of things and are thankful for whatever you do have. I'm still the same today, almost 90 years later.

Several famous authors have made their observations about Liverpool, a few of which are here for you:

> "My spirits rise on seeing the Mersey." *C.E. Montague*

> "It might have happened in any civilized place, or in Liverpool." *P.G. Wodehouse*

> "Liverpool, what a place to commit adultery!" *Edgar Wallace*

> "That rich and beautiful port." *Charles Dickens*

Liverpudlians are born with a sense of humour. It's all around them. I can remember a lot of the phrases we'd hear when we were little, in shops, or the doctor's office. Things like:

> "The doctor said I should get a second option."

> "He's one of dem plastered surgeons."

> "I took me prescription to the chemist. He's a smart fella. He's got all kinds of diplomats on his wall."

> "The other doctor told me to pollute it with cold water."

> "He needs to have his head X-raised."

> "She had all her overtures removed."

> "I was getting ejections."

> "I can't take them tablets, I'm lethargic to them."

> "It's just all around you, and you just can't help it sinking into your subconscious."

Then there's the schoolie ones, like:

> "He's been doing long decisions this term."

> "He speaks French fluidly. Er, what's French for Eau de Cologne?"

And on the religious side:

> "The Pope lives in a vacuum and is supposed to be inflammable."

I never did fathom why they called the police "the scuffers." Or "the bizzies." Maybe one of my readers will step up and enlighten me.

I've just remembered two more:

"I've never understood him. He's a complete enema to me."

"The police need to find some detergent for all this crime."

And then there's the oft quoted words of the legendary shawlies who used to sell fruit and flowers in Clayton Square:

"She's gorra smashing posh 'ouse, with all them muriels on the walls."

"E's gorra lip on 'im like a plumber's tool bag."

"She's so glamorous, she puts that cascara on her eyes."

It isn't possible to be a Scouser and not have a sense of humour. Now that I live in California, I often see that people are shocked at the way Ruth and I address one another. We have to explain to them that, where we come from, this type of insulting banter is a form of affection.

We were leaving a bar recently, and as I stood up to go, Ruth said, "Come on, er, what's your name?" A lady nearby said, "My God, that's her mother, and she doesn't know her name!"

I mean – c'mon.

Happy Birthday and other Liverpudlian Stuff

The first week of August, 2018 was the birthday of a city that is very dear to me. Liverpool celebrated 811 years since King John signed the historical documents in 1207 that had this fair city marked indelibly into England's DNA.

To the world, The Beatles seemed such a phenomenon. But not to us Scousers. It's only what we might have expected. There has always been such a wealth of talent, from musicians to comedians to actors to writers. So it was really no big surprise when the world found out what we Scousers had already known for a long time.

We couldn't keep them to ourselves and had to share them with the world. Some people haven't got over it; others have glowed with pride at what has come out of our huge little city that could.

Over and over, people from other countries and from other parts of England express their surprise at how hospitable Liverpudlians are. But it's in their DNA. And so is their sense of humour.

The throwaway remarks you can hear in any pub of cafe include such gems as:

> "Had a shockin' ferry across from Birkenhead. I was glad to get me feet on terra cotta."
>
> "I used to be left handed, but now I'm ambiguous."
>
> "He got real mad. He went Bismark."
>
> "I couldn't hear a word the priest said. The agnostics was so bad."
>
> "She's so skinny. I've seen more meat on a pair of knitting needles."

They just seem to roll off the tongue. And Liverpool now boasts some incredible restaurants and progressive chefs. It is truly a tourist mecca, and everyone who visits wants to return. I am not surprised.

No need to leave your heart in San Francisco, save it for Liverpool. You'll be glad you did.

Tea and History

All my life, the staple sustenance has been a good old pot of tea. My earliest recollection is of my Mum brewing a good old 'cuppa' in a brown teapot (a Brown Betty, they called it). It was from her that I learned the adage, "To obtain tea hot, first warm your pot."

Tea is the second most popular drink on the planet, I'm told. And in the United States, it's creeping up on coffee in terms of popularity. In my younger days, teabags were rarely heard of. Later, when we began to watch American films, we watched with interest when tea bags were used. But it would be several years before they became popular in England.

The history of tea has always fascinated me. And here we are in the 21st century with such a plethora of flavours. A good friend of ours, Kerry Dunne, was visiting from Arizona one day and asked aloud, "What's more British than a cup of tea? What's

Martin and Angie at a product demonstration at AJ's Fine Foods in Paradise Valley, AZ.

more British than The Beatles?" The proverbial light bulb went off in my head, and Mrs. McCartney's Teas was born – in America of all places!

We spent many hours researching and sourcing teas to ensure everything is fair trade, and hooked up with a very forward thinking and reliable distributor. Ruth and Martin built me a nice website. Inevitably, there is a Facebook page. Andreas Slavik of Vienna recorded a jingle for me with the Vienna Symphony Orchestra as a gift and a contribution to the project. I built a Facebook page and, voila, we were in business!

One of my first customers was The American Red Cross, who bought 4,500 variety packs (they contained five bags of each of the four flavours) to give away as incentives for people to donate blood. Will donate for tea.

Another early customer was John Paul DeJoria of Patron Tequila and Paul Mitchell Hair Care Products. He ordered 3,500 variety packs to put in their goody bags to give to all of the beauticians at their yearly get together at the Aria Resort & Casino in Las Vegas. I was so excited to be invited to this gathering,

Angie and John Paul DeJoria in Malibu, embracing a massive sample of his Patron tequila whilst sipping Mrs. McCartney's Teas.

where John Paul invited me up onstage. We talked about the tea, The Beatles, and my life. It resulted in a huge uptick in sales.

Use the QR code to see the video (link):

There are lots of interesting stories about the history of tea, which I sometimes talk about at various gatherings. Many Americans are big Anglophiles and always fascinated about anything British, and love our anecdotes. There is so much to talk about, including the protocol of serving afternoon tea. I have been fortunate to obtain a nice collection of teapots, silver teaspoons, tea strainers, and other accoutrements such as china dishes, two-tier cake stands, cake forks, and cake tongs, which lend a nice atmosphere to any tea party.

The origin of people putting the milk in a cup of tea first or last was after the plague in England, when disease was rife and people had to boil water to make tea. The posh (rich) people would put the milk in last to make sure the tea was brewed sufficiently. They used fine bone china cups. The working class and poor, who had less fine vessels to drink out of, were scared of the boiling water cracking their cups, and put the milk in first to diffuse the heat.

We sell our teas via our online site: www.mrsmccartneysteas.com. The teas are from many parts of the world, and are imported into the country via our distributor. They ultimately end up with me, when we arrange for them to be packed and mailed.

We have had fun talking to people at several food and wine events, spreading the word, and keeping the legend of tea alive.

So, that made me thirsty – guess I'll have to go and put the kettle on.

2018 Capitol Records

During 2018 and 2019, I had the distinct pleasure to visit the legendary Capitol Records Studios on Hollywood and Vine, the site of where so much musical history has been made, from Sinatra, to Dean Martin, The Rat Pack, our own Macca, and many more.

One of our very talented musical clients, Nick Marechal, has been working there with Grammy-winning producer Niko Bolas. Martin mixed a part of his Geist Musik Trilogy there too,

Angie hamming it up outside Capitol Records.

Angie admiring her hero, Frank Sinatra, at Capitol.

which was a big thrill for him, working with Niko and his stealth partner, known only as "Vladimir Johnson."

(If I told you who this is, I'd have to kill you.)

So when Nick Marechal arranged to work there, I was so jazzed to be invited to sit in on the sessions. And what a great photo op.

I have looked up at this ivory tower (actually it's supposed to look like a stack of records) for many moons, never dreaming that one day I could access its hallowed walls, and even visit its loo, and wonder, which famous bums had sat on that seat? The mind was boggling – Sinatra, Streisand, Ricky Nelson – who knows? I resisted stealing the lavatory seat.

But enough of my day dreaming.

We were treated to the full tour, seeing the studios where so much iconic music had been made, from movie stars, to soundtracks, to many artists whose names are emblazoned on their walk of fame. I am writing this little chapter so that I can drop as many names as can be, and I was privileged to sit on the stool that Frank used to sit on, hold the mic stand, see the John Lennon star on the Walk of Fame outside, and generally get my drooling over and done with.

To experience the incredible vibe that is Capitol, and the welcome of the lovely studio boss, Paula Salvatore, is to know that in addition to Streisand and Sinatra, people like Nat King Cole, Sammy Davis Jr., and even the Beach Boys laid down their magic there, and you feel that you have been just the tiniest fly on the wall of something "unforgettable." Sorry. I couldn't resist that one.

Check out Nick Marechal's music here (link):

TEAFLIX Tuesdays

Early in 2018, we were working with James Miller of Arizona, a business associate, on projects relating to Bitcoin. Martin filmed a small clip of Ruth and me talking about the subject, and James commented that he was so impressed with our chemistry that we should do a regular spot.

Angie, still hamming it up at Capitol.

And so, the idea of *TEAFLIX Tuesdays* was born. Martin created the concept, and we started a regular spot on my Angie McCartney Facebook page, going live on air at 11:30 a.m. Pacific time on Tuesdays. One of the early episodes resulted in me selling more Mrs. McCartney's Teas from one episode than I had in the previous year. We realized we were onto something.

When I look back over the episodes, I am constantly amazed at the reaction, starting out with just a few dozen of our "faithfuls" tuning in, to growing numbers of viewers. I have had a variety of guests, ranging from activists to musicians, authors, filmmakers, actors, chefs, winemakers, humourists, and business people.

The viewing figures have risen to as high as 13,000 plus, when I had as my guest Myriam von M from Germany. She is a cancer patient and activist in Europe, who has made numerous

Angie trying to look demure, preparing for TEAFLIX Tuesdays.

appearances and documentaries in her efforts to find a cure. We met her in 2015 when we all were guests on the Dancers Against Cancer ball, in Vienna, Austria. We have since stayed in touch. She was in Los Angeles a few months ago for meetings with TV and film people regarding her ongoing projects, so she joined us in the casa for a chat.

She is a colourful young lady, drawing attention to her great persona by wearing a variety of wigs and having lots of piercings, tattoos, and self-applied henna stars on her face.

See Myriam getting her MyAid Award for services to cancer research at Vienna's Hofburg Palace by scanning this code (link):

Online Passwords

One of the banes of my life is the whole security thing about logging into the bank and credit card accounts, which I do every morning.

I am very meticulous about this. However, in recent months it has become increasingly frustrating. It is time consuming to have my entries rejected, resulting in me being locked out.

This in turn means that I have to call the relevant institution (sometimes I feel like I'm ready to check myself into an Institution), and go through the entire rigamarole. This includes a security procedure, getting a temporary password, having it accepted (frequently this fails), and remembering the new password.

I am sure many of you will identify with this. My biggest problems are with two of the largest banks in the country, who have even informed me that we do not have any such accounts! Some days Happy Hour gets to start a little earlier.

I have a printout of passwords that reads like the *Encyclopaedia Britannica*. I have long since run out of pet's names, former home addresses, catch phrases, family "in" jokes, strings of numbers, and upper and lowercase alphabetical letters.

And to top it all off, Lifelock keeps running their scary commercials and warning us that every two seconds someone has their identity stolen.

Believe me, this password nonsense is becoming a job of its own. Do I expect too much out of life?

Then, in late September 2018, Facebook announced that many thousands of their passwords had been compromised. If only the hackers could use their skills for something productive. There we are, then ... where are we?

Robocalls and Other Digital Interruptions

Another of today's technical hazards is the robocall. I'm sure I don't need to tell you, dear reader, how frustrating it is that they always seem to know just when dinner is placed on the table.

And it's not only on the phones, but in emails and social media, too. For example, this morning I've already had an offer to extend my penis, choose a destination for the cruise I have just won, and be invited to submit my bank account details to a nice Prince in Nigeria who wants to send me a gazillion dollars.

Then, there are young men on Facebook who want to be my friend. Strangely enough, most of them say they are in the military in Afghanistan or somewhere similar, always divorced, and with a young son or a puppy dog on their lap.

Why on earth would they want to befriend an 89-year-old widow lady – and I use the term "lady" loosely. Perhaps they think I'm rich. Oh boy, have I got news for you.

The appeals for donations to many seemingly worthy causes are not always what they seem, either. It pains me to think that there must be some folks who fall for these, otherwise, why would these scam artists keep making these calls?

Then there are the threatening ones from a police officer who is concerned for my safety, and offers of free roof repairs (no thanks, just got a new one thanks to Sweet Alice Harris), back braces, personal alarms, and even dental implants.

I realize I have a way to go. I could get permanent eyelashes, butt implants, tattoos, vaginal blinging (ouch), and anal bleaching. The possibilities are endless.

A friend recently told us that his young son had come up with a great way to handle the dinner time calls. When the phone rings he answers, "Brown residence. How are you connected to the victim?" This usually stops them in their tracks. If they don't respond, he will continue, "This is an active crime scene. Your number has been traced and you may now be contacted as a person of interest."

When election time comes around, this is a particularly useful one. You may share it with my blessing. And only an hour or two ago, I was warned that I am about to be arrested by the Internal Revenue Service for my failure to pay my taxes, and that this was my final warning. So, I should bid you all a final farewell.

Oh wait, the phone's ringing. I'm gonna answer with, "Oooh you sound nice. What are you wearing?" That should scare them off.

The Changing Face of Advertising

So much seems to have changed in the advertising and media world, ever since we entered the digital age. I recently became aware of the talents of Amelia Conway directing commercials and music videos at the ripe old age of 14. She tells the story that she and a friend were bored, and decided to take her parents' camera, get dressed up, and go into the woods with flashlights. They went off and shot a bunch of unintelligible footage.

Later, her mom posted it on YouTube.com, and then voila! A star was born. It went viral. She directed her first commercial for Target when she was eleven and freely admits that she had no idea what she was doing and totally relied on the crew and performers to help her through it.

She didn't know what terms like "grip" and "action" even meant. So I am left to wonder, who was the genius who hired her? Didn't he or she know how many experienced Hollywood filmmakers were looking for work? A little later, she began to acquaint the old veterans with terms that were only familiar to her generations.

These ditties include:

Adulting
Based on the adjective "adult" and describes actions that
seem mature or grown up.

Extra

Trying too hard in a bad way. For example, calling your friend last night after you texted her at work was so *extra*.

HMU

Hit Me Up - an invitation to contact someone.

Thirsty

Coming off as extremely desperate in order to get someone's attention.

LMR

Like My Recent. Indicating you should refer to the sender's most recent Instagram.

Salty

When someone is angry, upset, or irritated.

Gucci

When some is really good or when you totally agree with someone. For instance: Your Uggs are SO *Gucci*.

Dench

This is now an adjective. I wonder if Dame Judi knows? The kids think she is cool since she teamed up with a rapper, so anything "Dench" is good.

Ticket to Ride

The world's fascination with all things celebrity related continues.

I can remember, when we used to stay at Paul's Cavendish Avenue house in the 1960s, there would often be evidence that people had rummaged through his trash cans on collection day. I wonder what they found, and what they did with it?

Paul's 1967 Lamborghini 400 GT was up for auction at Bonhams in the south of England in early 2018, but it failed to reach its reserve price. Given its provenance, that's a little surprising.

Then, his Aston Martin brought in big bucks at another Bonhams auction. The final price, with premium was said to be barely over $1.8 million, which fell smack in the middle of Bonhams estimate. It's an impressive price on its own, but more so when compared with its sale back in 2012. Back then, it was painted in the same blue as it had originally been, and only sold for $495,000, making this new sale more than three times higher. It was a 1964 model that had been made famous by James Bond (Sean Connery) in *Goldfinger*. Paul purchased it at the height of Beatlemania just after they finished filming *A Hard Day's Night*.

I remember going to a film premiere with Paul, Jane Asher, and Jim, and we were driven in his Hispano Suiza – which we used to call the "Elliott Ness Mobile."

Then there was Ringo's Mini Cooper, which went for a reported $133,000. It was bought by former Spice Girl Geri Halliwell.

And of course, the *Sergeant Pepper* gypsy caravan that had once belonged to John Lennon turned up in recent years, refurbished, and was auctioned for a tidy sum.

If it's had a Beatle behind the wheel, rest assured, it won't be a steal.

To see the Lamborghini – scan this QR code with your smartphone (link):

Ageing

Researchers are a step closer to understanding the secrets of "super-agers" – the lucky seniors who retain their memories, mental sharpness, and thinking skills much longer than their peers.

A team at Northwestern University performed brain scans on 13 super-agers whom they classified as people over 80. These amazing geezers scored as high in memory tests as those 15 to 30 years younger, and a dozen cognitively average counterparts. Over a period of 18 months, the researchers looked for changes in thickness in each participant's cortex, the outer layer of the brain responsible for thinking, memory and decision making.

They found that, while all the seniors lost brain volume, the super-agers retained twice as much as their peers. More research is now needed to understand what causes this lower rate of atrophy, reports CBS.

The most important aspect is to determine the possible genetic, social, and environmental factors that contribute to the super-agers' thicker cortices, said Paul Wright, Chair of Neurology at North Shore University Hospital in Manhasset, New York. This may unlock the key to successful ageing.

As I write this, I am pushing 90, hence my interest in the subject. It still amazes me that so much progress has been made in my lifetime, and hopefully will continue before I pop my clogs.

Recent research has concluded that when you get up in the morning, you should avoid your computer and cell phone for about three hours, and either read, walk, eat breakfast, or meditate, or do all four if possible. The brain evidently needs the early wakening hours to assimilate before honing in on the devices to which we are all slaves. I am going to give it a whirl. It's going to be a tough one though, as I always want to check email to see if anything startling has happened overnight, then check the bank accounts and credit cards.

When I was a kid, my mum told me that women usually only lived until about 48 years of age. Mind you, without washing machines, dishwashers, steam irons, and all the gadgets that we now take for granted, it's no wonder that the poor dames wilted before they hit the half century mark. And of course, birth control was unheard of.

And they dared to call them the Good Old Days!

Wet Behind the Ears

In August, 2018, we put out the word that we were going to hold a launch party at our house regarding an exciting new service we offered called, "McCartney Studios."

This announcement came to the attention of our old Brit friends, Eva and Nik Speakman, who regularly appear on ITV in London. They are psychotherapists who help people with their fears and phobias. They turned up at our party, and suggested that whilst in the States filming segments for their breakfast show in the United Kingdom, we shoot one on me and my fear of water and swimming pools.

This was duly set up, and a week later the Speakmans turned up with a film crew. We shot a very enjoyable segment, culminating in me taking a dip in our neighbour's swimming pool. This was major, as my terror of water started when I was about six years old. Of course, with good reason. Whilst at a holiday beach resort in North Wales, my brother Bob dug a hole in the sand and waited until the tide came in and covered it slightly. He then urged me to run towards him. I promptly fell into the hole and was completely submerged, damaged for life. Until now, that is.

Thanks to Nik and Eva and their therapy session with me, I was shown how to look at the experience in a completely different light. The show aired on ITV's *The Morning Show* in September, 2018, and again in August of 2019.

Not only was it a very enjoyable day, but a fruitful one. I can now approach the ocean and swimming pools with a completely different outlook – no longer wet behind the ears.

Looking back, their kids are now in their film crews and are all grown up – we've known this lovely family a while!

Angie getting her "water therapy" in Karen and Jay's pool, next door, filming a segment for UK's ITV Breakfast Show.

In My Life 269

The delightful Speakman family on a earlier visit.

Tongue Twisters

- She stood on the balcony, inexplicably mimicking him hiccupping, and amicably welcoming him in.
- Singing Sammy sung songs on sinking sand.
- The great Greek grape growers grow great Greek grapes.
- The thirty-three thieves thought that they thrilled the throne throughout Thursday.
- How can a clam cram in a clean cream can?
- I saw Susie, sitting in a shoe shine shop. Where she sits she shines, and where she shines, she sits.
- I wish to wash my Irish wristwatch.
- A skunk sat on a stump and thunk the stump stunk, but the stump thunk the skunk stunk.

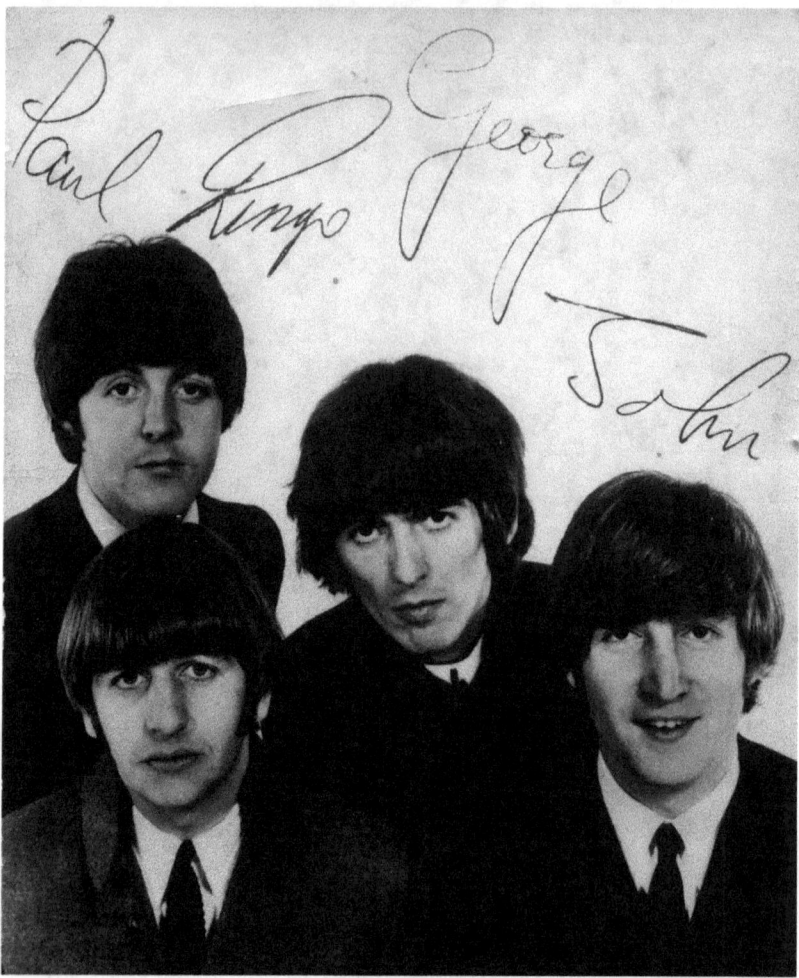

An original Beatles promotional photograph that resides in a secure fireproof safe.

- It wasn't the cough that carried him off, twas the coffin they carried him in.
- Gobbling gargoyles gobbled gobbling goblins.
- Did Dick Pickens prick his pinkie pickling cheap cling peaches in an inch of pinch, or framing his famed French finch photos?
- Seth at Sainsburys sells sleek socks.
- Seven sleazy shysters in sharkskin suits sold sheared seaskins to seasick sailors.
- I won't wish the wish you wish to wish.

12
And in the End...

I hope you have found something of interest, or maybe something to make you smile. You won't win any prizes for guessing that I am not a trained writer. I just write as I think, sometimes with the strange contents of my mature thoughts. I like the saying: The mind is a terrible thing to waste. (Also, its corollary: the waist is a terrible thing to mind.) Both, I think, are applicable in my case.

I sometimes wake myself up in the middle of the night laughing at some old joke of my father's, and considering that he died when I was seven years old, I mean *really* old jokes. Or, a wartime song that we used to sing in the air raid shelters during World War II. So the mind is like a filing cabinet, and it's probably time that some of the old files were put through the shredder. And a couple of nights ago, it was a dirty ditty that my brother Bob taught me when he was home on leave from his pastime as a Paratrooper in the Royal Corps of Signals, of jumping out of aeroplanes. I refrained from putting that in the book as I didn't want to run foul of the censors.

I thank you for your indulgence, and hope I haven't offended anyone (unless it was intentional). You just never know with me. So off you go now, to either donate this to the local book mart, or use it as a doorstop, or even pop it on your shelf. Just don't try asking for your money back – half your luck with that one.

I'll sign off with my favourite Monty Python ditty: Always Look On The Bright Side of Life. And remember to smile (while you still have teeth).

Warm and fuzzies, and if God spares me, and Dave Charlesworth and Marshall Terrill have not been led away drooling, there may even be a third masterpiece in the years to come. May good health, good humour, and good fortune stay ahead.

Dr. Angie McCartney, November, 2019

A Final Interruption by Ruth:

OK, OK Ange, that is enough, now knock it off and go and put the kettle on...

The Icing on Your Tea Cake

One of Mike McGear's friends, Ray Conn, has graciously allowed us to include several of his photographs. These photos have never been published before. Thank you, Ray!

Paul and the Lovely Lady Linda. Photo courtesy Ray Conn.

Young Stella already displaying her jewelry fashion chops, in her dad's arms. Photo courtesy Ray Conn

Mike and Ray Conn, 1981. Photo courtesy Ray Conn.

Mike listening to tracks he worked on with musician and photographer Ray Conn in 1981. Photo courtesy Ray Conn. You can listen to Mike and Ray by clicking the QR code (link):

Paul in a celebratory mood. Photo courtesy Ray Conn.

Acknowledgements

In Alphabetical order, to be Politically Correct:

Babs (Dame Barbara) Crawford and her darling family
who gave us a home when we ran away to Australia.

Barry & Megan Coffing
for turning their garage into a guesthouse and their entrance bell into a whistling fest.

Beryl Kendall (RIP) and The Kendall Cousins
who gave us our first home in America and helped us make a new life.

Betty White
who proves you can just keep doin' it!

Bill Kelly, Esq.
for all the legal eagle advice and rum drink recipes.

Bill Miller
my very favorite Virgin (ahem) person, and kitty concierge, who started so much.

Cynthia Lennon (RIP)
a lasting friend, who agreed to write the foreword to my first book.

David Skinner
Chef extraordinaire, wine maker of Mrs. McCartney's Wines, Raconteur and popular resort figure in his hometown of Kemah, TX where he runs a mind-blowing restaurant called "eculent." And that ain't all…

Dawn Bowery
my lovely British photographer friend, who photographed my cover picture for the first book.

Deven Parmar
my fellow Elk, Film Director and staunch friend and supporter, and his lovely Wife, Veronica for sharing him with us so generously.

Don Woods
my magnificent Wirral songwriting buddy whose video clips of Merseyside and The Wirral on YouTube.com constantly remind me of home.

Acknowledgements

Dr. Simon Mills and the long-suffering Molley (who is said to be a genuine alien)
> *for helping me receive my Doctorate in Business Studies, learn how to lose money on Bitcoin, and for managing to lead us all through far too many social activities, introducing me to Swannies, sharing his talents and social skills until I could take no more.*

Eric Belcher
> *for hiring me not once, but 3 times, and letting me quit instead of firing me!*

Ivor Davis
> *my Brit chum, who toured with The Beatles in 1964 and in 2019 published an amazing book covering the 50 years since the Manson murders (*Manson Exposed*).*

Jim Gath
> *my one time Boss (at* USA TODAY*), long time friend, brilliant writer, and savior of horses at Tierra Madre Horse and Human Sanctuary in Arizona .... and one FUNNY guy!*

Jim McCartney
> *who took us into his life and made a new world for us beyond belief.*

Joan Archer (RIP)
> *my big sister who taught me to be resilient in the face of a good air raid and a bristle scrubbing brush and who inspired me by recording her first CD at 82.*

Joan Jackson
> *a fellow author, who was a welcome guest on a recent edition of TEAFLIX Tuesdays, telling us about her books that relate to family matters and riveting subjects.*

John, Paul, George, and Ringo
> *who completely changed my world.*

Karotti & HD Schmitz-Nethercutt
> *for the gift of your lovely son, Martin, in our lives.*

Kerry and Cynthia Dunne
> *who encouraged me to start Mrs. McCartney's Teas. See – it's all your fault.*

Lisa Derketsch
> *thank you for the extra pair of eyes.*

Louise Harrison

for hanging in there, and being a fellow member of the Beatles' survivors club.

Mag. Raimund Carl

our steadfast leader at McCartney Sports in Vienna, whose thriving tennis division is our bright hope for the future.

Marc Linsey

one of our greatest supporters throughout many of our Texas adventures.

Mark Lapidos

for keeping The Beatles legacy alive and our friendship flourishing.

Mark Lewisohn

a good friend, and a true genius in all things Beatles related.

Marshall Terrill

genius writer, man of mystery, and brains behind this book.

Martin Nethercutt

my beloved son-in-law, who has guided me throughout this and other projects, and my life for the past umpteen years, with tolerance, kindness, loving support, and a dang load of technical know-how to bring it all together. (Good job Martin!) (Good night John Boy!)

Matthew & Gunnar Nelson

my recent new friends, their loyalty to their family legacy in music is incredible, and they are not exactly ugly!

May Pang

for old times sake.

Mel Haber (RIP)

for the old-fashioned, five-star inn-keeper standards at The Ingleside Inn in Palm Springs and those heavy pours at Melvyn's. Oh, and what about those stories? Mel is no longer with us, but is still in our hearts.

Nancy Lee Andrews

a stalwart friend, beautiful lady, and one helluva photographer.

Nashville Natives

Bob Mather, Blaine Hayes, Rob & Sally Hendrick, Ann Stokes and all the "deep fried pie" aficionados at South Street and Sammy P's.

Nick Marechal
for the many happy hours of music, for our in-depth discussions, and for the warm and loving friendship.

Niko Bolas
long time friend, musical genius, record producer, and engineer beyond belief, thanks for the love, the laughter, and liberal amounts of loquaciousness.

Paul Reitz
for being a great coach and a good SOLID friend! And for introducing us to QR codes.

Pauline Sutcliffe
for her encouragement, and help with Stuart's early artwork and fonts. Rest in peace Pauline.

Peggi Sturm
my salvation in the world of financials.

Rachel Jones
our lovely Vet who takes such good care of our kitties, and is always willing to go the extra mile. (How about putting in a good word for me with your Dad, Quincy, to produce my next album?) Just kidding.

Ray Conn
a good friend of Mike McGear's who graciously provided the photos in Chapter 12.

Ray Connolly
my rare and trusted journalist friend, for his encouragement over the years.

Ric Hollywood Wetzel
whose genius with my hair and make-up could make a Goddess from a sow's ear.

Richard Oliff
for helping me remember to clean with ... and not DRINK white vinegar, and having me on his UK radio show with our Dick's Domestics for umpteen years.

Rikki Klieman & Bill Bratton
a woman of strength and humour who should run for President with a magnificent husband who looks REALLY good in uniform! (I love a man in uniform.)

Ruth McCartney
: *my beloved daughter, my reason for living, my pal, my inspiration, my Digital Diva and fellow laundry folder.*

Saxophone Jones
: *my fellow author, who kindly invited me to write the foreword for his book, "Sax, Drugs & Rock n Roll."*

Shelly Goldstein
: *for her early encouragement, guidance, and loving support throughout the project.*

Steve Tyrell
: *for what else? The music!*

Team Paisley
: *Tony & Carol Busching, Alisa Allen, Kevin Stofer-Smith, Chris Kitch, and others, who have taught me so much and when to say "It's a wrap."*

Thom and Kennon Tran
: *who offered me the privilege of conducting their wedding ceremony.*

Tony Barrow (RIP)
: *who also knew the true stories, and who gave me so much support in reviving my memories.*

And all my loving friends, family, neighbours, fans of The Beatles, Tea fans, Facebook buddies, Senismag.com readers: your never-ending warmth and trust in me has helped me to keep going, often when I felt like giving up. But there ain't no stopping me now. So here goes book number two: *Your Mother Should Know*.

> Angie the Fearless!
> Four feet ten inches

In book one, I was four feet eleven and a half inches, but shrank down to four feet ten in the ensuing years.

> `Woof!`

Appendix 1: Foreword by Cynthia Lennon[1]

My friendship with Angie McCartney dates back many eons, and memories of times shared, laughs along the way, good times, and some not so good, but always our strongest bond has been the similarity of our relationships with our kids, mine with Julian and her with Ruth. Although Angie and I are ten years apart in age, our kids were only separated by three years, and so as Mums of young kids in the middle of Beatle madness, I think we immediately saw something in one another about trying to retain our Hoylake values. Angie was born in Hoylake and I grew up there so we had shared experiences on a few different levels.

She walked into our house, Kenwood, in St. George's Hill, Surrey one evening in 1965 with Jim, Paul, Jane Asher and some other friends, and immediately asked me if she could do anything to help in the kitchen. I said, "No thanks" and she went to sit on one of our 18-foot sofas, which seemed to swallow her up. But don't let Angie's stature fool you ... she's small but mighty.

Like me, Angie and Ruth have been around the globe once or twice, and they never failed to keep their sense of humour, work ethic, loyalty to each other, friends and family, no matter how dysfunctional. In fact, it was Angie who once told me she put the "fun" in "dysfunctional."

In the Seventies, I witnessed her devotion to nursing Jim, and the unselfish support of young Ruth who, as a teenager, was always by her side, helping in whatever way she could to ease his suffering. Ruth's school in West Kirby was close to our house and they would often stop by for a natter on the way home – and of course – a cup of Tea!

The Beatles fell apart but somehow we've always managed to stay in touch throughout the years and the miles. Since then, I've watched and read about their global travels, various

---

1   Originally published in *My Long and Winding Road* by Angie McCartney; used by permission.

jobs, projects, and company McCartney Multimedia, in sunny California.

When she asked me to write the foreword to her book, I was delighted, and although we now communicate across the miles by telephone, she never fails to make me laugh when we share experiences, and it will be fun to see the names of Lennon and McCartney together again – if only in print!

I sincerely wish her every success with this, her first book, which has only taken her a little over eighty-two years to complete, and she is even threatening a second one – I can hardly wait! Oh, but I do expect a signed copy!

Lovingly, Cynthia Lennon

Index

A

ageing 266–267
Alder Hey Children's Hospital 52–54
Aldrin, Buzz 251
  (photo) 251
All You Need is Klaus 86
Antonelli, Paul 157, 207
Archer, Joan 274
Archer, Paul 36–50
Archer, Peter 34, 96–97
Arendt, Tim 180
Around The World in 10,000 Bites 198–201
Artificial Intelligence 242–243
Asher, Jane 76, 121–123, 279
  (photo) 76
Asher, Richard and Margaret 80–81
Ask Angie 15
Aspel, Michael 103
Astaire, Fred 42
Atkins, Chet 4
Auger, Brian 78
Australia 150–154

B

Barker, Ken 106
Barrow, Tony 76, 86, 277
Bates, Nancy 84
Beatlefest 90
Beatles, The 6, 96, 100–102, 104, 252
  and Ivor Davis 236
  at Brian Epstein's memorial service 109–111
  breakup 115, 127–129, 143
  effect on culture 203
  fan mail 83–85, 89–91
  in Australia 101
  in Liverpool 97–99
  Liverpool statue 136–137
  Magical Mystery Tour 116–117
  tribute bands 183–184

Being John Lennon: A Restless Life 115
Beit T'Shuvah 219–221
Belcher, Eric 167, 274
Bell, Madeleine 79
Bensky, Lynda
  (photo) 238
Best, Pete 5, 98
Bevan, Buddy (Rev.) and Mary 63–64, 76
Big Data 241–242
Bills, Allison 243
  (photo) 245
Blackbird 4, 118
Bockmeier, Dieter 157–160
  (photo) 207, 208
Bockmeier, Fanny and Fonzie 160
Bolas, Niko 276
Borowitz, Mark 220
Bourdain, Anthony 198, 231–232
  (photo) 232
Bowery, Dawn 273
Braddock, Bessie 46–48
Bratton, William xi, 181–183, 276
  (photo) 181, 182
Briggs, Raymond 135
Bron, Eleanor 69
brown sugar 8
Burgin, Xavier 238
  (photo) 239
buttermilk 8

C

Cadd, Brian 171, 197
  (photo) 152
Cagan, Amanda 232–235
Calithumpian 161
Camilletti, Val 223–224
candles 202
Cannabis 14–15
Capitol Records 258–260
Caplan, Louie 95–96

Carl, Raimund Mag. 275
  (photo) 192
Carrog 76
Cassidy, David 172, 226–228
  (photo) 226
Cass, Mama 113
Cates, Morgan 184
Cavern Club 96, 98
Cavern Club Beatles 183
charity 249–250
Choi, Roy 231
Clapton, Eric 105
Clear Creek Winery 186
Cleese, Camilla 177–178
Cleese, John 174–180
  (photo) 175, 176, 178
Clubmoor Cinema 60
Coburn, Tony 191
Coburn, Tony and Jimmy 183
coffee 56
Coffing, Barry 186, 190–191, 273
Cogan, Alma 82–83
Come Back Milly 111
Concrete Utilities 35
Conn, Ray 272
Connery, Sean 140
Connolly, Billy 79
Connolly, Ray 113–116, 141, 276
Cooper, Kim 163–165
Cope's Tobacco Warehouse 83
Cotton Exchange 58–59
cotton trade 57
Country Hams, The 134
Cramer, Floyd 4
Crawford, Babs 273
Crawford, Babs and Willy 150
Crawford Family 25–50, 150–154
Crawford, Rory (photo) 152
Cryptocurrency 241–242
Curly Pool 153–154
cutting boards 56

D

Dale, Donald 180
Darnell, Tae 14

Davis, Ivor 236–237, 274
  (photo) 236
DeGeneres, Ellen 209–211
DeJoria, John Paul 256
  (photo) 257
Delap, Lucy 246
Derketsch, Lisa 274
des Barres, Pamela 218–219
Disney Aulani Hotel 209
Dooley, Arthur 136–137
Drake's Drum 73–74, 92
  (photo) 74
Drayton, Henry 245

E

Eastman, Lee 123, 128
Eastman, Louise 124
eculent restaurant 188
eggs 8, 202
Emerick, Geoff 229–230
  (photo) 230
Empress of Britain, The 51
Epstein, Brian 65, 86, 100–102, 106, 108–110, 123, 149
Ethel & Ernest (film) 135
Exchange Flags 58

F

Farrah Fawcett Foundation 212–213, 237
Fishwick, Frank and Edith 75–76
Fishwick-McCartney, Angie 77–79, 79
flowers 240
football clubs 48–49
Fourmost, The 86

G

Gath, Jim 274
Germany 160–163
Gibraltar 52
Gin Pancakes 185
GIs of Comedy Tour, The 214
Glitter, Gary 78, 138
Global Beatles Day 111

Gmeinwieser, Arno and Sherey 166
Good Ol' Freda 86, 88
Goons, The 33
Gordon, David 189
Gorman, John 74
Goss, Glenn 219, 221
Gowan, Lawrence 233
Graves, Elsie and Harry 103–104
Graves, Elsie (photo) 104
Greenslade, Roy 115
Gregory, Lyle 146
grocery cart 202

H

Hamburg Convention Centre 139
Hannay & Co 57
Harris, Alice
  (photo) 222
Harris, Alice ("Sweet Alice") 221–223
Harris, Ian and Jackie 131
Harrison, George 105–106
Harrison, George (journalist) 108
Harrison, Louise 106, 109, 275
Harrison, Louise and Harry 101
Harrison, Pattie 105
Hatton, Billy 86
  (photo) 97
headache 240
Heffelfinger, Ed 169
HELP! 66–70, 86, 100
  in Obertauren, Austria 191–192
Hendrick, Robert 172
herbs 55
Heswall Village School 71
Hey Jude 117
Hilbre 23
Hilbre Islands 19–21
Hollis, Strummer 234
Holton, Kennon 214
How I Won the War 112–113
Hoylake 17–19
Hurricanes, The 101

I

Ichiyanagi, Toshi 143

iFanz 85
I'm With the Band 218
In the Line of Fire 183
Instamatic Karma 145

J

Jackson, Joan 274
James, Dick 88–89
James Paul McCartney ITV Special 131–132
Jones, Brian "Saxophone" 78, 97
Jones, Paul 79
juice 8

K

Kargol, Nancy 121
Kargol, Nancy and Franck 250
Keats, Jon 191–193
Kelly, Freda 73, 84–89, 193
  (photo) 84, 88, 192
Kendall, Beryl 155–157, 273
Kendall, Jim 111
Kendall, Milly McCartney 65, 111, 119–120
  (photo) 120, 121
Kennedy, Ted 68
Kershner, Irvin 140
Kessie, Ken 94
King George 39
King's Lynn 137
Kingsway Tunnel 40
Kinnear, Roy 69–70
Klein, Allen 128
Klieman, Rikki xi–xii, 181–183, 247, 276
  (photo) 181, 182
Krusen, Bob 169
Krusen, Bob and Ann 171

L

Lane, Denny 133
Lapidos, Mark 275
Last Dance 170
Lennon, Cynthia 1, 144, 273, 279–280
  (photo) 26

Lennon, John 98–100, 141–142, 203, 266
  (birth) 2
Lennon, Julia 2, 3
Lennon, Julian 25
  (photo) 26, 145
Lennox, Annie 220-221
Lester, Dick 69
Let It Be 128
Lewisohn, Mark 275
Liverpool 39–41, 44, 57, 252–254
  show business legends 5
Liverpool Echo 47, 108
Liverpool Legends 107
  (photo) 107
London
  Christmas 80–81
  move to 139–141
Lulu 109
Lürtzer, Herbert 87, 193

M

Magical Mystery Tour 114, 116–117
Mainwood, Roger 135
Malta 52
Manchester, Melissa 234
Manly Ferry 153
Manson Exposed 237
Marechal, Nick 258–260, 276
Marshmallow Maiden 215
Martin, George 33, 229
Mather, Bob 171
McAlpine, Dr. 12–13, 19
McCartney, Benna 233
McCartney, Jim 57–61, 215–216
  (marriage) 61–65
  (photo)
  64, 65, 74, 112, 121, 134, 216
  (photo with his band) 134
McCartney, Keith 78
McCartney, Linda 123–126, 143, 146–149
  (photo) 147, 272
McCartney, Mary 2, 3, 61

McCartney (McGear), Mike 22, 72, 74–78, 78, 116, 273
  marriage 76
  photo 273
McCartney Multimedia 85, 169–173
McCartney, Paul 58–61
  and Drake's Drum 73–74
  and Jane Asher 121–123
  and Linda Eastman 123–126
  announcing Jim's birth 216
  automobiles 265–266
  birth 2
  chemistry with John Lennon 1–5
  meets Angie and Ruth 62
  playing piano with Angie 22
  receiving Grammys 128
  recording Walking in the Park with Eloise 133
  talking with David Cassidy 227
  visiting Alma Cogan 82–83
  working with Geoff Emerick 229
McClarty, Emily 37–39
McClarty, Mae 37
McGear (album) 77
McGough, Roger 74
McKern, Leo 69
Mellor, Chris 134
men 248–249
Merseyside 70–72
Mersey Tunnel, the 39
Millar, Gary (photo) 96
Mills, Simon (Dr.) 197, 241, 246, 274
mint 240
Mohin, Bill and Dilys 95
Moore, Dudley 185
Moptops, The 184
Morgan, Piers 228
Moylan, Sheena 72
Mrs. McCartney's Teas 186–187
Mrs McCartney's Wines 186–187
mustard 240
My Kid Brother's Band – a.k.a. The Beatles 107

My Long and Winding Road
  xiii, 1, 9, 85, 150, 279

N

nail varnish 240
Nashville 166–168
  moving to 167–169
National Lampoon Lemmings 238, 243–245
  (photo) 244
Nelson, Gunnar 235, 275
Nelson, Matthew 235, 275
Nelson, Ricky 235
Nethercutt, Martin 204–209, 275
  (photo) 206, 207, 208
Nicholls Ice Cream 71–72
Norden, Denis 140
Norris Green 11, 27, 34, 39
Nourpour, Fred and Mitra 213
nylon 31

O

Oakes, David 53
O'Heir, Jim 238
  (photo) 238
Oliff, Richard 78
Ono, Yoko 142–144
Our World 111
overseas travel 201

P

Pang, May 2, 144–146, 275
  (photo) 144
Parkgate 25
Parmar, Deven 273
passwords 262
Pavilion, The 30
Peace Tower 143
Pemberton, Lucy 18
Perez, Minerva 216–217
Pete Price, Name Dropper 150
Playa del Rey 173–174
Portnoy, Mike 232
pregnancy 49–50
Price, Pete 85–87, 136–137, 148–150
  (photo) 24, 71, 149
price tag stickers 240

Q

QR Codes xiv, 184
QR Reader xiv
Quarrymen, The 3
Queen Elizabeth II 43–44
Queen Mary 39
Queensway Tunnel 40

R

racism 44–45
Raider, Tom 184
Reitz, Paul 276
Rembrandt 26, 59, 61, 63, 65, 75, 90, 101, 105, 109, 114, 117, 118, 123, 131
  (photo) 59
River Mersey 17–18
robocalls 263
Rogers, Ginger 42
Romeo, Christine 213, 237
Rossetto, Harriet 220
Roundel Productions 139
Rowlands, Gill 72

S

Sachs, Andrew 140
salt stains 240
Sambrook, Barbara and Jack 250
Sambrook, Jane (Webster) 250
Sax and Drugs and Rock n Roll 78
Scaffold, The 74, 79
Scott, Gavin 235
Seiwell, Denny 133
  (photo) 132
Sensi Magazine 14
Shakespeare Theatre, The 30, 137, 149
shawlies 19
Shifrin, Sue 228
Sicily 52
Siegel, Ralph 159
Skinner, David 186, 187–191, 199, 273

Sorry Boys, You Failed the Audition 115
Southampton 51
Speakman, Eva and Nik 267
Speakman Family (photo) 269
spelling, UK vs American xiv
Spinetti, Victor 69–70
sponges 56
Springboard South 190–191
Springfield, Dusty 79
Standard, The 114
Starr, Freddie 78
Starr, Ringo 102–104, 110–111, 266
  knighthood 225
  swimming 69–70
Starr, Zach 102
Stefanelli, Joe 184
Stefano, Nando 213
Stern, Howard 129
Stewart, Alana 212, 237
Stewart, Margaret 84
Stopforth, Bob 11
Stopforth, Edie 118
Stopforth, Helen 11
Stopforth, Joan 20, 33–37
  (photo) 36
Stopforth, Mae 32–33
Stopforth, Peter 11
Stopforth, Richard 11
Storm, Rory 101
St. Teresa's Catholic School 19–20, 29
Sturm, Peggi 276
Sullivan, Ed 6
Sutcliffe, Pauline 276
Sutcliffe, Stuart 5
Swannies 246–248
  (photo) 247
Sydney Harbor 153

T

Taylor, Alistair 66
Taylor, Derek 116
tea and history 255–257
TEAFLIX Tuesdays 260–262
Tennessean, The 167
The Beatles and Me On Tour 236
The Wirral Way 18
Thomas, Betty 72
toothpaste 202
Tran, Kennon (Holton) 277
Tran, Thom 214–215, 277
Trembly, Cristy 89–90
tribute bands 183–184
Turkey 194–198
Twiggy 42

V

Vaughan, Frankie 137
vegetables 8
Victoria College of Music 22
VOKA 87
  (photo) 87

W

Walking in the Park with Eloise 4, 133–134
Waterworth, Roger 94
West Kirby 25
West Kirby Grammar School for Girls 25
White, Geoff 141
White, Ryan 86
Williams, Eddie 34, 35, 50
wine
  fast chill tip 202
Wings 128, 229
Wings Fun Club 130–131
Wingspan 126
Wirral Peninsula 26–27, 70–74
Wonderful Tonight 105
Woods, Don 18, 70, 273
Wooler, Bob 96
Woolley, Susan 246
World War I 11
World War II
  21, 24, 30, 38, 40, 43, 57, 143

Z

Zec, Donald 69–70

Publisher's Note

My wife Debbie and I met Angie, Ruth, and Martin at one of the "Meet the McCartneys" events at David Skinner's "eculent" restaurant in Kemah, TX. We published David's book, *Introduction to Decision Analysis*, 2nd Edition, in 1999. This got us started with the publishing business, which we have now operated for over twenty years.

David's book is now in its third edition; see our web site (link) using the QR code to the right! (See Ruth, I can be taught, it just takes a while...)

We publish business books about decision analysis, game theory, negotiation, and other business topics. Angie was thinking about writing another book, and was interested in finding a U.S. publisher. We had never published a biography before, but didn't see any reason we couldn't do it. David told her about us, saying, "He's slow, but he is honest." With that ringing endorsement, we all started down the journey to publish this book, bringing Marshall Terrill onto the team to help with editing.

On the one hand, this book was difficult to complete due to the layout's complexity (QR codes and lots of pictures) and the wide variety of topics and people that Angie talks about. However, it was also literally a labor of love for me, because...

I'm an engineer by profession, but have played in bands (rock, R&B, jazz, country, and contemporary Christian) all my life, beginning in the late 1960's. My high school bands could cover many of the artists of the day, such as The Rolling Stones, The Young Rascals, The Doors, The Yardbirds, Santana, Jethro Tull, The Lovin' Spoonful, and virtually all of the R&B artists (Isley Brothers, Sam and Dave, Wilson Pickett, Otis Redding, and so on). But we couldn't cover The Beatles' songs. Their harmonies were too intricate and Paul's bass was too difficult to emulate. To learn a song, we had to either pay $3.95 for the sheet music (which might or might not be correct) or spend hours playing the record over and over again to figure out and write down the chords and words. As Angie noted, times were different then!

Now you can get the chords and words and bass tabs off the internet for virtually any song. I think the first Beatles song I played in public was on the piano, backing up my girlfriend Julia singing "Let It Be" at our high school graduation. As I got older and my bands got better, occasionally we'd be able to cover a few Beatles songs, but again, it is not easy to replicate their harmonies or Paul's bass. I'll never forget listening to *Abbey Road* for the first time – I played it over and over again (and it sounds just as good today as it did back then).

When I work on the editing and layout of our books, I usually have Pandora playing in the background, and The Beatles are, of course, on my play list. The Beatles' music is integral to our entire culture (as the recent film, *Yesterday*, illustrated in detail). And, this is especially so for musicians.

So it was especially poignant for me to work on this book with The Beatles' music going in the background – reading Angie's stories about her life with Paul's father Jim and afterwards – stories that are funny, sad, positive, inspirational, and fascinating. Her journey with Ruth (and eventually Martin) is simply amazing.

So, thank you, Angie, for the chance to work with you on this project. And I sincerely hope that folks enjoy reading your book as much as I did.

>Dave Charlesworth, Owner
>Probabilistic Publishing
>Sugar Land, TX

PS: And thank you, Lisa Derketsch and Nancy Winchester for your help with this project!

Our Other Books

Here are abstracts of our other publications, some of which you may find to be of interest.

Introduction to Decision Analysis, 3rd Edition
by David C. Skinner

Mr. Skinner originally wrote *Introduction to Decision Analysis* as a handbook and guide for the Decision Analysis (DA) practitioner in 1995. The 2nd Edition was published in 1999 and quickly became an essential reference for industry as well as a graduate-level textbook for decision analysis courses at many universities. Feedback from students, practitioners, and professors was incorporated into the 3rd Edition, which was released in 2009.

Introduction to Decision Analysis is recommended for DA consultants, corporate DA practitioners, managers and technical professionals who are responsible for making effective decisions, and for MBA or other graduate-level students.

Introduction to Bayesian Inference and Decision, 2nd Edition
by Robert Winkler

The basic concepts of Bayesian inference and decision have not really changed since the first edition of this book was published in 1972. Even so, Bayesian inference and decision has been a very fertile and rapidly growing field, both in terms of theoretical/methodological research and in terms of real-world applications.

This book gives a foundation in the concepts, enables readers to understand the results of analyses in Bayesian inference and decision, provides tools to model real-world problems and carry out basic analyses, and prepares readers for further explorations in Bayesian inference and decision. In the second edition, material has been added on some topics, examples and exercises have been updated, and perspectives have been added to each chapter and the end of the book to indicate how the field has changed and to give some new references.

Why Can't You Just Give Me The Number? 2nd Edition
by Patrick Leach

Subtitle: An Executive's Guide to Using Probabilistic Thinking to Manage Risk and to Make Better Decisions

Patrick Leach draws on his extensive consulting and teaching experience to present a compelling, insightful, and understandable case for using probabilistic analysis as part of everyday business decision making. Practical examples and case studies are clearly presented.

Mr. Leach is an experienced conference speaker, business trainer, and consultant. He makes a clear, concise case for appropriate implementation of probabilistic analysis. Rather than get bogged down with equations and complexity, he shares his insight and the benefits of his experience (and some key research by others) in a way that is readable, useful, and memorable.

Game Theory for Business by Paul Papayoanou

Dr. Papayoanou has written a clear, complete, interesting, and concise guide to applying game theory in business situations. He takes a uniquely practical yet rigorous approach with both the book and his consulting projects. As a DA practitioner and having spent extensive time with Dr. Papayoanou's text, my conclusion is that DA is to checkers as Strategic Gaming is to chess: it represents a higher, more difficult, yet more powerful level of thinking.

Creating a Culture of Profitability by Rob and Aviva Kleinbaum

Subtitle: A Revolutionary Model for Managing Culture

Improving culture in business has been a "soft" and subjective topic – until now. Rob and Aviva Kleinbaum have used Lawrence Harrison's 30-year study of successful cultures as the foundation for a powerful and logical framework for analyzing and improving business culture.

Building on this research and integrating the work of others, the Kleinbaums have developed a conceptual model that is useful, based on data, and testable against experience. There are symptoms and metrics for the cultural ills that reveal problems before they become overpowering. They suggest reasonable and doable treatment plans that attack the symptoms and root causes.

There is a workable plan for getting started and integrating cultural management into the existing organization, without adding bureaucracy or overhead. Culture matters. Everyone knows that. But now something can be done about it.

Project Risk Quantification by John K. Hollmann

Subtitle: A Practitioner's Guide to Realistic Cost and Schedule Risk Management

Project Risk Quantification presents the most practical, realistic, and integrated approach to project cost and schedule risk quantification that is available today! It offers proven, empirically-valid methods and tools applicable to projects of all types and at all decision gates. The text is written for both the manager and the risk analysis practitioner. It will bring reliable accuracy and contingency determination to your capital project organization.

Problem, Risk, and Opportunity Enterprise Management by Brian W. Hagen

Subtitle: How to use language, data, information, and analytics that easily align with the ways we think.

Through decades of consulting practice, Dr. Hagen has tailored a decision-making process to correspond with the way that our brains actually function. This comprehensive book shares his methodology and the basis for it. He presents powerful insights and distinctions that are not found elsewhere.

The Business of Negotiation by Craig McKnight

Draw on Mr. McKnight's experience as a negotiator, attorney, CPA, decision analyst, manager, project manager, father, spouse, and negotiation instructor to get better outcomes for your negotiations, both in business and in life.

This book presents the clearest and most comprehensive guide to negotiations that is available today. *The Business of Negotiation* highlights many stories to help you understand all facets of negotiations in the writer's easy-to-understand conversational writing style. Mr. McKnight's presentation of negotiation as a process is foundational and is not found elsewhere.

My Mother Taught Me:

My mother taught me TO APPRECIATE A JOB WELL DONE.

'If you're going to kill each other, do it outside. I just finished cleaning.'

My mother taught me RELIGION.

'You better pray that will come out of the carpet.'

My mother taught me about TIME TRAVEL.

'If you don't straighten up, I'm going to knock you into the middle of next week!'

My mother taught me LOGIC.

'Because I said so, that's why.'

My mother taught me FORESIGHT.

'Make sure you wear clean underwear, in case you're in an accident.'

My mother taught me about CONTORTIONISM.

'Will you look at that dirt on the back of your neck!'

My mother taught me about STAMINA.

'You'll sit there until all those Brussels sprouts are gone.'

My mother taught me about HYPOCRISY.

'If I told you once, I've told you a million times. Don't exaggerate!'

My mother taught me about RECEIVING.

'You're going to get it when you get home!'

My mother taught me MEDICAL SCIENCE.

'If you don't stop crossing your eyes, they are going to get stuck that way.'

My mother taught me HUMOUR.

'When that lawn mower cuts off your toes, don't come running to me.'

My mother taught me about JUSTICE.

'One day you'll have kids, and I hope they turn out just like you!'

Angie's Biography

Liverpool-born Angie McCartney published her first book at almost 83 years old, and several years later, is doing the same again. She celebrated her 90th birthday in November, 2019, and she is already planning her 91st, and if her past parties are anything to go by, it should be quite a bash!

The interim years have seen significant changes in her life, from opening a fruit wine company, to performing a stint in the improv comedy world with National Lampoon's Lemmings, to delving into the world of Artificial Intelligence and learning more about the ever changing world of cyberspace (making plans to leave her brain behind when she finally "pops her clogs"). She figured that if Eleanor Rigby could leave her face in a jar by the door, she might do the same with her brain. Maybe it'll be a bigger jar though.

Along with daughter Ruth and aided and abetted by son-in-law Martin Nethercutt, she launched a weekly live show on Facebook called *TEAFLIX Tuesdays* early in 2018. The show has hosted a varied selection of guests, including writers, musicians, foodies, film makers, radio personalities, and even a thirteen-year-old young lady who introduced her to the world of slime. Yes, that gooey stuff that teens like to hurl at one another on Award shows. This second book has the added attraction of QR codes which readers can click on with their smartphones, to be linked to audio and video clips pertaining to the stories.

Angie has travelled to Europe and her home town of Liverpool, doing radio shows and appearances. She flew to Obertauern, Austria with Cavern Club co-owner Jon Keats to celebrate the fiftieth anniversary of The Beatles filming the ski scenes for *HELP!* This included meeting with the man who was Paul's stunt double on the ski slopes, and a hair raising ride up the alps on a ski mobile to his lodge at the peak, to being greeted by hundreds of carousing revellers. And there's a QR code of that, too.

Her weekly radio shows have continued with Pete Price at www.citytalk.co.uk, and Richard Oliff at www.harboroughfm.co.uk, to occasional appearances at venues to raise funds for charities.

She became one of Farrah Fawcett's Angels, participating in fundraisers for cancer-related charities. She is a member of the Westchester Elks Lodge, where she also contributes to their many children's charities and fundraisers, helping "Chef" Ruth, who cooks up a storm with well-liked British fare of the "bangers and mash" and "scouse" variety at many of their fundraisers. (What next - a series called "The Real Scouse Wives of Knotty Ash?")

Her social media friends keep her busy with orders for Mrs. McCartney's Teas, which she personally ships and tracks until they land safely at their destination.

November, 2018 saw her appearance in a music video, shot in a "Cuckoo's Nest" type venue for heavy metal band, "Heavy Justice," which was produced by the family's recently launched McCartneyStudios.com Production Company. She also does voice overs and writes a column for *Sensi* magazine in her spare time.

This latest offering inclues some of her heartwarming Beatles-related stories, which is what the majority of readers want to hear … maybe not for the first time, but as the Beatles phenomenon shows no sign of abating, she thought - why not?

Angie, Ruth, and Martin celebrate Angie's 90th birthday, November 14, 2019.